Dedication

To the memory of

Rear Admiral Berton Aldrich Robbins, Jr.,
U.S. Navy (Retired) and
Mary Patricia O'Meara Robbins

In their own distinctly different ways,
each contributed to our nation's
victory in World War II

Books by Wilbur D. Jones, Jr.

Forget That You Have Been Hitler Soldiers: A Youth's Service to the Reich, with Hermann O. Pfrengle
White Mane, 2001

Condemned to Live: A Panzer Artilleryman's Five-Front War, with Franz A. P. Frisch
White Mane, 2000

Arming the Eagle: A History of U.S. Weapons Acquisition Since 1775
Department of Defense Systems Management College Press, and Government Printing Office, 1999

Gyrene: The World War II United States Marine
White Mane, 1998

Giants in the Cornfield: The 27th Indiana Infantry
White Mane, 1997

From Packard to Perry: A Quarter Century of Service to the Defense Acquisition Community
Department of Defense Systems Management College Press, 1996

Congressional Involvement and Relations: A Guide for Department of Defense Acquisition Managers, Four Editions
Department of Defense and Government Printing Office, 1986–1996

Glossary: Defense Acquisition Acronyms and Terms, Two Editions
Department of Defense, 1987–1990

Visit his web site: *www.wilburjones.com*

Contents

Foreword

Wilbur Jones and his wife, Carroll, like most couples, probably feel the day they met was very special, but I call it special for another reason. It brought together a navy man with a penchant for writing (and writing well) and a woman with a great story to tell about Honolulu when the bombs fell and the war began. Central to this is Carroll's unusual mother, a destroyer officer's wife and already a professional news photographer, who somehow took care of her two children by herself in the midst of World War II, and at the same time photographed everything she could see.

The mother, Patricia O'Meara Robbins, was fortunate in being already a known professional with a camera. Someone understood that such pictures—the higher the quality the better—would be gladly needed, not only right then but also during the foreseeable future. Instead of being forbidden to take photos, for fear her pictures might fall into the wrong hands, she was given passes for her camera and herself, allowed to go almost anywhere, and to take all the pictures she wanted. So she always carried her camera, with official passes attached, took pictures whenever she saw one, and punctiliously turned them in. Many were widely printed during the war years and afterward. But being a human being and a fond mother, she posed her children also, wherever possible, in the middle of the damage and the carnage (she was not exposing them to "war-horror"; it was what everyone saw in Honolulu after the 7th of December). All the same, she probably took more pictures than were strictly needed to support the war effort. In short, many of them remained buried in her personal files, seen by no one.

So, when that dust cleared, the Robbins home was full of storage boxes of photograph albums, and sequestered among them were the Pearl Harbor Day, and the weeks and months after, remembrances of Patricia O'Meara Robbins' two kids. And then one day, years afterward, the older child, daughter Carroll, met Wilbur Jones, a lieutenant on her father's staff (yes, her father survived the war, though gravely wounded, and retired finally as a rear admiral), and natural events took their natural course—but not for 41 years, so far as the albums of old pictures were concerned.

It took Jones four decades to break down his wife's disinclination to look through their attic and talk about Pearl Harbor. "Let that old stuff stay buried" was her reaction to his approaches on the subject. But this, too, was finally overcome, and *Hawaii Goes to War,* with its poignant photographs of the "day of infamy" and the many desperate hours and weeks following, is the result. Some of the images will bring back some readers' own memories of having actually been there. Or, perhaps they will relive childhood recollections of where they were and how they took it aboard when Pearl Harbor first burst on their youthful sentience.

In American eyes, Pearl Harbor was undoubtedly the seminal event of the 20th century, transcending everything else. Its effect and controversies are still with us. I, for example, have become convinced that the army and navy commanders there should have received far more—and more pertinent—intelligence than they got. On the whole, however, in the long run Japan's surprise attack brought about good results, not that the high command of any of the Axis powers would have so stated.

One question well answered by Mrs. Robbins' photos has to do with the Japanese "bombing" of schools and churches. Our reaction, of course, was to become even more enraged—but some of her images show a somewhat different story, and this may explain why many were never published. The best evidence from that dreadful day is that, moving vehicles possibly accepted, Japanese aviators did not intentionally attack the populace of Honolulu. Schools, churches, and private buildings were hit and damaged, but not by Japanese bombs. What goes up must ultimately come back down, and it will hurt whatever it may hit. We did a lot of madly aimed shooting that day, and this is understandable, too.

But these things are only part of what this book is about. The pictures are there, and the stories from some of the survivors. But what about the people of Honolulu? How did they fare? There lies this book's principal message. It shows school students and teachers drilling for survival of a second attack, running into slit trenches and air raid shelters, for example. After Midway, the urgency for this kind of civilian preparation lessened, and gradually they were forgotten, although the air raid shelters remained in existence. Drills of this kind were never necessary on Mainland America, at least, during World War II, and the images only show how futile efforts of this kind would actually be today.

All of the above happened 60 years ago—a lifetime. Since then, the world has changed enormously. Today we hear about computer-controlled rockets that never miss their targets. That they may also carry nuclear weapons is a given. Guerilla warfare and terrorism will be with us for some time more, but all-out war, as an instrument of national policy, has seen its last days.

Captain Edward L. Beach, USN (Ret.)
World War II Submarine Officer and Author of
the novels *Run Silent, Run Deep;*
Dust on the Sea; and *Cold is the Sea;*
and
The Wreck of the Memphis; Around the World Submerged; United States Navy: A Two Hundred Year History; Scapegoats: A Defense of Kimmel and Short at Pearl Harbor; Salt and Steel: Reflections of a Submariner

Washington, D.C.

Preface

When Harold Collier, vice president of White Mane Publishing Company, asked me in a telephone conversation in October 2000 to write a book on Pearl Harbor, in a split second I knew exactly what to suggest. Let's do the aftermath, about what happened to the fleet and the people of Hawaii during the weeks and months after the 7 December 1941 damage was done, and the enemy had come and gone.

We could feature the remembrances of my wife, Carroll Robbins Jones, who as a girl witnessed the attack's second wave from Waikiki, and the hundreds of photographs of the aftermath taken by her mother, Patricia O'Meara Robbins, a professional photographer on assignment with the Associated Press using army and navy credentials. A pictorial history. We could discuss action by the Pacific Fleet, the ship salvage operations, and life on Oahu—how the armed forces and population lived fearing an invasion until the Battle of Midway fortuitously turned the tide. He wholeheartedly agreed.

The story of the Japanese attack on United States military and naval forces on Oahu, Territory of Hawaii, which launched our country into World War II certainly is well known. Most of the principal subjects have been well documented, exhaustively researched, widely debated, and voluminously reported. They include the diplomatic and political prelude, role of President Franklin D. Roosevelt, naval objectives in the Japanese Pacific strategy, handling of intelligence information, culpability of Admiral Husband E. Kimmel and Lieutenant General Walter C. Short, battle scenario and consequences, and eventual impact on American defense readiness. Consequently, there is no need to discuss those points in this book.

What has been inadequately addressed in collective detail under one cover is the aftermath of the attack—or, the first six months of the war through Midway in June 1942. Not enough has been written about the events and conditions existing in and around Hawaii, particularly its capital of Honolulu; the disposition and action of the U.S. Pacific Fleet principally operating out of Pearl Harbor, including the amazing salvage operations; the steady armed forces buildup; and civilian life under martial law and other extreme wartime impositions and shortages.

This work helps fill that historical void through vivid eyewitness remembrances of those who survived the attack and lived there in the aftermath. The most prominent remembrances are Carroll's, as she describes the incredible story of her mother's ambitious professional work schedule and the free-lance, no-school life of her two children who accompanied her wherever she went for the nine wartime months they spent on Oahu. The family had to do without her father, a naval officer off at sea.

Hawaii Goes to War also features some 126 photographs and other illustrations. Some of the photographs are familiar army and navy official credits of images taken of Pearl Harbor, Hickam Field, and elsewhere on Oahu, particularly regarding damage and salvage. Most images are Carroll's mother's, many of which have been published as "Associated Press" or with official army or navy credits. Some are unpublished. Each of her images depicts how the impending Japanese threat interrupted and changed normal life in Hawaii.

I am particularly pleased and proud to collaborate with Carroll on this book, a project I have hoped for the 42 years of marriage we might do "some day," certainly that she would tell her unusual story. What she recalls of the day of 7 December and the months thereafter in Honolulu are an exceptional addition to one of the war's principal sidelights. We believe the remembrances and photographs add a special new dimension to the study of Pearl Harbor and World War II history.

Her father, the late Rear Admiral Berton A. Robbins, Jr., U.S. Navy (Retired), as a lieutenant was the new executive officer of the destroyer USS *Shaw* (DD-373), whose magnificent white fireball explosion in dry dock became the battle's second-most famous image after that of the burning, dying battleship USS *Arizona* (BB-39). Thank God, he was about to board the ship when it took a Japanese bomb in the forward magazine and was uninjured. He went to sea immediately in the Wake Island relief expedition and then for two years on a cruiser task force staff. He became a highly decorated war hero and career officer, and later was my mentor and role model as I proceeded in my own successful naval career.

I met Carroll, then-Captain Robbins ("Pop"), and her mother, Patricia O'Meara Robbins ("Mutti" pronounced "Moó-tee"), in Naples, Italy, in 1958. I was his aide and communications officer in the U.S. Sixth Fleet. My interest in his wartime exploits and how the family existed in his continuous absence was peaked in long sessions of listening to their stories and looking at Mutti's incredible portfolio. As we show in her biographical information she was an extremely successful photographer of cultures around the world, Los Angeles society, and the Hollywood rich and famous. Carroll and I married in Naples in 1959, and the next year the navy reassigned me to shipboard duty in San Diego, California. It slipped my mind, and over the decades I lost track of the photographs' existence. Pop died in 1983, and Mutti in 1988. Carroll acquired many of her parents' papers and memorabilia, including the Hawaii photographs of 1941–42.

Carroll had always been reluctant, often quite recalcitrant, to discuss her remembrances of life during the war. She never forgot, but considered it too painful. The duty of her father, a Naval Academy graduate and truly dedicated, professional sailor, was to serve in combat. At Iwo Jima on 17 February 1945, the destroyer USS *Leutze* (DD-481) he commanded was hit by shells from Mount Suribachi. He was terribly wounded, and took three years to recover before returning to full duty. Mutti, Carroll, and her younger brother Berton remained in Hawaii until August 1942 while she continued to work for the AP with army and navy credentials. Then they sailed for Los Angeles, the O'Meara family home, where the kids were raised for the rest of the war.

After Carroll and I retired from the Washington, D.C., area where we lived for 28 years and moved to my hometown of Wilmington, North Carolina, in 1997, I chaired a year-long tribute to the local area's role in the World War II war effort and the men and women who served, called Wartime Wilmington Commemoration, 1999. As 7 December approached, word of her experiences prompted the county's Cape Fear Museum to ask her to speak on the subject and exhibit some of her mother's images. For the first time ever, she did, and her talk and exhibit were one of the Commemoration's highlight events. I was so proud that she had at last opened the door to this portion of her childhood and its significant addition to history. I was pleased she shared with me, her family, and many others what it was like to live without a father for virtually the entire war, and with a mother bent on pursuing her professional career meanwhile.

After the event, we put the photographs and the remembrances back in a storage box, not knowing when or if we would ever share them again. Then along came Harold Collier's phone call. Now here they all are for the world to see and know, and we hope to enjoy and appreciate. Thank you, White Mane.

Hawaii during World War II was a U.S. Territory and went by the title "Territory of Hawaii (TH)." Qualified residents had U.S. citizenship and rights under the U.S. Constitution. It was admitted as the 50th State on 21 August 1959.

The authors use the format of military times and dates (e.g., 0755, for 7:55 a.m.; and 7 December 1941).

A mini-glossary of some words and abbreviations is in order:

GIs—U.S. soldiers, or military personnel in general
Haole—Person from Mainland, Caucasian
IJN—Imperial Japanese Navy ship
Islands (capitalized)—The Hawaiian Islands
Liberty—Navy and Marine off-duty time away from a ship/station
Mainland—Continental United States (48 states)
MPs—Army/Marine military police
ROTC—Reserve Officer Training Corps
Snafu—Situation normal, all fouled up

Wahine—Native Hawaiian girl

USO—United Service Organizations

USS—United States ship

The authors make two references to men from Wilmington and New Hanover County, North Carolina, who were present at Pearl Harbor and the Battle of Midway. These men, particularly the Midway fliers, add a personal, local note to the Hawaii story, and are essential to the book I have recently written on the Wilmington area's contributions to the war effort during World War II, titled *A Sentimental Journey*.

Wilbur D. Jones, Jr.
Captain, U.S. Naval Reserve (Retired)

Prologue

7 December 1941

Sometime in the early part of 1941, my father, a navy lieutenant on board the destroyer USS *Tucker,* sailed for Hawaii. During most of the spring and early summer of '41, the Pacific Fleet moved from home ports such as San Diego and Long Beach along the California coast, to Pearl Harbor, Oahu, Territory of Hawaii. History has shown that a conflict with Japan was anticipated by the military but *when* and *where* was unknown. Because the ships were not technically "home ported" at Pearl Harbor, the navy did not authorize the transfer of dependents (wives and children), so most families remained on the "Mainland."

My mother, Patricia, brother, Berton, and I lived on Marguerita Avenue on Coronado Island, across San Diego Bay, when Dad left for Hawaii, not an unusual occurrence as we were used to his being gone much of the time. The separations had become hard for Mother, so she devised a way to get "official" passage to Honolulu, and of course Berton and I were part of the package. First, we moved to Los Angeles, where Mother was born and raised and enjoyed the familiarity of a large, well-known family involved in the early years settling the city and state. She had begun to develop a reputation as an outstanding photographer, winning a number of awards for advertising and still work in both New York and Los Angeles exhibits. We lived in an apartment on Wilshire Boulevard during this short time and loved being near family friends and favorite relatives who indulged us and joined in our childish activities.

For me, school was not a favorite activity, possibly due to very bad eyesight, and being teased for wearing thick glasses and, for a few hours a day, a black patch covering the lens of "the good" eye, which was supposed to force sight for the weak one. I was not encouraged to develop after-school chums at this time since "we will not be here long," and consequently Berton and I and our grampa O'Meara, and uncles Bill and Carroll O'Meara were playmates. Mother was busy finalizing details on two assignments for photo stories in Honolulu, one for *Mademoiselle* magazine, the other for *Look* magazine. There was conflict in "THE FAMILY" about my mother dragging us kids off to that "pagan place" with iffy schooling and her working with "the Kodiak craze" (Grampa's terminology), and our not experiencing a normal childhood. I don't believe they quite trusted Mother's maternal instincts or her gypsy life and felt we kids would be better left in Los Angeles, attending St. Brendan's School, eating regular meals at specific times, under the watchful eyes of all of Hancock Park and Windsor Park residents, insuring that we would learn all the "right" traditions of FAMILY!

We sailed from Los Angeles on the SS *Mariposa*, one of the three Matson Lines luxury passenger ships, and arrived on 25 November 1941. The ship was headed for Australia with remaining passengers and those who boarded in Honolulu. We later learned the *Mariposa* was sunk en route with no survivors. The only thing I recall with certainty about our trip over is being terribly seasick. Dad met us all with mounds of leis, and the heavy scent of the flowers, coupled with a still rocky equilibrium, brought on more nausea.

Finding a permanent place to live was evidently more difficult than Mother anticipated. Rentals were few and most did not take children. We did not qualify for navy quarters, and we could not stay long in our temporary accommodations at the Moana Seaside. I'm sure our parents knew somehow they had minimum time together, and with Dad transferring to the destroyer USS *Shaw* as executive officer on 6 December, and expecting to go out on patrol after they left dry dock, and Mother making her contacts on the island, they settled on a furnished place at The Comstock Apartments Hotel in Waikiki, two blocks from the beach and the Royal

Hawaiian Hotel. Mother and Dad could be together without the encumbrances of setting up house, and Berton and I had a great new world to explore that included learning how to become Hawaiian. I was seven and one-half years old, and Berton five.

Very early Sunday morning, 7 December, Berton and I were listening to someone reading the funnies on the radio, as our parents slept. We paid no attention to an announcer repeating something about "this is no drill..." until Dad literally burst into the room and loudly demanded we turn up the volume. Our normally low-voiced, even-tempered father was abnormally agitated and tight jawed. It seems in my mind that it was only moments before he literally ran out the door carrying his jacket over his shoulder, perhaps trying to put it on. As he left he called to my mother to keep the radio on and not leave the premises. I have no memory of seeing him again for more than two years, but I know he returned for a few hours. Dad had just finished transferring his things from the *Tucker* to the *Shaw* the day before. The *Shaw* suffered a direct hit through the forward magazine while in dry dock. One of the most published photos of that day depicted this event.

The rest of the day, although very clear in my mind, has no sequence to the events. It is almost as if I am mentally seeing a kaleidoscope of images, watching movie flashbacks in vivid color, but somehow devoid of great emotion. I never remember feeling fear; perhaps too much was happening all at once to experience intense feelings of any kind. Perhaps because we didn't understand what was happening, only that nothing made sense except for Mother, who ran into the apartment, soon appearing with one camera slung around her neck and carrying her bag containing at least one other and supplies. This was *not* unusual and almost comforting to us, seeing her remain in character while others around us behaved strangely, such as the woman who went to pieces threatening "if one more bomb drops I'll scream." It did, and she did. Her 13-year-old daughter danced around clapping her hands singing "goody, goody, goody, no school tomorrow." A man emerged from one of the upstairs apartments holding some liquor bottles and loudly announced to all that as long as we were going to be bombed he might as well do the job himself. Not until years later did I understand that one. This man eventually fell off the balcony rail where he had been sitting, and amazed everyone by struggling to his feet and retiring for the day.

One of my clearest recollections is of standing in the grassy area in back of the building where all the residents congregated and hearing a drone that became louder and louder. Someone pointed to my right yelling "here come the Japs!" We all seemed to stand woodenly, afraid to move, staring at the sight of formation after formation of *Zeros* flying low enough to see the heads of pilots in the cockpits. Someone uttered a "my God," in awe rather than fear, and we were rooted until they passed over. I could clearly see the faces of the pilots as they passed low overhead, their white ceremonial scarves flapping in the open cockpits, a vision I will never forget. This had to have been the second wave that came from around Diamond Head.*

Rumors were flying around about planes landing in the mountains, another impending attack, about saboteurs coming ashore aboard submarines, spies already on the island ready to set fire to important buildings and blow up hotels and telephone and telegraph offices. Mother cautioned us not to talk to anyone or listen to all the talk. She was right, of course, but this whole scene was just too bizarre not to notice. Mother tried reaching some of her friends with the wire services and a fellow from *Life* magazine, on the island with a bunch of reporters and a photographer for a "Life Goes To A...," the popular pictorial story and regular magazine feature. They were to do a Ti-Leaf skiing party, quite a popular local event, but had been partying the night before into the small hours of the morning and were in no condition to cover anything.

Sometime during the day on the seventh, one of the Associated Press people found us and asked Mother

* It was indeed the second wave, consisting primarily of Lieutenant Commander Shigekazu Shimazaki's 6th Attack Unit of 27 Nakajima B5N2 *Kate* torpedo-bombers from the carrier *Zuikaku*. It came from the north, then turned south, then turned sharply at Diamond Head back in a northwesterly direction. It passed Carroll on Waikiki about 0845 and struck Hickam Field and surrounding area from 0850–0930, including the *Shaw*. [With appreciation to, among others, Carl Smith, *Pearl Harbor: The Day of Infamy* (Oxford: Osprey Publishing Co., 1999)]

to work with the AP, along with Army Headquarters and Naval Intelligence. Many of the full-time photographers (not military) with the newspapers and wire services were of Japanese descent and had to be rounded up with other known Japanese in the Islands. The *Life* people were indisposed, and Mother was always known to be "on assignment" and always ready for a challenge. This was, for her, like catching the brass ring.

Mother had to wait a couple of days for proper credential, but managed to shoot pictures that first day of events around us. It seemed that almost immediately either soldiers or Civilian Defense people appeared telling all civilians not to leave the area in which they lived, that there would be a strict curfew, and no lights after dusk. Many wives gathered their children and headed for the docks, trying to get passage to the mainland, while others ran to the hills for a few days, some hid under beds, and some gathered together to form a group comfort zone. In hindsight, there was reason for not leaving your home area, whatever it may have been. If a loved one had been killed, or gone to sea for an undetermined length of time, or came home, how could the family members be notified?

People were asked not to drive cars that day in order to leave streets free for emergency vehicles. Also, many streets in residential and tourist areas were pitted and potholed from gun shells and bomb debris. I later learned that no Japanese bombs were intentionally dropped on civilian areas, as the planes generally carried one or two bombs and would naturally have a higher priority target. It is apparent that some of our own U.S. weapons may have been responsible for residential damage. Only a block from our apartment, a bomb dropped causing a crater in the street, and flying shrapnel tore chunks out of the apartment building on the corner. I do remember hearing the sound of the bomb getting louder and louder, a sort of whistling noise. Once someone tried arguing that a falling bomb *does not* make such a noise, but there are many, me included, who would vehemently disagree. Never having heard such a noise before, I was without fear, only curious. The fear finally came after being told that a man crossing the street diagonally had been killed, and I saw the missing building chunks and window glass and other debris. My fear increased when a few more people became hysterical, some children began to cry, and the MPs arrived and announced we were under martial law. Whatever that was, it sounded ominous, and, I thought, had something to do with gunslingers and cowboys.

I have no memory of my brother, nearly two years younger, being scared either. Hungry, yes. Scared, no. Berton was always hungry, but this time he really must have been. Seems we had all forgotten to eat. Food was never a priority with me in those days, but even I felt emptiness as it was well along into the day. There wasn't much food in the little apartment kitchen, and no store open. Someone passed the word that the drugstore a couple of blocks away would stay open until they ran out of everything edible. We ran down there and sat on the high stools that twirled around while Mother negotiated for whatever they had. I don't remember what it was, but after a few bites I threw up all over the yellow dress with brown and white checked pockets and neck piping. Berton ate my portion. Angst had finally set in. Mother talked her way into buying as many Hershey bars and chewing gum as possible from the store owner, declaring chocolate was nearly a whole food, and for her children (yea Mom!), and the gum was for her so she wouldn't eat the candy, and to keep her from smoking. She ate the candy along with us, we chewed the gum along with her, and she didn't stop smoking for another twenty-plus years.

In no particular order that day, we ran with Mother as she snapped pictures of a burning truck, a car stopped by MPs in the middle of the street checking the passengers, and army trucks lumbering down the street carrying uniformed soldiers or quickly-pressed-into-duty Civilian Defense personnel. As the day began to fade, the realization set in that no one had seen Dad. How would he get home? No busses were running and no one was supposed to drive a car. If we couldn't have lights, how could he see his way? If there was no food, how could we all have dinner? And the one question none of us wanted to ask and didn't know the answer to, was he still alive? How bad was it at "the base"? Tears finally came to all of us. That night was hard. Mother and the others gathered on the steps to listen to a radio with some kind of cover so no light from the dial could be seen. To add to the frustration of some adults, no smoking was allowed outside as the ash light could be seen miles away. I well remember my mother with a cigarette burning most of her waking hours. She was a naturally high-strung woman, impatient, aggressive, creative, and extremely intelligent, who used a cigarette as her pacifier. This must have been hell for her.

Sometime during that first night Dad returned for only a few short hours, bringing with him the burned, bullet-riddled American flag flown on the *Shaw* during the attack. The Harris tweed jacket he had worn that day had a burn hole in one of the pockets and a bullet inside. Mother never had the jacket repaired and, of course, it was not worn again. Dad later gave the flag to the U.S. Naval Academy, and it is on exhibit in its museum in Annapolis, Maryland. They kept the jacket for a number of years until it disappeared in one of their many moves. Mother had the bullet mounted on her charm bracelet, which I now have.

In some ways, this book is also a story of my mother. She was indeed a one-of-a-kind for comparison as I raised four of my own. My brother, Berton, and I never understood that Mother was not your average mom until a few years later when we were exposed to real kids, real families living real everyday lives that, although dull in comparison, were somewhat envied for the protection, the comfort of knowing just what to expect daily, even hourly. In spite of all our envy of normalcy, we relished the nonconformity of living with our mother and conspiring in pranks with our grampa, a master at outwitting "them," all the boring people.

Throughout this book I have inserted my remembrances in italics to embellish the historical story being told.

My parents unfortunately left no memoirs, but my mother's article in the February 1944 *Popular Photography* magazine is at least a suitable and informative substitute. The article is reproduced as part of this front matter. I was able to retrieve only a few personal papers after the sale of their Vista, California, house where Mother died. The buyer had thrown them out, and a curious and helpful neighbor salvaged some and notified me.

Carroll Robbins Jones

Acknowledgments

The authors wish to thank the following persons for their assistance with this project:

To Jean Hort, Director of the Navy Department Library, a historian's "most-valuable friend";

From the Naval Historical Center, Bernard Cavalcante, Dr. Edward Marolda, John Reilly, Jeff Barlow, Jack Green, and Bob Cressman;

Dr. David Winkler of the Naval Historical Foundation;

To then-Director Janet Seapker and staff, particularly Jennie Ashlock and Suesann Sullivan, of the Cape Fear Museum, Wilmington, for producing the "I Remember Pearl Harbor" program in connection with Wartime Wilmington Commemoration, 1999, which gave Carroll Robbins Jones a forum for sharing her remembrances for the first time;

And the marketing, editorial, and production staffs of White Mane and Beidel Printing House for accelerating their typical highly professional responses in helping to produce this book.

Introduction

Somehow, as through prophetic timing or sheer coincidence, and without authorization, a World War II Japanese Mitsubishi A6M *Zero*, resplendent in battle colors and big red circles splashed on fuselage and wings, swept no more than five hundred feet overhead down the length of the USS *Arizona* Memorial at Pearl Harbor. The date was Sunday, 7 December 1975. The hour was precisely 0755. Ordinarily, this might be a bonafide living recreation of that historic event. Except that this time, it flew directly over the president of the United States, who was stepping off an admiral's barge on to the Memorial landing.

Such aircraft action under those circumstances was absolutely forbidden by the Federal Aviation Administration. But it mattered little. President Gerald R. Ford, my boss, just returned from China, had gone to the *Arizona* to participate in the 34th anniversary commemoration of the attack that plunged the nation into the war, the "date of infamy." As his advance representative for the event, I had worked hard to coordinate all pieces for his arrival on the very day and hour the first planes appeared over Battleship Row. Neither the Secret Service nor I, however, had any idea that some local vintage-plane owner would add an unusual depth of realism to the morning. What realism! As the *Zero* roared into view, the agents' immediate reaction was to reach for their holstered revolvers from underneath suit jackets. Stunned, my reaction was to pop my head skyward and watch him zoom across toward the SubPac piers. We saw him no more. A surprised but settled president, First Lady Betty Ford, chief of staff Dick Cheney, Pacific Fleet commander Admiral Noel Gaylor, and their small entourage and agents then proceeded into the Memorial. I closely followed. Normalcy quickly returned to Pearl Harbor, but my advance duties continued.*

The Attack

The Imperial Japanese Navy (IJN) dispatched two separate task forces to attack Hawaii. On 26 November 1941, the principal group, the Pearl Harbor Strike Force, commanded by Vice Admiral Chuichi Nagumo, and the Combined Fleet battleship support group, commanded by its fleet commander Admiral Isoroku Yamamoto, began departing Japanese waters. Of the 31 Japanese ships, the Striking Force contained the six large carriers, and the support force two battleships. An Advanced Expeditionary Force included 28 submarines, with five midget submarines attached. The carriers and their ultimate destiny were:

IJN *Akagi* (Nagumo's flagship)
Sunk at Midway, 4 June 1942

IJN *Kaga*
Sunk at Midway, 4 June

IJN *Soryu*
Sunk at Midway, 4–5 June

IJN *Hiryu*
Sunk at Midway, 4–5 June

IJN *Shokaku*
Sunk at Philippine Sea, 19 June 1944

IJN *Zuikaku*
Sunk at Leyte Gulf, 26 October 1944

Nagumo launched 353 attack aircraft in two waves from two hundred miles north-northeast of Oahu. The first wave reached the U.S. Pacific Fleet headquarters base at Pearl Harbor, the main target, at 0755 on Sunday, 7 December 1941,† achieving

---

* Later I heard that federal authorities had gone after the pilot for violating restricted air space. Otherwise, I have no idea what was the disposition. SubPac, by the way, stands for Submarine Forces, Pacific Fleet, headquartered in Southeast Loch.

Of the approximately 50 events I advanced for President Ford in 1975–76, two had a particular historic significance I will always remember. The most momentous was the visit to New York Harbor on 4 July 1976, our Bicentennial day, and the other was to the *Arizona* Memorial. I felt honored and privileged to be chosen to help lead these events.

† In Tokyo, the date was the eighth. In Washington, D.C., the hour was 1255.

complete surprise. The Japanese also attacked airfields at Hickam, Kaneohe, Ford Island, Ewa, Bellows, and Wheeler and other military installations at the same time, and then withdrew. Three types of naval aircraft comprised the principal striking force:

Mitsubishi A6M5 *Zeke*
Fighter-bomber

Mitsubishi A6M11 *Zero*
Fighter-bomber

Aichi 3A2 *Val*
Dive bomber

Nakajima B5N2 *Kate*
Torpedo-bomber

Ninety-six U.S. ships were present. Seven battleships, the primary targets, were moored alongside Ford Island in Battleship Row, and the eighth, *Pennsylvania*, was in dry dock across the channel. The battleships and their immediate status after the 110-minute attack were:

USS *Nevada* (BB-36)
Damaged, got underway, grounded on side of channel

USS *Oklahoma* (BB-37)
Sunk and capsized at berth, rested with superstructure on bottom

USS *Arizona* (BB-39)
Sunk at berth, blasted apart, burned

USS *Tennessee* (BB-43)
Damaged

USS *California* (BB-44)
Sunk at berth

USS *Maryland* (BB-46)
Damaged

USS *West Virginia* (BB-48)
Sunk, settled in shallow water at berth

USS *Pennsylvania* (BB-38)
Damaged

Other ships sunk or damaged included: three cruisers damaged, four destroyers damaged, one minelayer (USS *Oglala* [CM-4]) sunk, one auxiliary (USS *Utah* [AG-16]) sunk (capsized) and one heavily damaged. All ships sunk or damaged were later salvaged, rebuilt, and saw further action against the enemy except for *Arizona* and *Utah. Oklahoma* was raised but not rebuilt. The United States had 394 aircraft in Hawaii, many obsolete or under repair. Losses were 97 navy and Marine Corps, and 72 army air forces (total 169), and 31 navy and 128 army air forces (159) damaged.

United States personnel casualties included 2,403 dead: 2,008 navy (most of them in the first 10 minutes, and half were on the *Arizona*); 218 army; 109 marines; 68 civilians. Wounded were 1,178: 710 navy; 364 army; 69 marines; 35 civilians. Decorations awarded included 16 Medals of Honor, 51 Navy Crosses, four (Army) Distinguished Service Crosses, and 53 Silver Crosses.

Japanese casualties were minimal: approximately 185 killed (55 air crewmen and the rest naval personnel) and one captured, a midget submarine commander who became America's first prisoner of war. The attackers lost 29 planes, one large sub, and five midget subs, one of which was taken intact and later shipped around the country for war bond rallies.*

Hawaii was but one of Japan's targets in launching the Pacific War. Air raids hit the U.S. possesions at Wake Island and Guam, and ships bombarded Midway in the Hawaiian Archipelego. On the 8th, troops landed in Malaya and near Luzon, Philippines, and on Hong Kong, and aircraft struck U.S. forces elsewhere in the Philippines, destroying most of the B-17s and P-40s at Clark Field.

Wilmingtonians at Pearl Harbor

On a personal note, at least 20 men—15 navy, 3 army air forces, and 2 army—from the area of my hometown of Wilmington and New Hanover County, North Carolina, were on duty at or near Pearl Harbor. Three were killed in action on board ships. One more, a naval aviator, sank the first Japanese vessel, a submarine, engaged in action following 7 December.

Those who died were:

USS *Arizona* Signalman First Class Harvey Howard Horrell, of 914 North 4th Street, previously reported as missing in action, was

* The midget submarine finally got to Wilmington for a few days in May 1944. I remember being thrilled to get close to it while on exhibit at Front and Market Streets downtown.

killed in action. His mother, Maggie J. Horrell, "was in tears last night as she spoke matters pertaining to her dead son. 'He enlisted in the navy at the age of 18 and almost since the time he received his preliminary training at Norfolk, Virginia, he has been stationed at places far distant from Wilmington.' For that reason, she said, she had not seen him for about 12 years." He was unmarried but had two brothers.[1]

Boatswains Mate Herbert Franklin Melton, son of Mr. and Mrs. Franklin Melton of Masonboro Sound, "died at his post aboard a U.S. vessel," according to a message his mother received. Melton, 25 (his birthday was December 7), graduated from New Hanover High School (NHHS) in 1936 and entered the navy that year. His wife and young son lived in Long Beach, California. He had two brothers and five sisters in North Carolina.[2]

USS *Shaw* (DD-393) Radioman Second Class Clyde Carson Moore, 23, an NHHS graduate, had served in the navy since 1939. His wife, Maie Waters Moore, of 215 Dawson Street survived him. Moore, "the second New Hanover County man known to have been killed while fighting for his country, died instantaneously in an explosion aboard his ship, a destroyer." His brothers Robert H. and Ralph E., both serving on ships in the Pacific, wrote letters home about it. His parents were Mr. and Mrs. J. R. Moore of Castle Hayne, "who are believed to have the distinction of having had more sons in the United States Navy than any other family in North Carolina." Six sons had enlisted in the navy. Two served in the 1920s. Another brother, Jack, was stationed elsewhere. Moore, one of 128 aboard *Shaw* who died, was buried in the St. Louis, Missouri, National Cemetery in August 1949. None of the bodies in that group was identified, and they were interred together. His wife remarried.[3]

Lawrence Homer Henderson of Hampstead, near Wilmington, was a seaman second class on board *California*. Taylor Marion Jeffords of Wilmington was a baker on the *West Virginia*. Civilian Justus Sistrunk of Wilmington, recently discharged from the army in Hawaii, was employed at Hickam Field. Wilmington army air forces Captain Colonel Brooke E. Allen, a B-17 pilot, took off from Hickam about 1140, circled around Diamond Head, and was airborne for about seven hours searching for the departed Japanese fleet. "Allen reported being sent out with information that there were two Japanese carriers to the south, but he found very shortly after takeoff one American carrier to the south. Then, following his personal feeling that the Japanese would have come from the north, he put his compass on 'N' and headed straight north. How close he ever came to the carrier task force he never knew but 'returned with minimum fuel and a heart full of disgust that I had been unable to locate them.'" His was one of 48 sorties that went out searching that day.[4]

Wilmingtonian Lieutenant Clarence Earle Dickinson, flying an SBD-3 Dauntless of Scouting (Squadron) Six off the USS *Enterprise* (CV-6), on 10 December, divebombed and sank the damaged and surfaced submarine I-170. It was the first enemy ship sunk after the Pearl Harbor attack.*

Pearl Harbor was the United States Navy's greatest disaster. The Hawaiian fleet was staggered but not crippled. For all its losses, American naval and military forces in Hawaii and the Pacific Fleet immediately began rebuilding for an uncertain and desperate future. The sneak attack—a national psychological shock wave—banded the citizens together as few other acts could have done. It catapulted the expression "Remember Pearl Harbor!" into a war-rallying cry. The Japanese gamble was a tactical victory but long-term strategic mistake. By design and

* The first U.S. ship to sink a Japanese vessel was the destroyer USS *Drayton* (DD-366) which dispatched a submarine on 24 December.

good fortune, the U.S. carriers had been at sea, and none were damaged. The Japanese lacked the U.S. sustained industrial capacity to build modern battleships and fast carriers, to produce carrier aircraft, and to train replacement carrier pilots. The principal decisive action in the subsequent Pacific naval war, therefore, would be between carriers and not battleships, a war of attrition the Japanese were incapable of winning.

Yamamoto, who had advised his government to avoid war with the United States, but believed the surest early road to military success was through the attack on Hawaii, warned after 7 December that Japan had "awakened a sleeping giant." Four days later Germany declared war on the United States, and the Allies had achieved through Axis belligerency what U.S. isolation and diplomacy had only deferred. America had been drawn into the war in both the Pacific and European theaters.

History will long remember what happened at Pearl Harbor and the president's "Date of Infamy" address before Congress on 8 December. As historian Walter Lord wrote, FDR's "speech was over in six minutes and war voted in less than an hour, but the real job was done in the first ten seconds. 'Infamy' was the note that struck home, and the word that welded the country together until the war was won."[5]

WDJ, Jr.

The Robbins Family

Rear Admiral Berton Aldrich Robbins, Jr.
U.S. Navy (Retired)

Berton Aldrich Robbins, Jr., called "Bob" or "Robby" by friends, was born on 27 August 1908 in Inwood, New York. In 1926, following high school graduation in his home town of Malden, Massachusetts, he enlisted in the Marine Corps. Appointed to the U.S. Naval Academy from the fleet in 1927, he was commissioned as an ensign in June 1931. His first assignment was on the battleship USS *Oklahoma* (BB-37), followed by service in the Asiatic Fleet in China on the tender USS *Black Hawk* (AD-9) and the gunboat USS *Whipple* (DD-217) from 1933–36. After duty on the heavy cruiser USS *Portland* (CA-33) from 1936–38, he served on the USNA faculty teaching ordnance in 1938–39. He returned to sea on the destroyers USS *Kilty* (DD-138) and USS *Tucker* (DD-374) whose station was moved from California to Pearl Harbor in 1941. On 6 December he was transferred to the destroyer USS *Shaw* (DD-373) in dry dock at Pearl.

When the *Shaw* was put out of commission during the Japanese attack, Robbins was temporarily assigned to the seaplane tender USS *Tangier* (AV-8) for the aborted Wake Island relief effort in December. Shortly thereafter he became a staff officer for the Pacific Fleet's Cruiser Task Force, commanded by Rear Admiral William W. "Poco" Smith, on the USS *Chicago* (CA-29), where he participated in the raid on Lae-Salamaua (Papua, 10 March 1942) and the Battle of the Coral Sea (5–7 May 1942). Smith shifted his flag to the USS *Astoria* (CA-34) for the Battle of Midway (3–6 June 1942) and the early Aleutians Campaign (summer 1942). Later, CRUTASKFOR commander Rear Admiral C. H. McMorris shifted the flag of the Cruiser-Destroyer Task Force, on which Robbins was serving, to the cruiser USS *Indianapolis* (CA-35) for the 1943 Aleutians Campaign (U.S. occupation of Adak, Attu, Kiska, and Amchitka), the Battle of the Komandorski Islands (26 March 1943), and later to the cruisers USS *Detroit* (CL-8) and USS *Richmond* (CL-9).

In November 1943 Robbins was assigned as prospective commanding officer of the new-construction destroyer USS *Leutze* (DD-481), with leave and training schools en route. He arrived at *Leutze* in the Bremerton, Washington, Navy Yard in February 1944. The ship was commissioned in March 1944 and entered Pacific service in August in Destroyer Squadron 56. *Leutze* participated in the amphibious assault on Peleliu (Palau Islands, September 1944); the Leyte Campaign (Philippines, October–December 1944), including the Battle of Surigao Strait (Leyte Gulf, 25–26 October 1944); the Lingayen Campaign (Luzon, Philippines, January 1945); and preparations for the amphibious assault on Iwo Jima (Volcano Islands, 17 February 1945). Here *Leutze* suffered a direct hit on the bridge from an enemy battery on Mount Suribachi, seriously injuring Robbins and four crewmen. He was removed for hospitalization at the Aiea Naval Hospital on Oahu and the Long Beach, California, Naval Hospital, where he arrived in April 1945.

He was recuperating and on limited duty at Long Beach until July 1947 when he was assigned to the Armed Forces Radio Service in Los Angeles. From March 1951 to June 1953 he served as commander, Rhine River Patrol and commander, U.S. Naval Facility, Schierstein, Germany, at the end of the occupation. In August 1953 he assumed command of the attack transport USS *Pickaway* (APA-222) in Transport Squadron One, in Korean waters. He served as director Far East Region, Office of the Assistant Secretary of Defense for International Security Affairs, from March 1955 to August 1958. His final assignment until retirement in November 1959 was as commander Service Squadron Six/Commander Service Force Sixth Fleet on board USS *Mississinewa* (AO-144) in Naples, Italy.

Robbins was promoted to lieutenant (junior grade) in June 1934, to lieutenant in July 1938, to lieutenant commander in June 1942, to commander in November 1942, to captain in April 1950, and to rear admiral on retirement.

He received the following decorations: Navy Cross (for Leyte Gulf), Silver Star (Iwo Jima), Bronze Star with Combat "V" (Lingayen Gulf and as *Leutze* commanding officer), and Purple Heart (Iwo Jima). The Navy Cross citation reads: "For extraordinary heroism as Commanding Officer of the USS *Leutze* in action against enemy Japanese forces in the Battle of Surigao Strait on October 25, 1944. Participating in a night torpedo attack against an advancing column of enemy battleships, cruisers and destroyers, Commander Robbins directed his ship through intense and prolonged enemy gunfire to launch a well executed attack and succeeded in retiring without damage to his vessel...(contributing) to the decisive defeat of the hostile force...." (*Leutze* is credited with helping to sink the battleship IJN *Fuso*.)

Mary Patricia O'Meara Robbins

Mary Patricia "Pat" O'Meara was born in Los Angeles on 8 September 1911, one of seven children of William Patrick and Katherine McCormick O'Meara, members of an old California family. Her maternal grandfather, Patrick Joseph McCormick, built the first railroad from San Diego to San Francisco. The work of her parents' German chauffeur, also an amateur photographer, fascinated her. Relatives gave her a German folding camera for her seventh birthday, and from that time on, she "worked at it." She shot all her classmates at St. Mary's Academy in Los Angeles, took pictures for the school yearbook, and kept a pictorial record of the debutante parties the year she made her debut at a gala party in the Los Angeles Biltmore Hotel.

She began photography as a hobby as a child. Her hobby might have remained just that had she not met her naval officer, Ensign Berton Robbins, at a society dance in Long Beach. Immediately after their marriage on 11 July 1933 they left for China on a navy transport where he would report for duty on a ship on the Yangtze River patrol station. She took shipboard pictures and after arriving in China learned enough Chinese to "wander around" by herself taking photographs. She ventured with camera to the Great Wall, into Peking's Forbidden City and Imperial Palace, and took pictures of Princess Der Ling, the last lady in waiting to the Empress Tsu Hsi (the "Old Buddha"), who became a close friend. She studied China and its people, history, and customs. From China, the Robbinses lived temporarily in Manila, Philippines, from where she added more photographs in her travels. She exhibited her pictures of China, and sold some, entered and won several national contests; and began working on assignment for national advertising agencies doing illustrative photography. She was well on her way in a new career.

She and her family had just moved to Honolulu when the Japanese attack changed everyone's life. With her husband's future duty uncertain after the *Shaw* blew up, she immediately began taking images of the attack's aftermath. Army Headquarters and naval intelligence issued her special passes and identification allowing her open access around Oahu. Because she was already under contract with Associated Press and had agreements to do several mainland newspaper and magazine layouts, she had a free run of Oahu. She took her two children along everywhere as she shot pictures of death and destruction, community life, the war effort, and civilian defense. Many of the photographs normally associated with the aftermath not taken at Pearl Harbor and the military bases are hers. The credits are given, however, to the Associated Press or as official army or navy photographs.

After she returned to California in August 1942, Pat continued to shoot Los Angeles society and Hollywood celebrities, many of whom became good friends. Her images over the years were published in national magazines including *Popular Photography, Look, Mademoiselle, Collier's*, and *Saturday Evening Post,* and in numerous newspapers.

The Robbinses had two children: Carroll Eloise Robbins, born in Shanghai, China, on 28 April 1934, and Berton A. Robbins III, born in Los Angeles on 23 March 1936.

After his retirement from the navy, the Robbinses lived in Palm Desert, Los Angeles, and Vista, California. He died on 4 December 1983, and Pat on 8 May 1988. Berton III, a 1958 Naval Academy graduate and career naval officer, died on 10 April 1992. All three are buried at Arlington National Cemetery.

Carroll Robbins Jones

Carroll Eloise Robbins married Lieutenant (Junior Grade) Wilbur D. Jones, Jr., in Naples, Italy, on 11 August 1959, where he was serving as her father's communications officer and flag lieutenant. They have three children: Patricia Jacobson of Champion, Michigan; David of Raleigh, North Carolina; and Andrew of Wilmington. They have raised their only grandchild, Carrie Jones, a Wilmington high school student, since she was two.

She and Wilbur have lived in Naples, Coronado, and Los Angeles, California, and Alexandria, Virginia, the latter for 28 years. In 1996 she retired following a 20-year career in the residential real estate business in Northern Virginia. In 1997 the Joneses moved to Wilmington, his native home town. She is a member of the Stamp Defiance Chapter, Daughters of the American Revolution, serves as a volunteer eucharistic minister for St. Mary Catholic Church, participates in local investment and book clubs, and enjoys gardening and reading. She is employed as a "full-time part-time" research analyst in Special Collections of the William Madison Randall Library, University of North Carolina at Wilmington.

"Pin-Ups from Home"

by Patricia O'Meara Robbins
Popular Photography Magazine, February 1944

War wives at home have an ideal opportunity to make photography a practical and worthwhile hobby. It is a mystery to me why more of us haven't taken it up in order to keep our faraway husbands posted on how Junior looks with a missing front tooth, or how his face beams as he tries on that new navy uniform he bought with the money Daddy sent him, how little Sue can undress all by herself now, or how fervent she looks when she kneels to say her prayers.

Besides, many of us have been blessed by being able to follow our husbands to other interesting lands where we saw many colorful sights and people. (I say "follow" our husbands because the typical navy wife usually catches up with her husband to find out that he is leaving for somewhere else the next day.) My own experience is typical of the photographic opportunities presented to navy wives. My husband was an ensign fresh out of Annapolis when we were married ten years ago, and he was immediately assigned to China. I tagged along.

I had been taking pictures ever since I was seven years old and had studied art. I loved the drama and color of old China, and spent much time capturing, both with still and movie cameras, the quaintness, the Oriental color, and the slow-moving pageant I found there. However, it was very difficult to obtain pictures of the Chinese themselves. They have a superstition that your little black box will capture their souls along with their images. Most of them would hide their faces or turn their backs when I approached with one of my Graphflexes ready for action. It didn't take long, though, to find some who would gladly let me "capture their souls" for a small coin.

I followed my husband over most of the Orient—usually finding that Uncle Sam wanted him somewhere else just as I caught up with him. From Shanghai I played follow-the-leader with him to Hong Kong, then to Peking, Nakow, Tsingtao, Chingwangtao and Shankaikuan, where the Great Wall reaches the sea, clicking my camera shutters merrily all the way.

My daughter, Carroll Eloise, was born in Shanghai a year after we were married, and almost immediately I began keeping a camera record of her week-to-week changes. My husband and I did manage to make a trip together over the Great Wall of China by sedan chairs, and I made a film record of this colorful trek.

Then on to Manila where I was on hand to take movie shots of the historical first landing of the China Clipper in Manila Bay. Then more playing hop-scotch from place to place—Olongapo, Cavite, and Baguio in the Philippines, and on to Tokyo, Yokohama, and Kobe in Japan. Altogether we spent three years and hundreds of pieces of film and dozens of flashbulbs in the Orient. Since then there have been Guam, Midway, Wake, and four trips to Hawaii. I have my own photographic exhibits in many of the countries I have visited.*

I was in Hawaii when the war broke out and was fortunate to be able to help record a bit of history in the making there. I made pictures for Associated Press as a pinch hitter until they could get a staff photographer. (It seems their regular cameraman was Japanese and authorities had impounded his camera when Pearl Harbor was bombed.)

For a couple of weeks after the outbreak of war, my life as a newspaper photographer in Honolulu

* Of course, Carroll accompanied her mother. Ripley's *Believe It or Not* in 1935 featured Carroll as the youngest white child ever "to take a chair" on the Great Wall of China. She was present for Manila's China Clipper flight. In the Manila Hotel, the Robbinses lived next door to General Douglas MacArthur and his sister-in-law, Mary MacArthur, widow of Admiral Arthur MacArthur, who acted as his hostess between marriages.

was rather a ticklish business. No one was allowed to carry a camera on the streets without the army's OK. I had to get permission and a photographer's card from army intelligence. More than once when I was out taking pictures, a "doing his duty" soldier came running at me with his rifle aimed squarely at my stomach. From the looks on the faces of these soldiers, they were just about ready to shoot first and ask questions afterward. (I always thought I would feel very foolish perforated—people could see through me easily.)

My habit of doing my own developing and printing—even in far-off lands—has found me mixing my solutions in some of the oddest places, and projecting by means of such queer contraptions that only facetiously could be referred to as enlargers. I had my two-by-four bathroom blacked out in Hawaii and borrowed an enlarger that looked like a shoe box with a strange bulge at one end and some sort of lens at the other. A good hot day spent in such a cubbyhole, coupled with the anticipation of seeing whether the next negative would bring a salon print or just an everyday shot, plus the excitement when I would on occasion find a print that had possibilities, left me a bit moist and not a little wilted.

The only way my husband, who has been in virtually every major naval engagement in the present war, has been able to keep well-acquainted with his children is through photography. He takes great delight in receiving pictures of his children from me regularly—and I have taken hundreds of them since birth—since he has had to be away from home so much of the time. In the past three years he has been able to be with us only two months. I try to mirror my husband's America—his family—for him. I try to capture every new expression on our children's faces, every new trait—especially when these traits are in any way characteristic of their Daddy. But I try particularly to take pictures of the children *doing* something rather than obviously posed shots.

I have done many morale shots and publicity photographs as one of my contributions to the war effort, but how better could I add to navy morale than by making pin-ups of my family (and including myself occasionally) for my navy man? Pictures of his children mean more to him than all of Hollywood's glamour girls or Varga's filmily-clad curvaceous creatures.

How better could my husband get his mind off the rigors of a heavy siege of duty as an admiral's aide in action at Midway...or after strenuous days in the South Pacific and more recently in the Aleutians—than by opening a fresh package of photographs of his children to find one showing his son "bulging" the muscles of his right arm to an admiring sister or mischievously popping his sister's soap bubble? One photo, I know, interested him especially. It showed his son wearing one of his Dad's navy officer's caps and looking into a mirror that he compared with the picture of his Dad on the table in front of him. Another which found a soft spot in my husband's heart was a shot of the two youngsters standing on a wharf with their backs to the camera, Daddy's ship put out to sea. Daddy's ship, of course, could be seen in the background.

Other pictures in the photo-books I sent my husband show scenes taken during the precious minutes we were able to be together—our trip over the China Wall, and a shot taken at home showing both children with outstretched hands while their Daddy reached into his pockets for a coin for them. These pictures, I know, mean almost everything to my husband. Time changes youngsters fast, but these pictures have kept him up to date.

I have trained the children to pose ever since they were babies, and consequently they now fall automatically into a pose that looks as natural as a ship standing in the harbor. My children, who are now about seven and nine years old, have their own cameras and have made wonderful headway learning to develop and print. The thrill my husband gets out of receiving pictures taken and finished by Berton and Carroll is mirrored in the enthusiastic letters he sends them...and his praise of their work is one of the high spots of their lives.

And the photo-sending isn't all one-sided either. Prints my husband sends us keep our memories of him always fresh and intimate. Witness my son's rather touching remark to a friend: "I do too know what my Daddy looks like—I see his picture on momma's dresser." *(Ugh! We* never *called her momma. Those were* her *words, not ours.)*

"Navy Wife Tells Life in Hawaii—

Everything on Islands Geared to War Effort and Under Martial Law"

"There is no social life in Hawaii today," reported the *Los Angeles Times* in a 22 August 1942 interview with Pat Robbins. "Everything there is geared to the war effort and people have readjusted their lives to conditions under martial law 'most admirably.'"

"With the vanishment of the social scene in Honolulu went the once gay and carefree set of 'navy wives'; instead of cocktail parties at Waikiki Beach they attend first-aid and other emergency defense classes. People of the islands have had a taste of the horrors of war and are fighting back 'with all they've got.' The picture of Honolulu and other islands of the Hawaiian group was given yesterday by Mrs. Berton A. Robbins, Jr., wife of a navy lieutenant commander, who recently arrived in Los Angeles. She was accompanied by her two children, Carroll, 8, and Berton A. III.

"The paramount problem in the islands today is the entertainment of the armed forces and the vast number of civilian defense workers, according to Mrs. Robbins. 'The United Service Organizations have done all within their means, but their means are limited,' she said. 'The job of entertaining those thousands of men is a tremendous one and one we have to do."

SATURDAY MORNING. **Los Angeles Times** AUGUST 22, 1942.

Navy Wife Tells Life in Hawaii

Everything on Islands Geared to War Effort and Under Martial Law

There is no social life in Hawaii today; everything there is gea[illegible]o the war effort and peo[illegible] readjusted their lives to [illegible]s under martial law [illegible]imirably."

[illegible]he vanishment of the social scene in Honolulu went the once gay and carefree set of "Navy wives;" instead of cocktail parties at Waikiki Beach they attend first-aid and other emergency defense classes.

People of the islands have had a taste of the horrors of war and are fighting back "with all they've got."

This picture of Honolulu and other islands of the Hawaiian group was given yesterday by Mrs. Berton A. Robbins Jr., wife of a Navy lieutenant commander, who recently arrived in Los Angeles. She was accompanied by her two children, Carroll, 8, and Berton A. III.

Lieut. Comdr. Robbins was executive officer of the destroyer Shaw at Pearl Harbor when the Japanese made their treacherous attack, but escaped unhurt, Mrs. Robbins said.

The paramount problem in the islands today is the entertainment of the armed forces and the vast number of civilian defense workers, according to Mrs. Robbins.

"The United Service Organizations have done all within their means, but their means are limited," she said. "The job of entertaining those thousands of men is a tremendous one and one we have to do."

Mrs. Robbins is a native of Los Angeles and attended St. Mary's Academy in Inglewood and Ramona Convent in Alhambra. She is visiting her mother, Mrs. W. P. O'Meara, at 129 S. Van Ness Ave.

VISITORS FROM HAWAII—Mrs. Berton A. Robbins, wife of Navy officer, yesterday told how social life in Hawaii has vanished under war conditions. She's visiting here and is shown with children, Carroll, 8, left, and Berton A. III, who is 6. Times photo

Los Angeles Times article and photo, 22 August 1942, after their return to California.

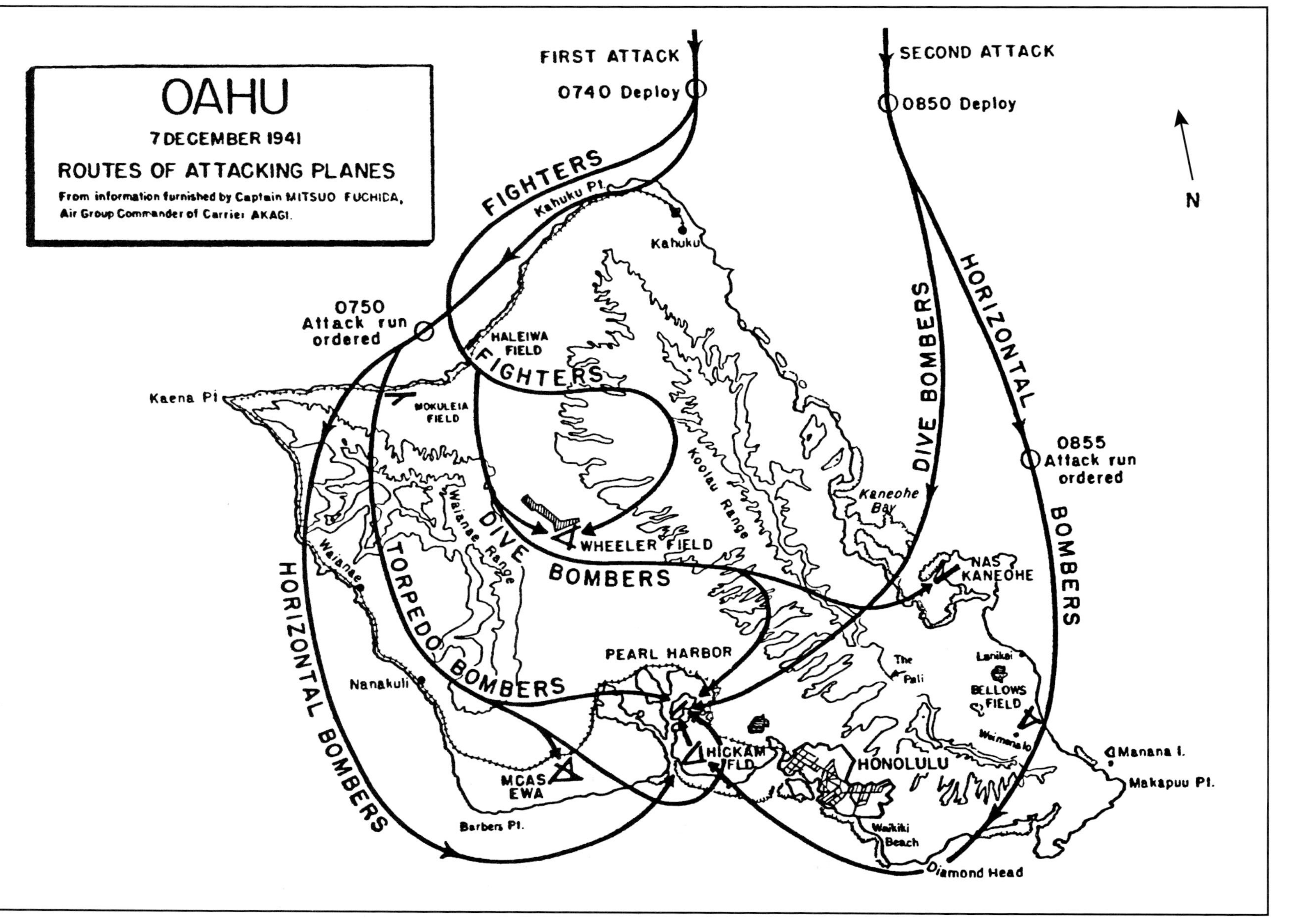

Oahu. Map of routes of attacking Japanese aircraft, 7 December 1941.

Naval Historical Center and others

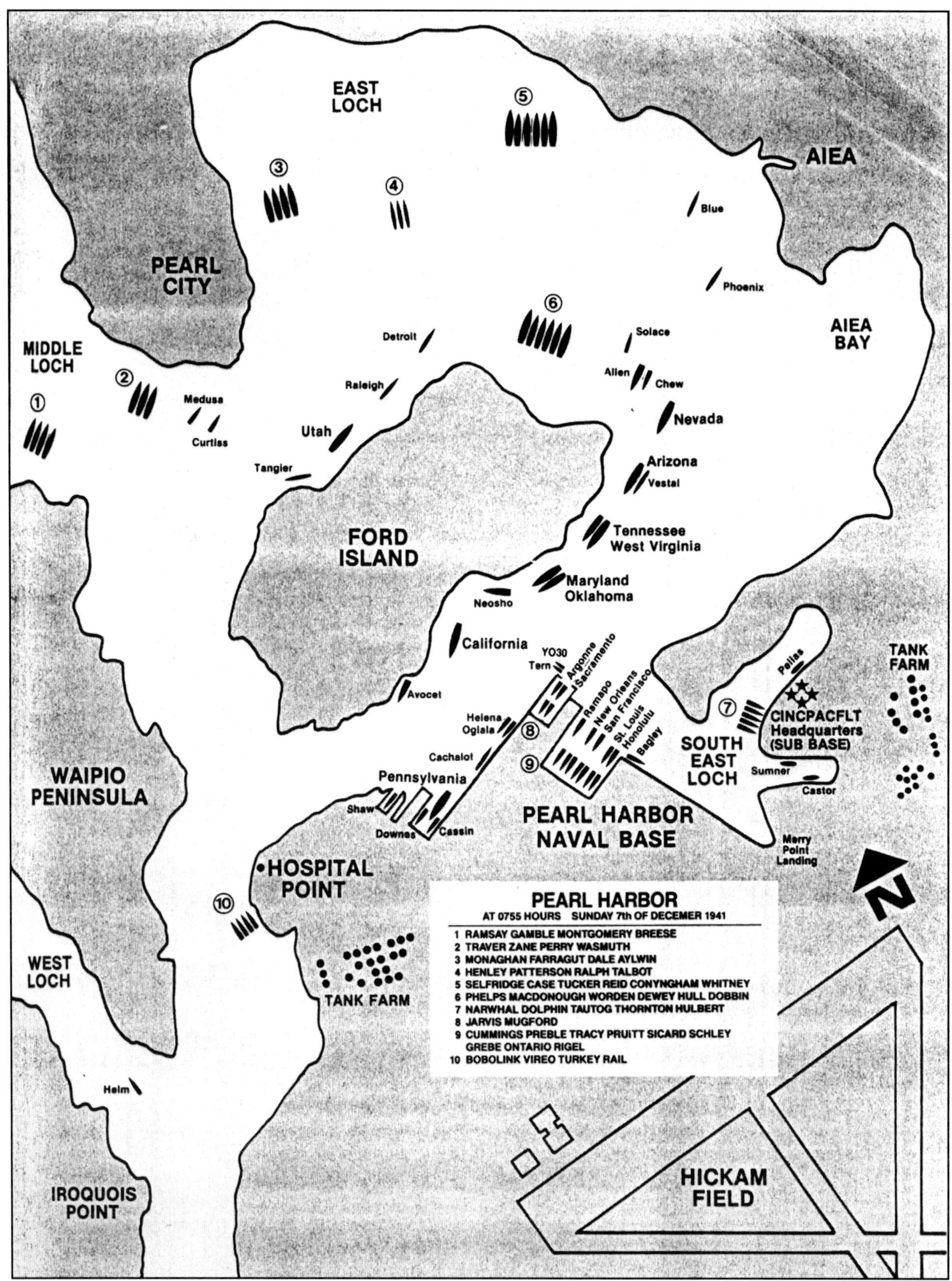

Pearl Harbor. The fleet in port at 0755, 7 December 1941.

Naval Historical Center and others

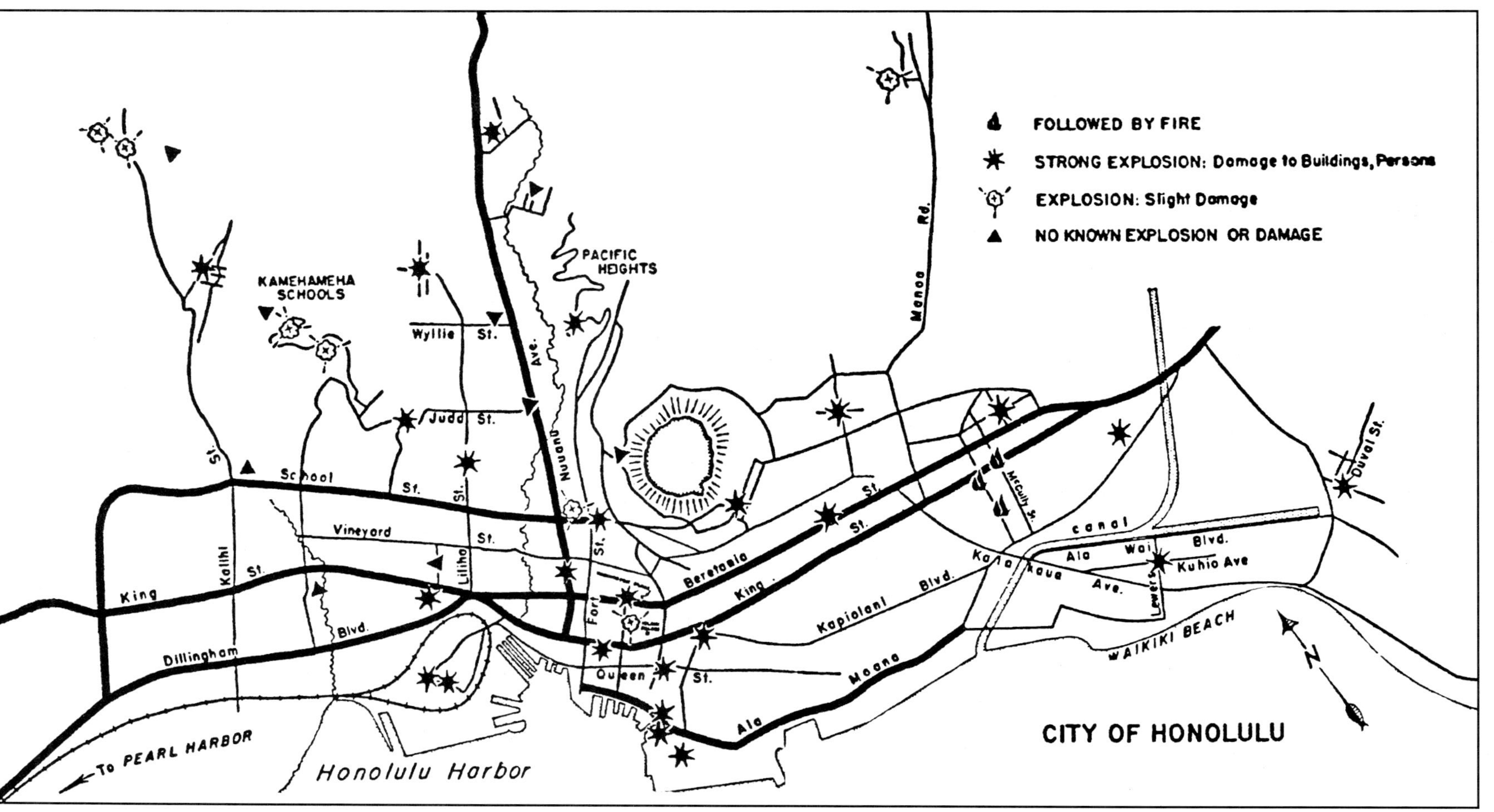

Honolulu. Projectile impact areas on 7 December 1941.

Gwenfread Allen, *Hawaii's War Years*, and others

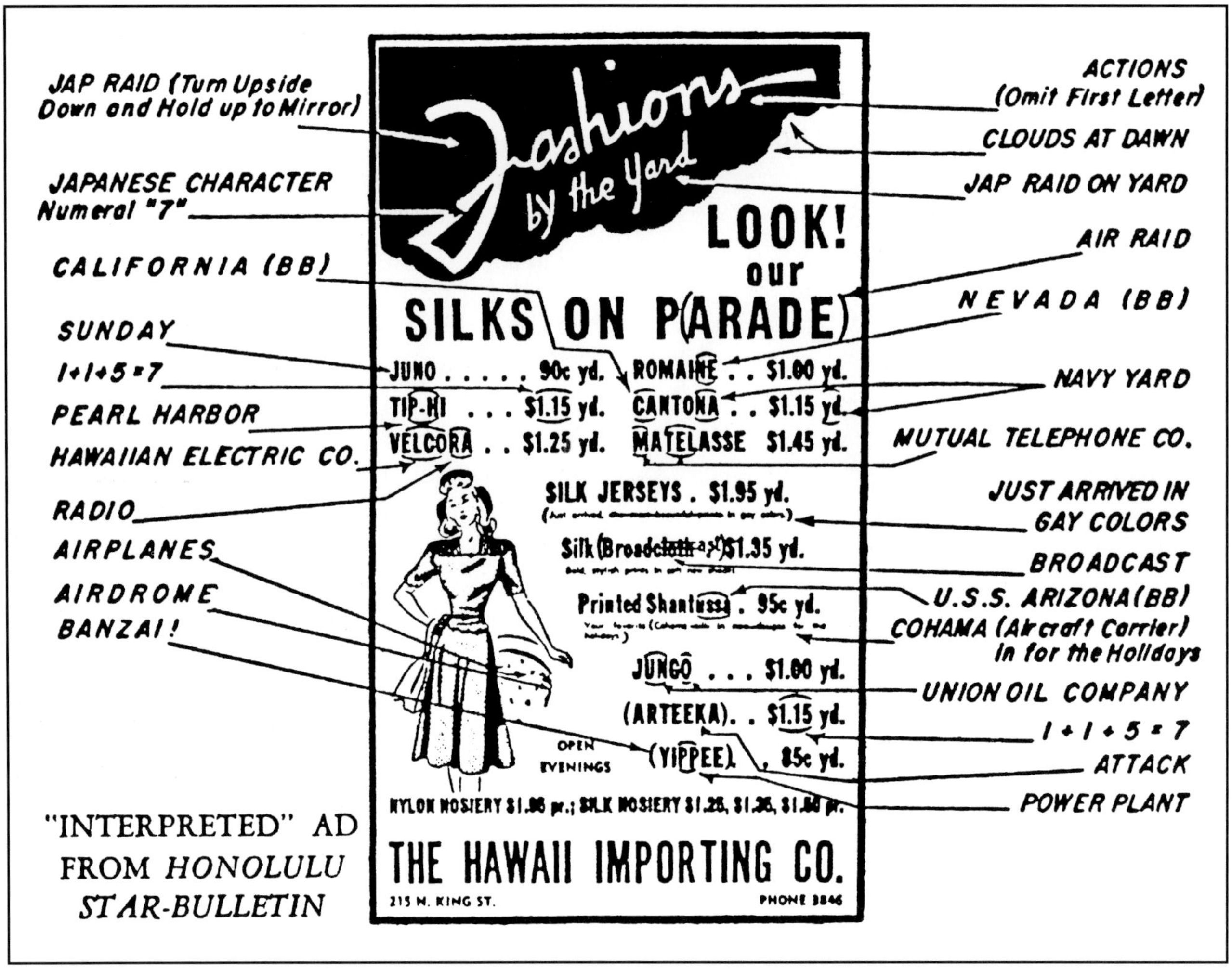

JAP RAID (Turn Upside Down and Hold up to Mirror)
JAPANESE CHARACTER Numeral "7"
CALIFORNIA (BB)
SUNDAY
1+1+5=7
PEARL HARBOR
HAWAIIAN ELECTRIC CO.
RADIO
AIRPLANES
AIRDROME
BANZAI!

Fashions by the Yard
LOOK! our
SILKS ON PARADE
JUNO . . . . . 90c yd. ROMAINE . . $1.00 yd.
TIP-HI . . . $1.15 yd. CANTONA . . $1.15 yd.
VELCORA . . $1.25 yd. MATELASSE $1.45 yd.
SILK JERSEYS . $1.95 yd.
Printed Shantussa . 95c yd.
JUNGO . . . $1.00 yd.
(ARTEEKA). . $1.15 yd.
(YIPPEE) . 85c yd.
OPEN EVENINGS
THE HAWAII IMPORTING CO.
215 N. KING ST.

ACTIONS (Omit First Letter)
CLOUDS AT DAWN
JAP RAID ON YARD
AIR RAID
NEVADA (BB)
NAVY YARD
MUTUAL TELEPHONE CO.
JUST ARRIVED IN GAY COLORS
BROADCAST
U.S.S. ARIZONA (BB)
COHAMA (Aircraft Carrier) In for the Holidays
UNION OIL COMPANY
1+1+5=7
ATTACK
POWER PLANT

"INTERPRETED" AD FROM *HONOLULU STAR-BULLETIN*

Advertisement interpreted as Japanese intelligence mechanism.

Honolulu Star-Bulletin

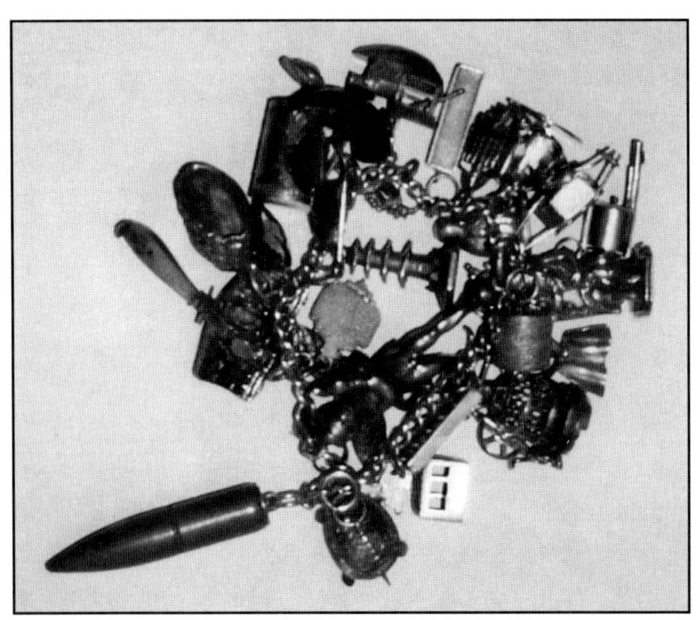

Patricia O'Meara Robbins' charm bracelet showing 30-caliber bullet, *lower left*, found lodged in her husband's jacket on 7 December 1941.

Authors' Collection

Chapter 1

"A Time of Fear and Anxieties": The Immediate Post-Attack

When the last Japanese planes broke off their shattering assault on Pearl Harbor, they headed northwest to overtake carriers that were already speeding back to Japan. In the pattern of destruction they left behind, survivors of the attack tended to their wounded, battled the fires and counted their dead. Surrounded by wreckage and human suffering, they felt stranded and defenseless—"like you had four flat tires out in the desert," as one soldier put it. Looming in their minds also was the threat of invasion—the pervasive fear that the Japanese would follow their raid by landing in the islands. "They could have come in canoes and we couldn't have stopped them," said another soldier. Invasion rumors and false reports were everywhere. Japanese paratroops were said to have landed on the big island of Hawaii. Word spread that Honolulu's water supply had been poisoned. The capture of the midget submarine...escalated the invasion fears: perhaps it was on a reconnaissance mission to pave the way for landings.[1]

Arthur Zich in the informative *Time-Life* Books series on World War II poignantly stated the situation in Hawaii after 7 December: near desperation, bewilderment, and fear. The tensions were legitimate. Hawaiians had no way of knowing that less than 48 hours after the attack, Combined Fleet commander Admiral Isoroku Yamamoto had ordered his staff to prepare plans for the invasion, setting in motion the most ambitious Japanese operation of the war.

"It was a time of fears and anxieties, justified and otherwise," wrote Stanley D. Porteus in 1947, "of precautions, both foolish and necessary; of altruism and selfishness; of sudden bursts of irritation and flashes of wry humor. Jitters were not apparent, but the underlying strain showed itself at odd moments and in unlooked-for ways. Though it may have been the valor of ignorance, civilian spirit stayed high. But, without a doubt, rumor took a firm hold on the Armed Forces. There must have been treachery somewhere, thought they, or this horrible thing couldn't have happened. Many of the utterly false statements then current on the mainland could only have had their origin here."[2]

Oahu in early 1942, 3,900 miles from Tokyo and 2,300 from San Francisco, was rapidly becoming the pivotal U.S. base between the Japan's imperialist expansion and the U.S. West Coast. "The conquest and occupation of Hawaii constituted an important part of the Japanese Empire's war strategy," wrote historian John J. Stephan. "Seizure of the entire archipelago was a major objective in the Combined Fleet's long-term plans from the day after Pearl Harbor until the Battle of Midway....Well into 1943 [Japanese] civilians prepared scenarios of Hawaii's political administration, economic reconstruction, and social transformation under Japanese occupation."[3] Not only wôuld occupation essentially place control of the Pacific in their palm and force America to protect their own shorelines, but Japanese officials realized that Yamamoto's "sleeping giant" would use Hawaii as the ideal springboard for what was certain to be its future counteroffensive.

We witnessed total destruction of houses in the Pearl City area, and knew children must have lived in them as bent and burned remnants of toys were scattered in the debris. We saw trucks reduced to flattened metal, almost unrecognizable, and a car riddled with bullet holes still containing several dead bodies. The smell of burning oil was pungent and hung in the air for a long time. I recall seeing oil slicks from the deck of the troop ship we sailed on more than eight months later when we returned to California.

On 9 December, Chief of Naval Operations Admiral Harold R. Stark told Admiral Husband E. Kimmel at Pearl he expected the Japanese to occupy Midway, Maui, and the island of Hawaii before Oahu. Kimmel replied his carriers were all right, Pearl fuel farms and workshops were intact, morale and determination were high, and that if abandoned or lost, Oahu had no substitute as a U.S. forward base. He asked immediately for more weapons, aircraft, troops, and workmen to defend and rebuild the Islands. Kimmel wrote, "...The loss of battleships commits us to the strategic defensive until our forces can again be built up. However, a very powerful striking force of carriers, cruisers and destroyers survives. These forces must be operated boldly and vigorously on the tactical offensive in order to retrieve our initial disaster."[4]

Any likely attack on Oahu would come on the northwestern side. Defending it was the army's job, taking the fight to the Japanese was the navy's. The army was organized as the Hawaiian Department for defensive purposes only. The army air forces in Hawaii soon became the 7th Air Force at Hickam Field and its satellite fields at Wheeler and Bellows. Pearl contained dry docks, oil tanks, 58 miles of roads, its own railroad and a huge ammunition depot, naval air base, a marine railway, submarine base, radio communications center, and anti-aircraft batteries. As soon as the smoke lifted, workers began a 24-hour schedule of repairs and new construction. The shipyard expanded to seven times its prewar capacity of storehouses, shops, new equipment, and production capability, with more than seven hundred ships receiving repairs during the war.* Ship berthing capacity doubled to seven miles.

The Japanese essentially left Hawaii alone, most definitely after the Battle of Midway. Several instances of submarines firing on the other islands were reported for a few months. On 3 March 1942, two long-range four-engine seaplanes from Wotje refueled from a submarine at French Frigate Shoals en route to bomb Oahu. Bad weather and effective anti-aircraft fire chased them away, and their several bombs dropped unobtrusively in the Tantalus Mountains.

The Immediate Reactions

Oahu had two immediate priorities: to rescue the civilian and military wounded and the dying, and to prepare for a possible invasion. Security agents began picking up enemy aliens considered dangerous, including 370 Japanese, 98 Germans, and 14 Italians. Most of the civilian property damage (estimated at $500,000) had been caused by falling anti-aircraft shells, not from Japanese bombs.† Civilian casualties on the seventh were 170.

The next weeks were hectic learning how to live under strict martial law and making the most of daylight hours. Mother was able to borrow a not always reliable car from an unmarried classmate of Dad's gone to sea. It was evidently common to buy an old jalopy for transportation from someone rotating back to the mainland, and then selling to a newcomer. Our Buick had been left in storage in Los Angeles, and at least this noisy pile of tin was a means of getting around. We kids thought it was funny and called it the "Ooga Ooga," named for the sound of the horn—when it worked. We must have been cause for a lot of humor; a nice-looking young professional photographer taking pictures for the Associated Press, naval intelligence, and army headquarters tooling around restricted areas with two wise-guy kids insisting they were Hawaiians, in a half-broken-down jalopy that shook, rattled, and wheezed as if dying.

The six-month-old Major Disaster Council was the first civilian volunteer agency to begin operations, renamed by Governor Joseph B. Poindexter as the Office of Civilian Defense.‡ Medical supplies

* Perhaps the most dramatic ship repair job was the sensational 72-hour turnaround of the carrier USS *Yorktown* (CV-5) from Coral Sea battle damage in May 1942 to being available for the Battle of Midway in June.

† One eyewitness may have seriously understated the damage. "Honolulu's scars consisted of a couple of buildings destroyed, a few others partially destroyed, some splattered with blast fragments, and a few inconsequential craters on the road sides." [Stanley D. Porteus, *Blow Not the Trumpet: A Prelude to Peril* (Palo Alto, Calif.: Pacific Books, 1947), 183]

‡ In February 1942 the territorial OCD employed 3,013 full-time staff augmented by 14,000 volunteers. By November, with the danger of imminent invasion passed, the OCD cut payrolls drastically, stopped construction projects, reduced or eliminated subsidies to other agencies, and replaced many paid workers with volunteers.

and blood plasma were in short supply, but soon blood donors were lining up. Honolulu Police Chief W. A. Gabrielson's first radio message to the people was to "stay calm and stay home."[5] The police and the fire departments asked for volunteers and were so swamped with the response they could not utilize all the untrained men.

The OCD placed guards at every crossroad and bridge armed with clubs, knives used for cutting sugarcane, and obsolete guns. By midnight 8 December, 3,800 volunteers were on duty in Oahu and thousands of others of the other islands. Officials feared that public utilities would be sabotaged and painted some buildings and structures with camouflage colors (including the famous Aloha Tower on the waterfront), built dummy plywood airplanes and dispensed them in fields. "But there was no purpose in arming the home guard with fake guns. Personal revolvers, pistols, rifles and shotguns, antique or not, were now in demand as first-line weaponry....Hawaiians themselves were too busy for the most part to complain" about shortages, even though the belief was Europe was the [Allied] priority.[6]

"Once it got dark, it was almost worth your life to go outside," one observer remembered. "What with the impact of the attack itself and the rumors, there were a lot of itchy trigger fingers around....One heard more than just a few rifle shots ring out on those first couple of nights after the attack."[7] For weeks thereafter, whenever a sliver of light punctured a blackout some people took the opportunity to fire a few rounds. Some offenders were punished. Try putting toothpaste on a brush or taking a bath in the dark, more than one person moaned.

In his diary entries of 12 December, Marine officer Cornelius C. Smith, Jr., wrote:[8]

> ...I got a chance to see the civilian population at war....Soldiers abound downtown, and there are guards everywhere. The Hawaiian Gas & Electric Company on Kamehameha Boulevard all sandbagged and protected with machine guns. The Matson docks are heavily guarded. The telephone company on Fort Street is alive with uniforms, and so are King Street, Beretania, Bishop and the Ala Moana. All of the stores have butcher tape on their windows. They are interesting. Some are strictly utilitarian in design; others are patterned works of art; geometric designs, floral patterns, 'Vs' (for 'Victory,' I suppose), and so on. A marvelous thing is the human spirit.
>
> Stores are closing at 3:30 p.m. now. There are only cash sales. Gasoline is rationed, 10 gallons per month to each customer. In the Piggly Wiggly chain store the shelves were only half-filled. The town is under martial law, and the Army Provost Marshal has superseded the Territorial Judge. Blackout offenders and petty criminals are hit with a heavy hand. The blackout was novel for a day or two, but now it's a bore. You don't dare let a light show. Civilian Defense people are roaming streets at night shooting out lights in houses. Willful offenders may be fined $5,000 and jailed for five years. Early offenders (those being picked up now) are held on $100 bail. Most are poor and can't pay, but that is the way of it. There is no more liquor available, and the pubs are all padlocked. Lau Yee Chai's, Waikiki Tavern, The South Seas, Trader Vic's—all have bolted their doors and shuttered their windows. Pity.

Initial requests from islanders to the Mainland were for maps of Hawaii, flashlights, and batteries. Merchants helped by providing residents with whatever they had of blankets, flashlights, emergency equipment, candles, and blackout material. Authorities closed grocery stores for a day while stocks were inventoried, and halted liquor sales. Restaurants had to close for blackouts, and canteens fed volunteers.

Food was a major anxiety. In December Hawaii had enough food to last about six weeks for the civilians until the army canceled many purchase orders and fed its troops on field rations. Because Japanese submarine interference was negligible, food and other supplies soon began arriving from the Mainland in some quantity.

Finding food had become increasingly difficult as the very few shipments coming in gave priority to military personnel, hospitals, pregnant women, and real small children. We didn't seem to fall into any category. We would go to the store with Mother and find the usual powdered milk, canned peaches, some kind of gluey cereal mixture, brown bread, canned fish, canned peas, and sometimes Spam. There were other things from time to time, but I lost weight the first few months until regular shipments began to arrive. To this day I gag at the thought of powdered milk, pimento cheese, and any kind of tinned meat (not Spam).

We were having these items for dinner sitting at a little table by the window that overlooked the street and sidewalk. It was becoming dark but the blackout curtains had not been drawn in order to feel the breeze from outside. We heard running steps and what must have been an MP or Civilian Defense person yell for the runner to stop. We had all been warned that in the beginning of experiencing strict rules of martial law, there were no second chances, and if caught, identify yourself. The running steps began again and then a loud bang, a pop really. It seemed to be right outside our window, but actually was down the street. A man had been shot for not following rules. A male defense worker who lived in our building, Dick Pennington, had gone to see what happened, and because our apartment was on the corner overlooking this area, stopped by to see if we were alright, particularly us kids. This is when we learned the man was dead.

Authorities began censoring outgoing U.S. mail, cables, and phone calls within two hours after the attack. The incoming mail was interesting. Submarine officer Lawson P. Ramage remembered, "I was absolutely amazed at the attitudes of the mothers telling their sons to get out there and kick you-know-what out of the Japanese. They were really belligerent, and they hadn't seen the thing up close the way we had....I never expected that something could stir up such emotion across the country."[9] The Marine Smith added, "I guess that years from now kids will see it in the history books, and maybe some kid will raise his hand wildly, wanting to tell how his grandfather shot down a Jap plane, or got wounded, or caught a spy. And the teacher may be an unimaginative soul who will shut the kid up—but that all belongs to another day."[10]

Censorship was intended to prevent information of military value from leaving Hawaii. People were warned not to speak of aircraft, ships, troop movements, the weather, morale, or the like. Censors tried to listen to every phone conversation. Callers had to notify censors in advance of their calls including any names to be mentioned, and could speak in English only. Censors also examined radio program scripts in advance and temporarily banned audience participation shows. Who were the censors? Retired teachers and business people, society girls, housewives, concert pianists, interior decorators, and others. "The postal censorship was by all odds the biggest task and that of which the average resident was most aware."[11] The necessary imposition nevertheless caused business difficulties, delayed the mail, and retarded the Mainland from understanding what was actually happening in Hawaii.

In spite of long lines for everything, being cut off most of the time from news of family and friends on the Mainland, the shortages of most daily necessities, curfew, blackout, having to always wear our ID bracelet or tag around the neck, and of course being forced to carry the cumbersome gas mask at all times, people continued on making the best of the situation, perhaps to the point of a live-today-to-the-fullest-for-tomorrow-may-never-come attitude.

Rumors circulated with the speed of light. The Japanese had landed at Barbers Point, Kaneohe Bay, Mount Tantalus, and Midway, Guam, and Wake had fallen. Dead Japanese pilots wore University of Hawaii or Honolulu McKinley High School rings. A renegade radio station was jamming U.S. military messages. Enemy battleships and cruisers were off Oahu's beaches and incoming landing craft were being taken under fire. The military fired at a large school of fish, thinking it was submarine. (One of the shells fell short and wrecked the Barber's Point railway.)* "Everybody felt silly after it was all over, but nobody had been hurt and everybody profited

* On New Year's Eve 1941, Japanese submarines shelled the islands of Hawaii and Kauai, causing little damage. Two weeks prior subs hit a pineapple cannery.

to some extent by the realistic battle practice," an observer noted.[12]

"A great many Mainland Americans believe that most of the Japanese in Hawaii are hiding in the sugar fields, ready at a signal to leap out and cut us down with their cane knives," wrote Blake Clark. "Most of these [rumors] were spread over the Mainland by a press correspondent from Hawaii before checking his information with official sources."[13] Why not? "Saboteurs Land Here" was a headline of the 8 December *Honolulu Advertiser*. During the first week of war, commercial radio stations were off the air. Citizens listened to the police radio for news and accepted factually reports of suspicious characters, burglars, prowlers, and more. Arrows had been cut in cane fields to point toward Pearl Harbor. Hawaiian Japanese had known about the raid in advance, and Japanese maids failed to go to work that Sunday morning. Newspaper advertisements carried warnings and instructions to local Japanese.

Flustered military wives returning to the Mainland in early 1942 found gullible listeners to their many rumors and opinions, and in no time the 48 states of course knew what was taking place. Perhaps the most amusing rumor was the report of a citizen to the police that a neighbor's dog was barking at night in code that sounded Japanese. The officer told the man it was more important that he find the dog receiving the signals. And, Hawaiians were certain the Japanese would attack again on 11 February, a holiday for the imperial family. After this did not materialize, rumors seemed to dissipate. As the spy mania died down, good humor returned.

Navy wife Evelyn W. Guthrie was a Red Cross volunteer. After Pearl Harbor, "we all plunged into activity. We were busy at the Red Cross headquarters and also involved in the urgent business of delivering surgical dressings to the naval hospital and to Tripler." Guthrie described picking up sailors from their ship that just arrived to take them into town. They passed cane fields and the airport where Hawaii National Guardsmen were posted. They were of Japanese descent, "and I could see the look of consternation on the faces of my passengers. A chief petty officer with four gold hash marks had the courage to speak up, 'Gosh, Ma'am, did the Japs win?'" They all laughed.[14]

Always we carried with us our ID cards, on a string around our necks mostly, and could not wander too far without our gas masks. For a number of months we had air raid drills, and several times they were not meant to be drills but thought to be the real thing. The sirens could go off at any time, and we were supposed to run for trenches, or at least get inside against a wall. This was a constant worry for our Mother when she was working and we were not with her. Being separated in case of attack must have been a recurrent nightmare. The sound of the sirens stayed with me for many years and always made me shake. Sometimes later in the war I would wake in the middle of the night in the house on Van Ness Avenue in Los Angeles and hear the wail of either a police car or ambulance and go cold with fear and lie for a long time remembering so many things.

There were air raids over the next several months, at least one at night. We kids were always told they were practice raids, but later I learned that at least two were not, and that enemy planes had been sighted approaching the island. I don't recall if the planes actually did anything or even flew over land, but given the jittery climate at that time an air raid based on the smallest rumor would have been plausible. We kids never really believed they were practices anyway, and Berton and I and our small friends had spent hours defending the island against "the Raiders" and were prepared. How strange and aggressive we children would be to the "politically correct" mothers of today who shield their children from warlike toys and games and therefore harm and corruption. Oh how they protect their children from unpleasantness, aggression, and loss of any kind (a game, a friend, a toy). My brother and I and our friends grew up to be stable, loving, morally and mentally competent, law abiding, tax paying, and compassionate citizens, who learned early and learned well a responsibility to our families, schools, communities, and ourselves, not seen in the overly protected young person today. Most of us were products of "single parent" homes, or "single mom" homes, and lived under a cloud of never knowing when and if we might ever see "Dad" again. Many did not. We expected only what we deserved, made the most of our own entertainment, and knew that we were privileged just to be Americans, proven by scenes of destruction and death and starvation seen in the movie newsreels, and Life *magazine.*

Martial Law

Martial law and blackouts went into effect on 7 December. Constitutional guarantees allowed citizens of the Territory of Hawaii were ignored. Territorial courts were closed from 8–16 December when they reopened for certain civil cases. In January 1942 the army allowed them to act as "agents of the military governor" in holding non-jury trials. For the first two weeks the public was satisfied with the imposition of martial law and provost courts system. But soon the realizations became apparent. Except in Honolulu the courts were secret, defendants received no copy of the charges and were often convicted of violating the "spirit" of some nebulous general order issued by the military. By the time Secretary of the Interior Harold Ickes appointed Ingram M. Stainback as governor in the late summer of 1942, replacing Poindexter whose term expired, it was obvious the federal government was displeased with military encroachments into Hawaiian civilian authority.*

People became well aware of the army provost marshal, Lieutenant Colonel Neal D. Franklin, "a big, black haired, six-footer, [who] brought informality into the court and human interest stories into the public press. Colonel Franklin is tough...fair and impartial." In the first six months he levied some $60,000 in fines, with a daily average of about one hundred cases, mostly blackout violations.[15] Military courts dispensed swift and often perceptive forms of justice,† sometimes arousing public protests about the military's authoritarian manner.

Hawaii's military governor assumed control of all three branches of the territorial government. His executive officer established headquarters in the Iolani Palace. The district troop commanders on the other islands became the military governor's deputies. The provost marshal forbade sales of any device that could be associated with espionage, including radio and photographic equipment, and forced ham radio operators to relinquish their equipment. Civilian film could be developed only with a permit, enforced by censors at all firms in that business. The most frequent such violation was photos of barbed wire; photographing any installation nonexistent before the war was prohibited.

In the days to follow we were fingerprinted, given identifications to wear at all times, inoculated for I can't remember what, blood-typed, and eventually issued gas masks. We watched as bomb shelters and trenches were built in every vacant lot, and as sand bags were loaded in front of shelters, along ridges of the trenches, in front of some buildings and even in some areas along the beaches. Store windows were taped, some with big "V For Victory" logos, makeshift blackout curtains were hung at windows, and barbed wire appeared both in town, at the hotels, and in some locations of the beach. We were instructed to pay particular attention to the barbed wire when we played up and down the beach, as it could really be dangerous to us. There had always been wire netting beyond the coral reefs to keep out the sharks, but now we had to contend with more boundaries. The beach was our playground and we spent hours wandering Waikiki, getting to know the "beach boys," the snack bar workers at the Outrigger Canoe Club and Moana Hotel, some regulars with surf boards, and even some of the entertainers (piano players and singers) who would sleep in the sun during the afternoon. These were our friends, as we had no other children to play with on a regular basis. Looking back on those months of no school and adventurous days, we must have been tagged "wild things" by more structured parents.

In the meantime, Mother seemed always to be busy taking pictures and having to drag us along much against our will. It was boring for us while she set shots, lighting, etc., and to stand around waiting to hand her something from her bag or hold a light (ugh). She had no choice of course, and I do recall her litany of

* By March 1943, civilian authorities had assumed most of the military governor's former functions. "Some people have called Hawaii's wartime government the only true fascism which has ever existed on American soil," a historian wrote in 1950. "Moreover, they see a complete return of civil rights...a tribute to the American form of government and way of life." [Gwenfread Allen, *Hawaii's War Years 1941-1945* (Reprint: Westport, Conn.: Greenwood Press, 1971), 183]

† For example, a person arrested and tried for speeding in an automobile would be sentenced by an army officer to donate a pint of blood.

admonishments to us about behavior. It was just as hard on a five going on six and seven and one-half year old not to become antsy after awhile. Having raised four children I find it remarkable she didn't lose her mind. Her temper, yes, and often!

Civilian Defense

On the morning of the seventh, the Hawaii Territorial Guard was activated, including the University of Hawaii ROTC, the Guard's nucleus, and several high school ROTC units. By nightfall it numbered 35 officers and 370 enlisted men. With their activation, Civilian Defense measures, some planned and some ad hoc, began implementation.

The blackout, essentially a preventive measure, "was, by all odds, the most telling consequence of the war, as far as the civilian population was concerned," Porteus remembered. "How many families it cemented, how many it disrupted, there is no telling...." but it probably brought them closer together. "...In many Honolulu homes the arguments were endless—which room to black out, how best to do it, who left the door open, who mislaid the flashlight, and so far into the nights or at least as late at ten o'clock when all Honolulu and his wife (but not his dog) went to bed. By military order, dogs were put to bed at dark."[16]

Berton and I were convinced that most of the children we knew close to our age were boring, which drew us closer together. We even reverted back to a kind of "pidgin Chinese" between us, which came very naturally to me especially. I was born in Shanghai, China, and until four and a half years old was raised by a Chinese amah who traveled to California with my parents and me. Ah Qwai was with us through the birth of my brother and stayed until 1938 when it was no longer possible to renew her work permit in spite of all the arm twisting from my grandfather with his friends in the Senate and Congress. War was inevitable and it was through Grampa's intervention she was able to enter the United States for the two-plus years she remained. Her sole responsibility was child care, period. My mother never bathed nor changed a baby. Nor did she ever get up in the middle of the night for a feeding. I spoke Chinese before English, which caused me to speak with an accent, mixing my "L's" and "R's" especially. Some of these part-Chinese, part-English words worked their way into our family vocabulary to stay. My brother learned enough Cantonese before Ah Qwai returned to China to participate in our special language. This drove Mother crazy, and frustrated everyone else. As a result of my Chinese pronunciation of words, I was forever after known in our large family as "Callo," and referred to myself as "Callo Lobbins," instead of Carroll Robbins as a little girl. Not until after starting school was it apparent I "talked funny" and was often teased; however, having a special language could also be very comforting.

Officials recruited block air raid wardens. One such warden, an elderly retired pipe fitter, "impressed by his sudden rise in importance, became something of a minor dictator in enforcement of regulations." Navy wife Peggy Hughes Ryan wrote that "peering through our windows in the dark, he would distinguish the glow of cigarettes or the radio tubes. At once he would startle us by pounding on the house and shouting 'Out those lights out!' Frantically we would throw a blanket over the radio and crush the offending cigarettes while our zealous warden threatened fines and jail sentences."[17] Another observer noted, "In some homes only one room was blacked out and the entire family huddled in it from dusk to bedtime, every half hour or so putting out the lights and opening the windows for fresh air. Blackout materials were scarce and many ingenious schemes were improvised. Paper tape and Christmas wrapping materials of blue cellophane rapidly disappeared from the stores."[18]

The army established curfews to keep unauthorized people off the streets, highways, parks, and beaches, to prevent subversive signaling, and reduce potential sabotage and danger during air raids. Between 1800 and 0600 lights were not allowed to be visible from the outside. So that people could get home before dark, the army ordered most Oahu business to close by 1630. Later the hours were staggered to reduce the "rush-hour" congestion on Honolulu streets. "When you visit friends in the evening, you go prepared to spend the night," a Hawaiian said in 1943. "The consequences of getting caught after curfew are too serious to risk."[19] Authorities went so far as to urge expectant mothers to go to the hospital during daylight if possible to avoid having "blackout babies." Sometimes the police or Red Cross Motor Corps had to drive them at night anyway.

Conditions gradually relaxed according to the sunset hour and seasons with an extension to 2100 for pedestrians and in September 1942 to 2000 for cars. Still, headlights had to be painted black except for a small circle of blue. For more than the first year, street lights did not burn, and persons hesitated to enter the intense darkness. Then they were fewer and dimmer than before the war. In July 1942 the total blackouts were reduced to dim-outs of 25-watt bulbs, many of them converted Christmas tree globes blackened except for a one-inch circle at the bottom, which could burn during blackout hours.*

Other measures taken such as bomb shelters, preparations for incendiary and other air raids, use of gas masks, and public education programs, were primarily protective measures. Old trucks and cars dotted potential aircraft landing areas such as parks and fields, including the Diamond Head vicinity. The civilian "Kiawe Corps" helped string barbed wire and cut brush to clear fields of fire on possible landing beaches. The army took over civilian airports and grounded all private planes. Rattling windows and momentary qualms were the result of frequent test gun firing.

In late January 1942 Mother's pictorial story on "Hawaiian Houseparty" was printed in the Los Angeles Examiner, *and a longer version in one of the national ladies magazines, possibly* Mademoiselle. *The story featured the same young women living together on Diamond Head with our friend Harriett Weaver. They all had jobs, but were post debutantes at heart, however, after the bombing really involved themselves in any helpful way allowed. Some married handsome young naval officers, and Berton and I happily participated in these weddings. We loved Diamond Head. Going up there meant party time, and that meant lots of FOOD, music, but mostly that Mother would have a good time and for a short while at least be happy. We kids were pretty much left alone and allowed to roam the beach within a reasonable area. Almost immediately after the Japanese raid on 7 December, barbed wire had been stretched along certain sections of beach along with small artillery embankments. This deterred not only would-be enemy invaders, but the Robbins kids from "accidentally" finding themselves in the surf.*

Occasionally we spent the night with Hazel Lewis or Harriett, or one of the other friends we visited, but more often we had to return to our apartment after dark. That became a fun game of "dodge the police," as this would always be after curfew and in darkness. My brother and I learned the rules quickly, but really had no idea what a dangerous game this was. We had dodged Civilian Defense on foot several times returning to our apartment from visiting a great lady, Betty Smith, wife of Rear Admiral William W. "Poco" Smith, who lived only a few blocks from us. We would run silently, stopping behind bushes, making sure no one was on foot patrol close by. This meant having to be very, very quiet, no coughing, no talking, no laughing, and absolutely no cheating to see who could get home before the others. Mother, Berton, and I would move as one, and never got caught. Mrs. Smith didn't like our doing this, but it became an accepted practice for the younger adults after dark trying to get home. I recall clearly how young wives would gather at our apartment for an evening, and send out a scout to see if all was clear before leaving. Coming down from Diamond Head was altogether different as it meant releasing the car brake and coasting down curves with no lights, seeing how far we could get before trying to turn over the engine on the Ooga Ooga. We were stopped a couple of times by MPs, but Mother flashed her press credentials inventing some story as to why we were late returning home. When questioned about our being with her under these circumstances, her stock answer was "what am I supposed to do with them, drown them?" She used this one for many years in various situations.

The islanders' biggest concern was over the requirement that every person must build a "scare puka" (hole) bomb shelter. Some residents dug their own, other hired contractors. "There was little to do at the office, so everyone hurried home, donned old clothes, and started to burrow in clay or volcanic ash, or to chip his way through layers of blue lava. The work was fine as mental hygiene and helped to cement neighborly relations."[20] A navy wife remembered digging. "But this cool, damp spot

* All blackout regulations ended in July 1944, but the 2200 curfew remained for another year.

was soon taken over by scorpions and the huge island toads known as 'buffos.' We absolutely refused to go there during air raid warnings, preferring bombs to crawling, jumping things."[21]

The OCD built community shelters near the waterfront, at hospitals and first aid stations, and near schools, stores, theaters, churches, and recreation centers. Because many parks and vacant lots had been taken for military use, finding spots for shelters was difficult. Volunteers dug numerous trenches (almost 10 miles worth) all over Honolulu and other populated areas, including school playgrounds, beautiful park lawns, and pineapple fields to be harvested, using zigzagged patterns in places of best possible cover. The trenches also served to thwart possible aircraft landing zones. Lava and coral rock and high-water levels in the heavily populated Waikiki district and others presented construction problems. Construction continued until January 1943, resulting in the capacity for 70,000 in 159 shelters in Honolulu and 95 elsewhere in Oahu. The most extensive structure to be bombproofed and sandbagged was the Mutual Telephone Building, the hub for the entire Pacific telephone system.

Numerous volunteer organizations sprung up besides the OCD and Hawaii Territorial Guard.* They included the Organized Defense Volunteers, "a unique group in the military history of the United States. They were recognized as part of the armed forces of the Central Pacific area, and each member took an oath agreeing to serve on his home island 'whenever...invasion is imminent.'" Called the "last ditch soldiers," with plantation workers as the nucleus, they numbered 20,000 in nine units.[22] Three Honolulu groups were the Businessmen's Military Training Corps, the Hawaii Defense Volunteers, and the Women's Army Volunteer Corps. The BMTC restricted its 1,500 membership to Caucasians. The HDV was for non-Caucasians and Hawaiians and numbered 800. The 400 members of the WAVC, organized in August 1942, drove army buses, performed emergency stenographic work, and assisted in government agencies. The OCD established a women's division in May which organized neighborhood groups and conducted courses in home protection. In October 1,500 men formed the Hawaii Air Depot Volunteer Corps to help at Hickam Field. The army discharged Japanese members of the Territorial Guard in January 1942. Those who wanted to continue to serve their country were allowed to form a labor battalion, the Varsity Victory Volunteers.

The army considered the mass of the male groups as the equivalent of one division capable of replacing regulars for offensive assignments. Altogether, the volunteers logged many thousands of hours as guards at military installations, helped reassure the people, and converted patriotism into practical applications. Boy and Girl Scouts with their bicycles and motor bikes assisted police and the OCD by carrying messages to plantations and wounded to hospitals, helping with rescue squads and firefighting, and painting headlights black.

One of the most irritating, constant reminders of Civilian Defense to cope with was the army requirement to carry gas masks. On 10 December distribution began: 400,000 to adults, 72,000 to children, and 32,000 "bunny masks" to infants, and instructions were given to adults. "If you think that was an easy job to work hour after hour fitting masks to people of all nationalities, and all degrees of emotional control, putting the instructions into all types of pidgin English, and helping mothers with scared and almost hysterical children, then you should unmask your own imagination."[23] About the size of a leg of lamb, as one wearer put it, the canvas bag was supposed to go everywhere. Beginning in late December, Oahu residents received typhoid and smallpox shots, were fingerprinted, and were issued registration cards which were required to be on the person at all times.

An 18 December front-page story in the *Honolulu Advertiser* informed that "War is no bar to marriage nor obstacle to true love." The story indicated more than one hundred applications had been filed in Honolulu during the first three days of this week. After days of nothing but censored war news, the newspaper resumed its society pages.[24]

My brother and I were suddenly in frequent demand as ring bearer and flower girl in a forgotten number of weddings. The script always seemed to be the

* Other volunteer groups formed included the Women's Ambulance Service Patrol, Women's Air Raid Defense Group, and Hawaii Rifles.

same, which suited us fine. We wore the same clothes, walked side by side behind the attendants at each affair, with me dropping flower petals en route, and my brother carrying something with a ring attached to it. Once, there was no ring due to it being a hurried event, and instead perched on the little pillow was a shower curtain holder with glitter on it. We thought it beautiful! The best part was the food and music after the ceremony, always Hawaiian musicians usually wearing all white, playing Hit Parade *tunes until the mood became charged after a few "pineapple" drinks, and then a switch to some fast-moving, hip-swiveling island songs. The triple whammy of romance, drink, and beat of native music could,* and did *loosen the inhibitions of most guests. And a good time was had by all.*

We were always the only kids at these affairs and used to getting attention and being asked to dance either to the island music or with an adult. We were not shy and would usually comply, which seemed to bring laughter from everyone. I think we understood we were not being laughed at, *but rather we brought humor or happiness to the celebration. After awhile we became show-offs and would sort of hot-dog the dancing part until Mother gave us a pretty clear message. I have wondered since how many of those hurried-up marriages lasted. After the weddings, after the young men left for somewhere in the Pacific, and the young women went back to their jobs or hoped for a vacancy to the Mainland, and the long months, sometimes years, of waiting to be together became monotonous. How many of their men survived?*

Hawaii prepared for its new role. "If the Japs come again," a citizen forecast confidently, "and General [Delos C.] Emmons has warned us that they will—they are going to a find a Hawaii that is not only alert but spoiling for a fight....They will not find hangars filled with planes nor runways covered with closely grouped machines. Each plane is now sheltered in an earthwork embankment so that no matter how perfect the attacking pilot's aim, he can damage but one plane with a single bomb. As you drive past Hickam, Wheeler, or any of the many new airfield that have been built in recent months, you never see a plane unless it is landing or taking off."[25] Fortunately, it was all for naught.

Notifying the Home Folks[26]

"One of the pressing problems after the attack was how to get word to one's family," recalled naval officer Paul Backus in Paul Stillwell's *Air Raid: Pearl Harbor!* "Knowing that all the military [radio] circuits would be jammed for days with operational and logistic traffic, I telephoned Patricia Goepp, a girl I had been dating, and asked her if she would try to get a cable out for me. She acted on faith, because I had no money at the time to give her. Also, from nowhere, I obtained a Navy issue postcard from which I was allowed to mail and did so on 9 December. (If war was not expected immediately, why were these cards so readily available?) In the meantime, my family had been in touch with both our senator and congressman. They were working through the Navy Department, trying to find out if I had made it. Patty's cable got through about four days after the attack and before any word came via the members of Congress. The postcard arrived a few days later. My mother kept it, and I now have it."

Hickam Field Civilian[27]

Justus Sistrunk, a 1939 graduate of New Hanover High School in Wilmington, North Carolina, was employed at Hickam Field on 7 December. As a member of the army air corps, he had been sent to Hickam in 1940. When his job was civilianized in October 1941, he had the chance to get out and resume his job without a uniform. He lived in Waikiki on Kakeo Avenue with a couple of men who also worked at Hickam. On that day they went to work but he didn't. He heard the announcement but thought it was an alert because there was one the day before. But when he heard blasts nearby he knew something was up. His job was in the station supply office on the hangar line. "We got hit pretty bad. It took us about a week until we cleaned it up so we could work in it [building]." He and his mates worked day and night cleaning and getting records back in shape. He sent a telegram to his parents living in Wilmington saying he was okay.

After the attack martial law was instituted, with blackouts from sunset to sunrise, and military patrolling residential areas. "All we could do was sit and wait and see what would happen, and that's what we did. There was barbed wire on Waikiki, never went swimming there, but did on other side of island. Wasn't much night life, most people stayed in at night, couldn't drive on streets without a pass, and headlights were almost completely blacked out. It was no fun living over there. You were frozen to your job. We couldn't join the service if you wanted to."

He had different supply jobs and was promoted. "It was just a routine job. You couldn't go anywhere." A few months after the war started he got a "dear John letter" from his Wilmington girlfriend—she married someone else. In August 1942 he married a co-worker named Thelma whom he had known only a few months. She lived downtown near King Street. He would walk to see her from Waikiki every night. Finally they figured it would be easier to get married. She continued working there during the war. After their wedding they lived at the corner of Punahou and Beretania Streets. People were not supposed to be out during blackouts and the curfew. They would often walk to a movie theater on the corner of King and Punahou a block away. One time she forgot her identification card, and the military police wouldn't let her go back and get it. They booked her at the police station. Later they moved into housing on Hickam.

(Sistrunk retired as an air force civilian in Hawaii in 1971 and now lives in Wilmington.)

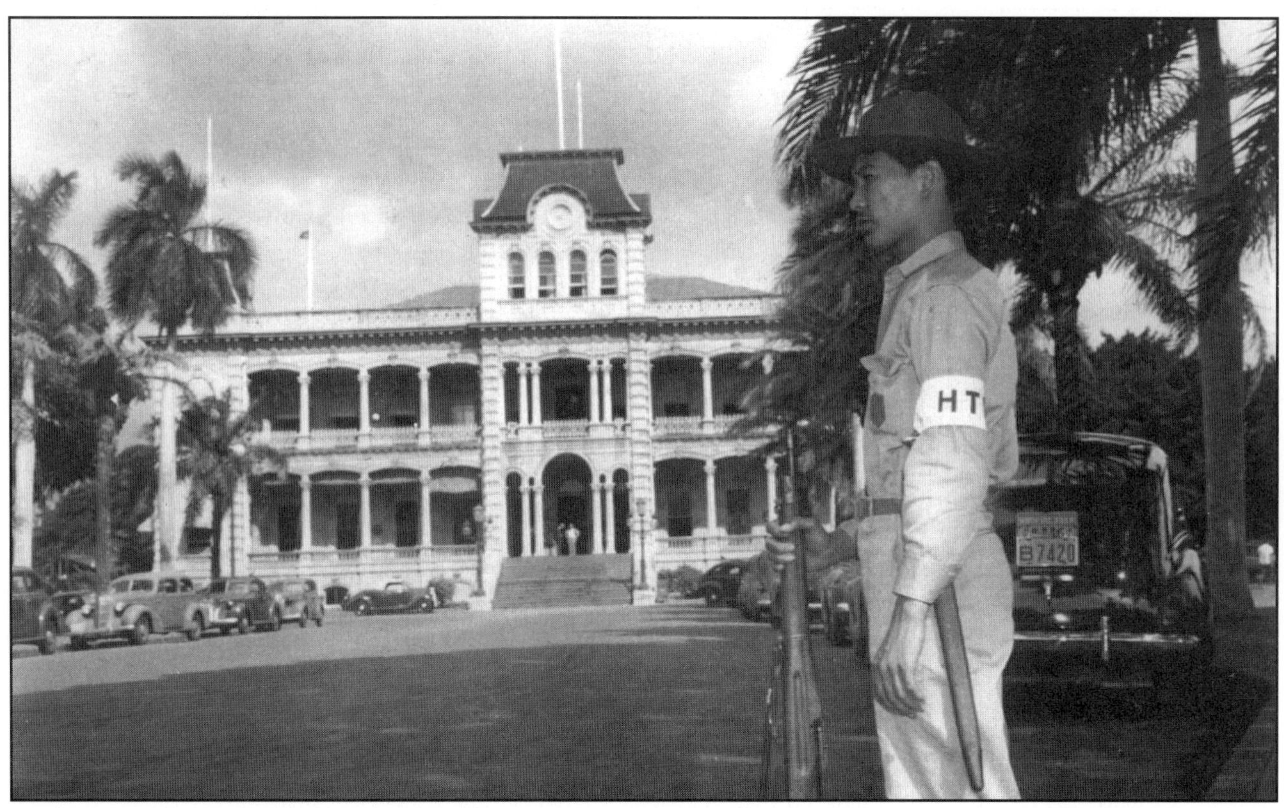

Guards were everywhere. This one is from the Hawaii Territorial Guard with Springfield rifle model 1903, in front of Haleokalani Palace, also known as the Governor's Palace.

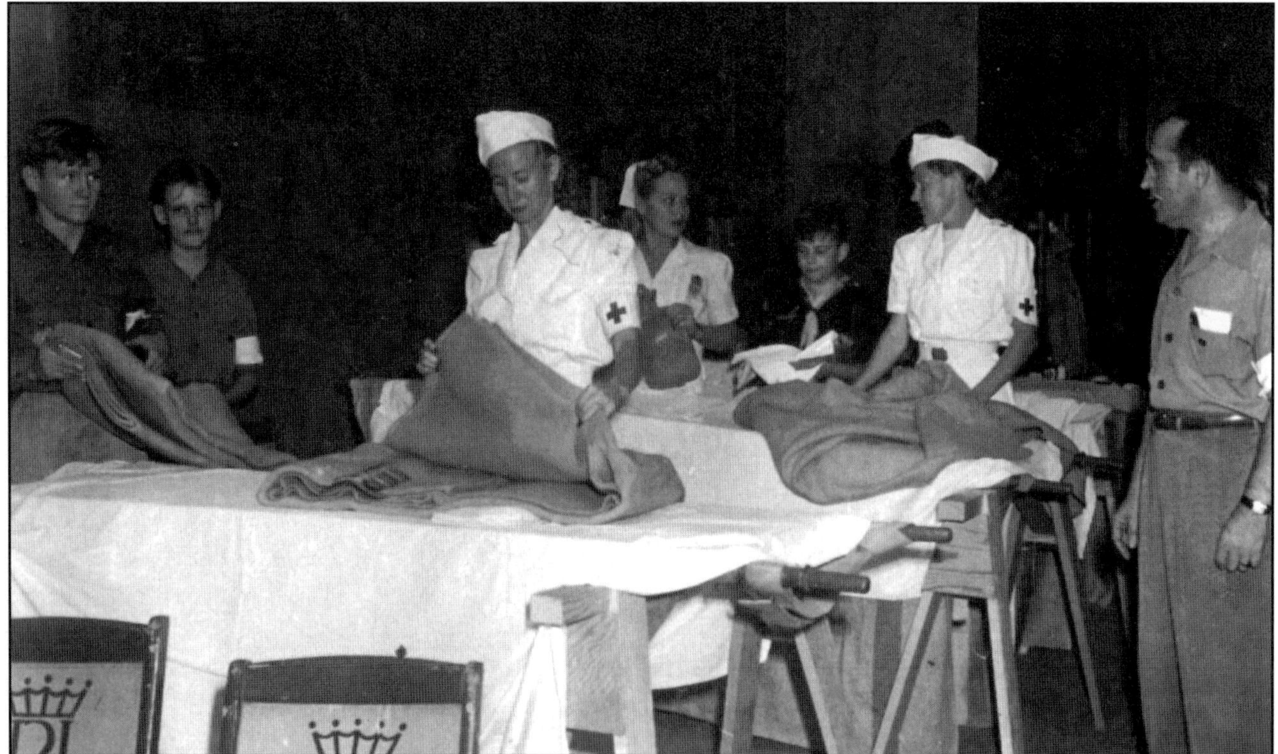

The Royal Hawaiian Hotel was used for Civilian Defense, the Red Cross, and other emergency aid activities.

Barbed wire barricades manned by MPs appeared overnight.

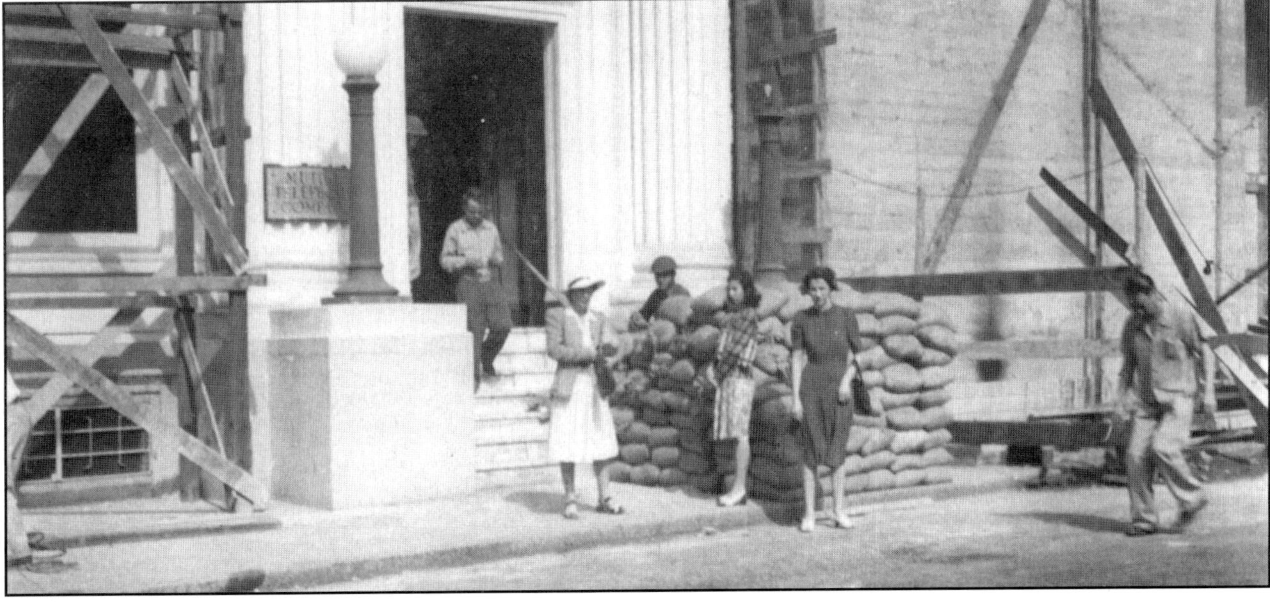

Sandbagged guards at the entrance to the damaged Mutual Telephone Company, provider of the Islands' telephone service and hub of the Pacific network.

Brother, Berton, tinkers with jalopy carcass placed in field near Diamond Head to thwart Japanese landings.

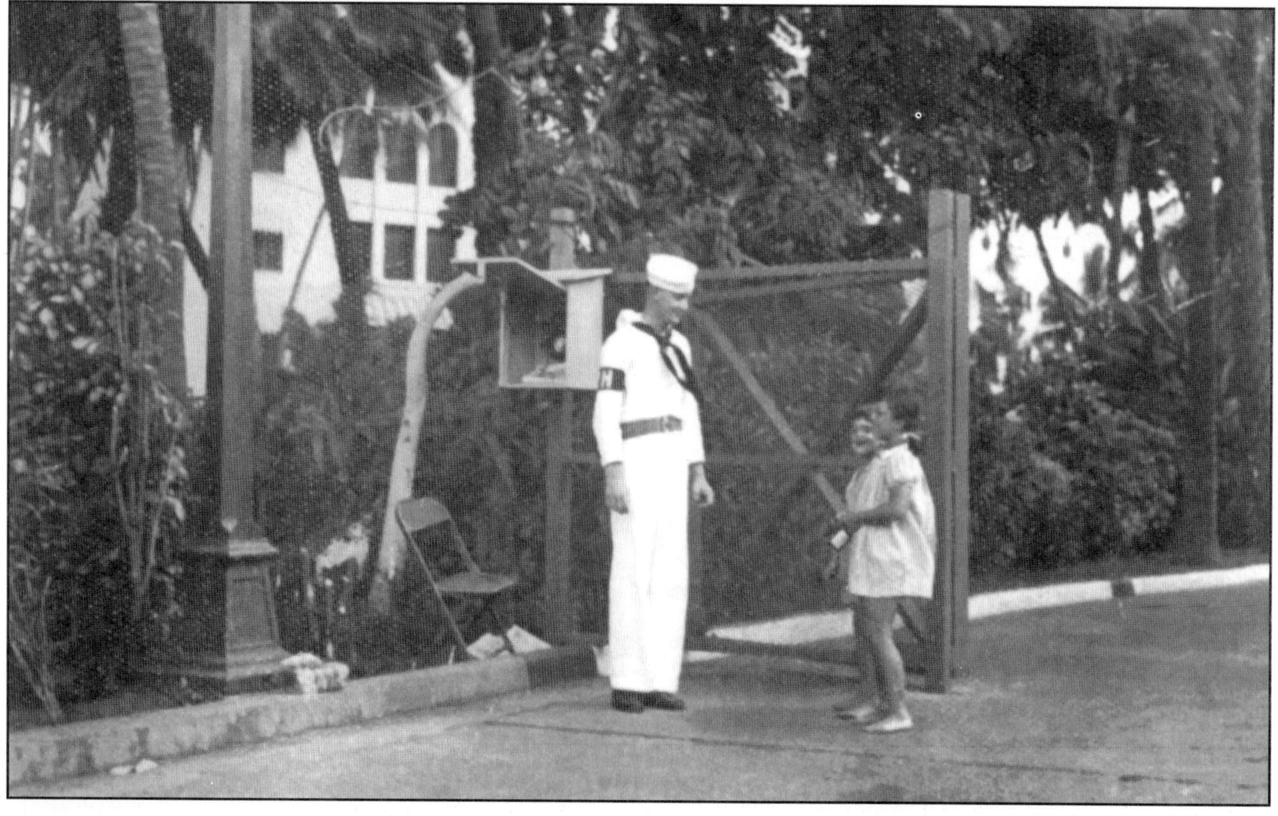

Berton and I visit with navy sentry at the Royal Hawaiian Hotel. We had begun our transformation to native style by going without shoes.

In front of *The Honolulu Advertiser* building.

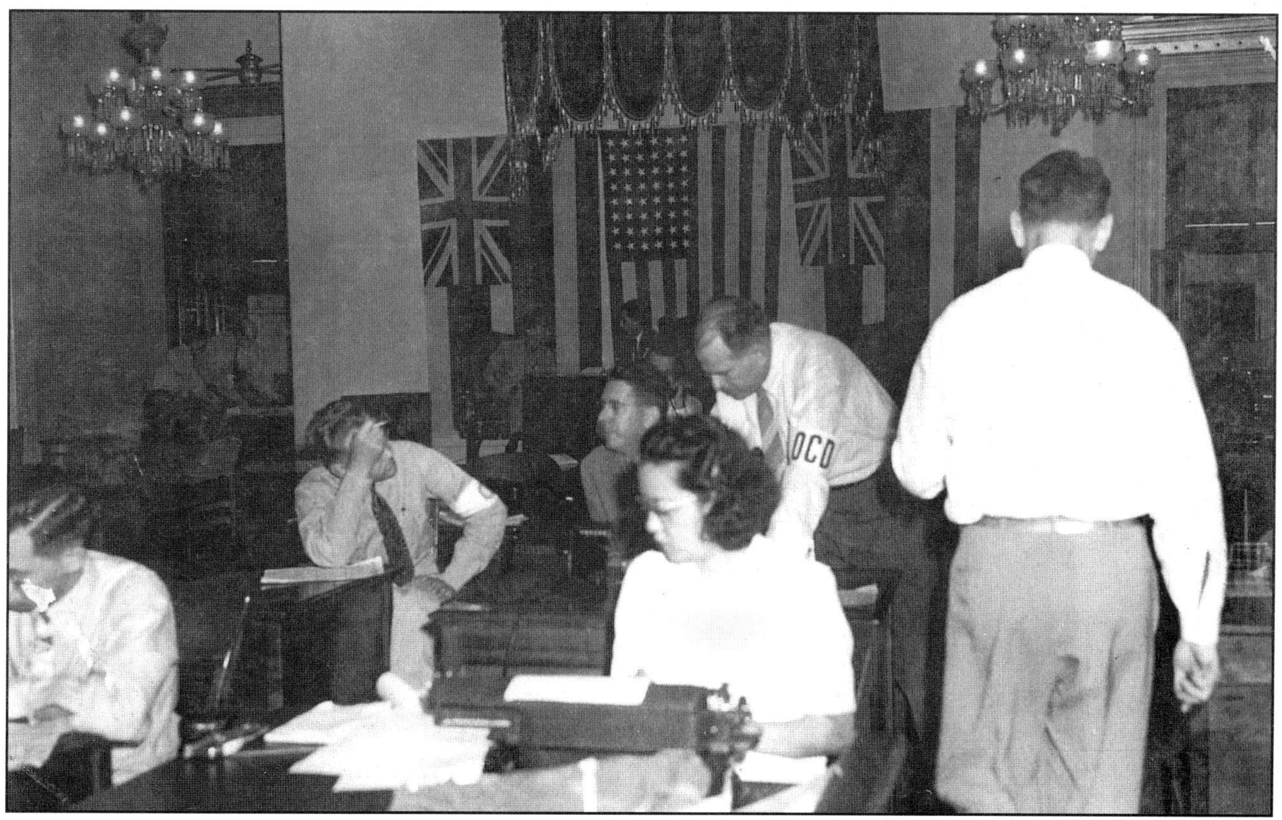

Full-time and volunteer workers in the Office of Civilian Defense in City Hall worked around the clock. Other flags in background are of the Territory of Hawaii.

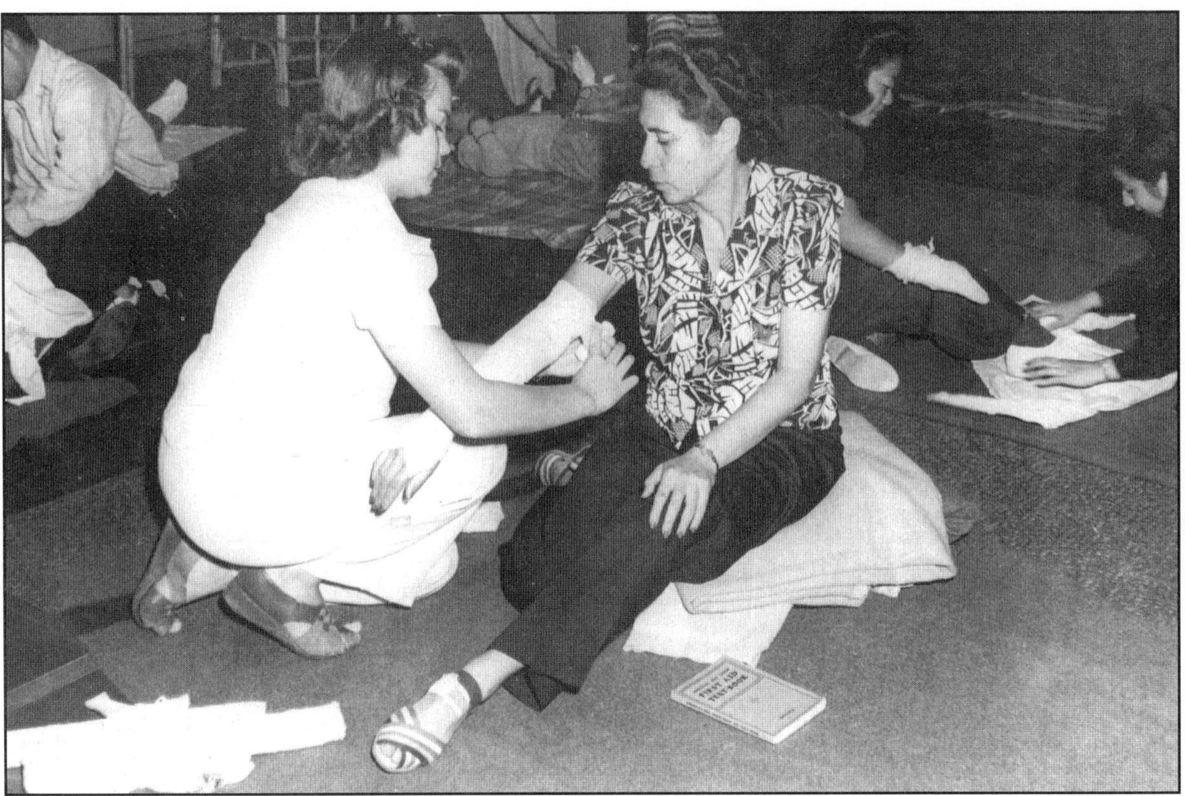

First-aid classes sprang into action immediately.

Ramona Petrie on the job as the mayor's secretary. Note the Spartan furnishings. The wall poster says: "They [enemy] are wise—so don't you be the monkey that tells everything he knows...."

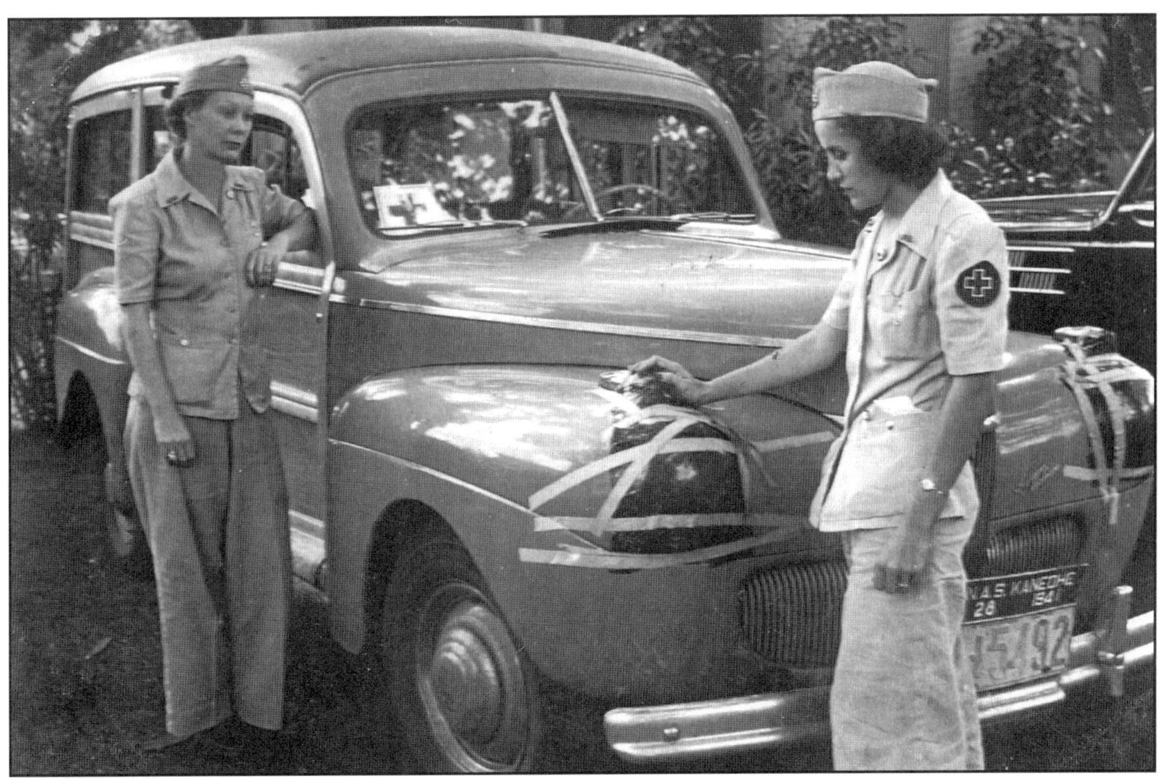

Red Cross Motor Corps volunteers taping blackout covers on headlights. Note the Naval Air Station Kaneohe tag.

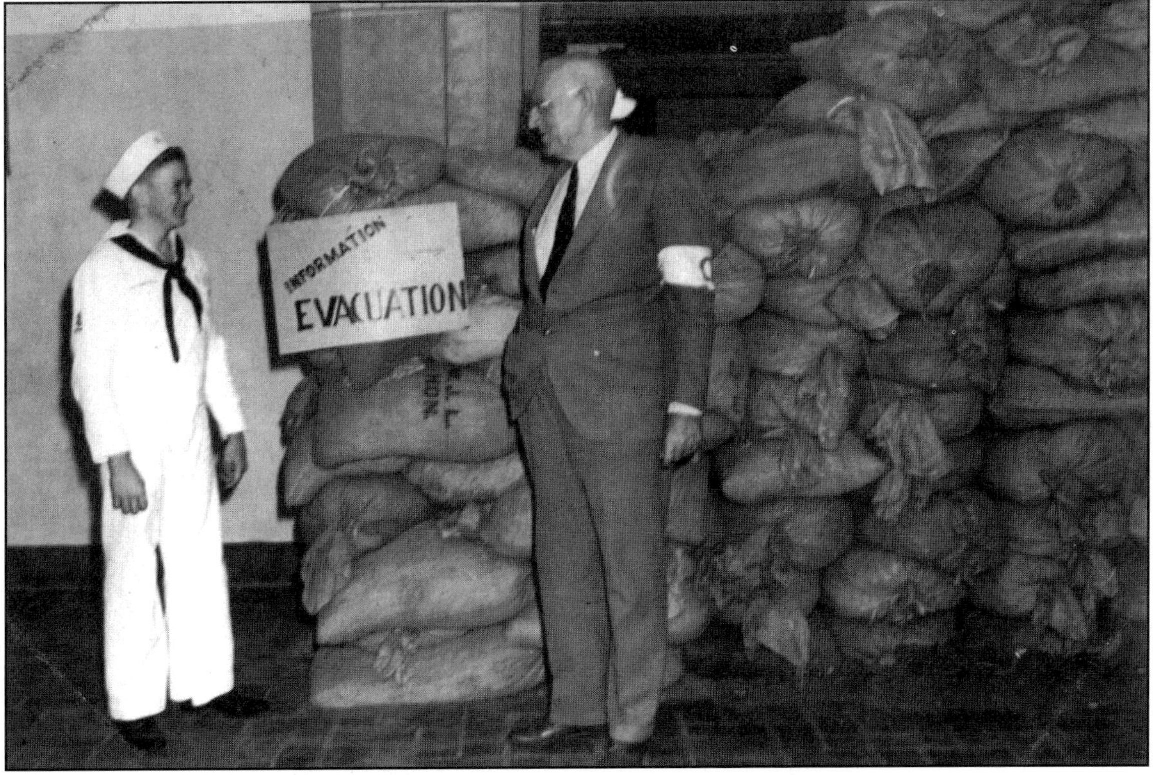

Mayor Lester Petrie with sea cadet in front of sandbagged city hall.

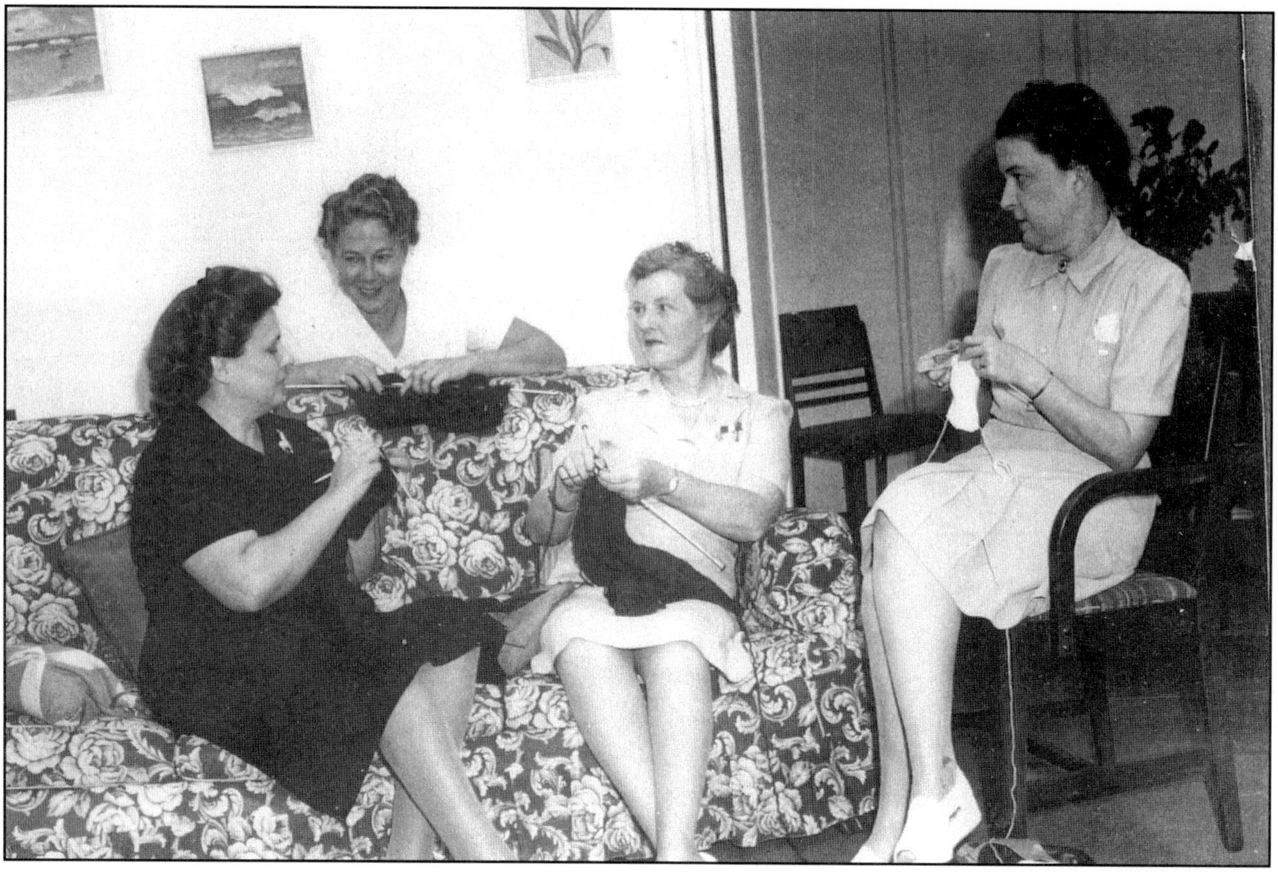

Betty Smith, *second from right,* wife of Rear Admiral William W. "Poco" Smith, commander of the Pacific Fleet's Cruiser Task Force, and ladies knitted socks, gloves, and scarves for the sailors. My father served as Admiral Smith's aide on the cruisers USS *Chicago* (CA-29) (Battle of the Coral Sea), USS *Astoria* (CA-34) (Battle of Midway), and USS *Indianapolis* (CA-35) (Aleutians).

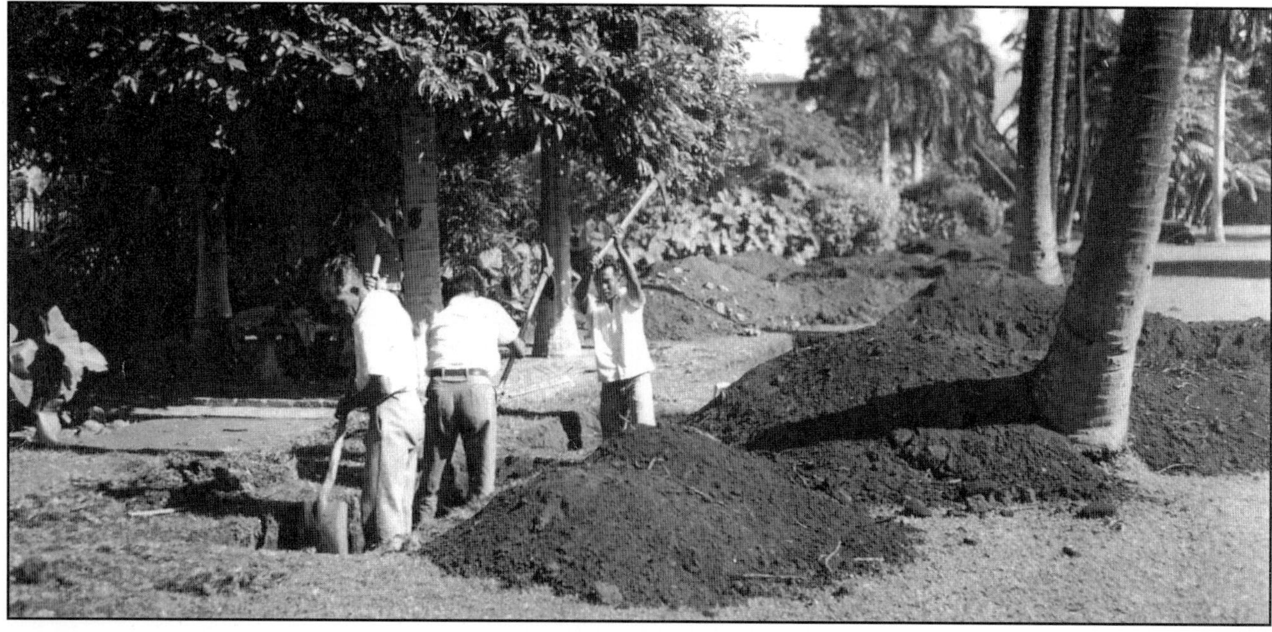

Inmates from Oahu prison digging air raid trenches throughout downtown.

Berton and I collected empty bottles and tins to recycle. The liquor store owner was our friend and gave us Orange Nesbitt drinks. Shoes? What shoes?

Everyone was fingerprinted for an identification card which was to be carried at all times.

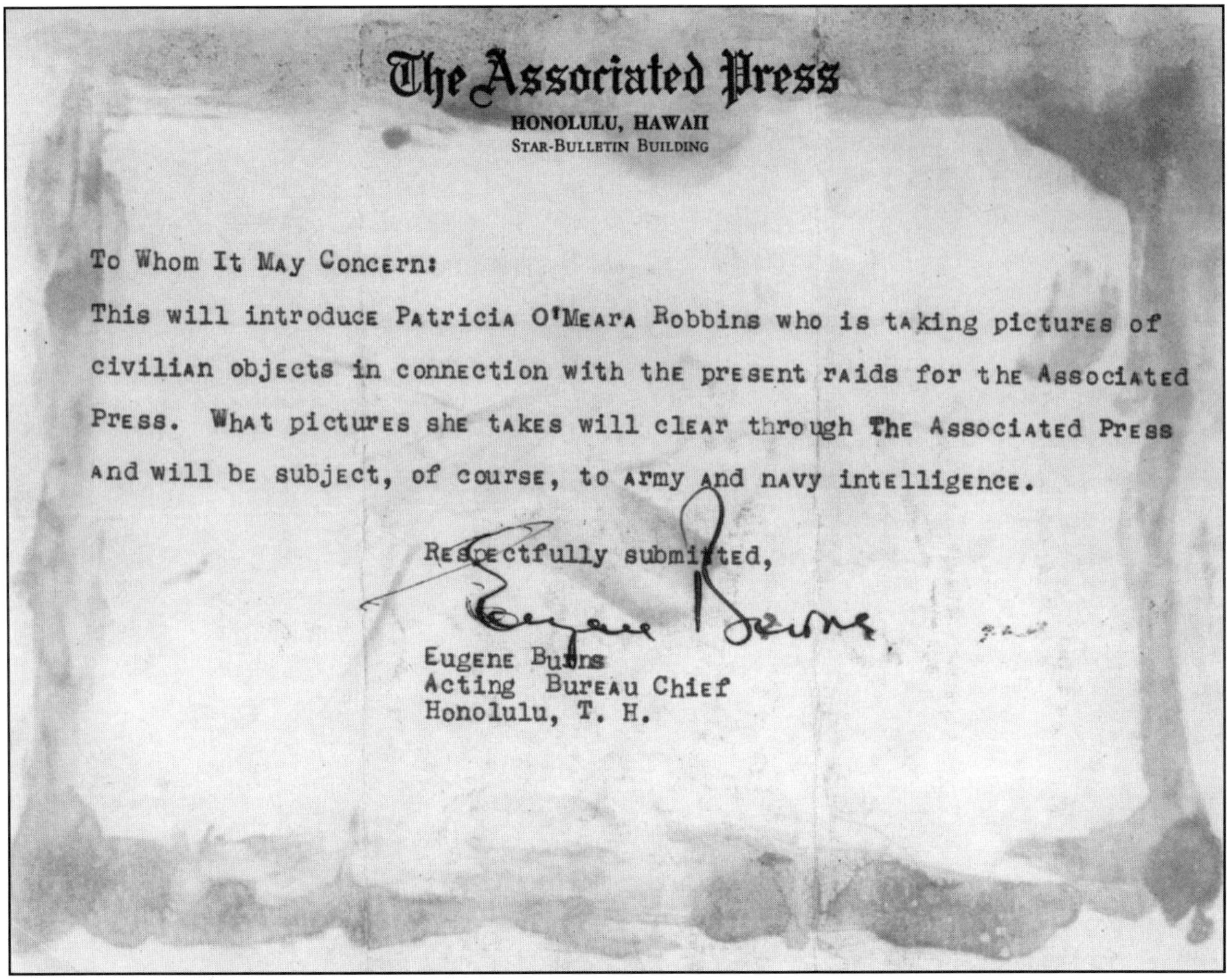

The Associated Press
HONOLULU, HAWAII
STAR-BULLETIN BUILDING

To Whom It May Concern:

This will introduce Patricia O'Meara Robbins who is taking pictures of civilian objects in connection with the present raids for the Associated Press. What pictures she takes will clear through The Associated Press and will be subject, of course, to army and navy intelligence.

Respectfully submitted,

Eugene Burns
Acting Bureau Chief
Honolulu, T. H.

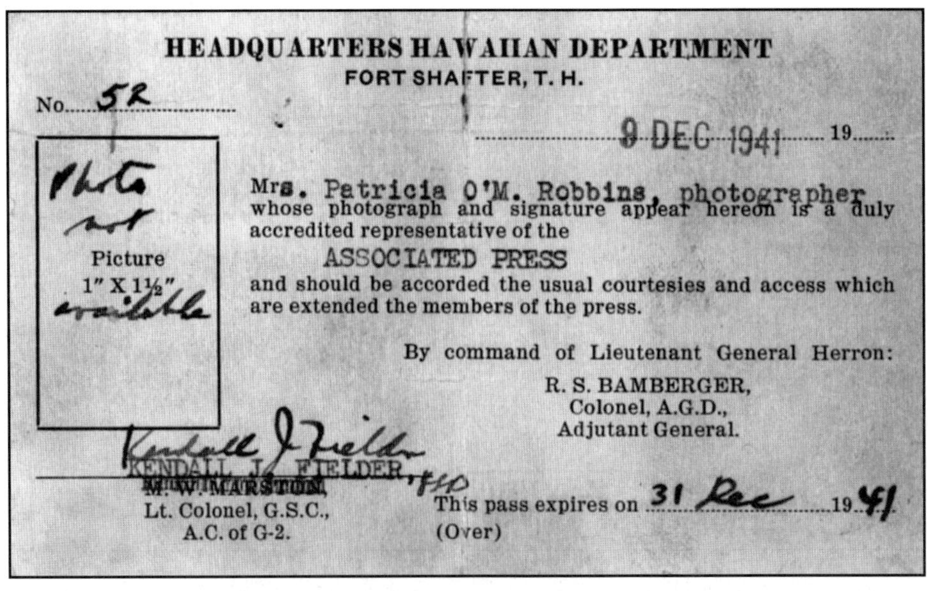

HEADQUARTERS HAWAIIAN DEPARTMENT
FORT SHAFTER, T. H.

No. 52

9 DEC 1941 19

Photo not available
Picture 1" X 1½"

Mrs. Patricia O'M. Robbins, photographer whose photograph and signature appear hereon is a duly accredited representative of the ASSOCIATED PRESS and should be accorded the usual courtesies and access which are extended the members of the press.

By command of Lieutenant General Herron:
R. S. BAMBERGER,
Colonel, A.G.D.,
Adjutant General.

KENDALL J. FIELDER
~~M. W. MARSTON~~
Lt. Colonel, G.S.C.,
A.C. of G-2.

This pass expires on 31 Dec 1941.
(Over)

Credentials issued by Associated Press and Army Headquarters Hawaiian Department for introduction of Patricia O'Meara Robbins, and permission to take photographs around Hawaii after the attack.

Authors' collection

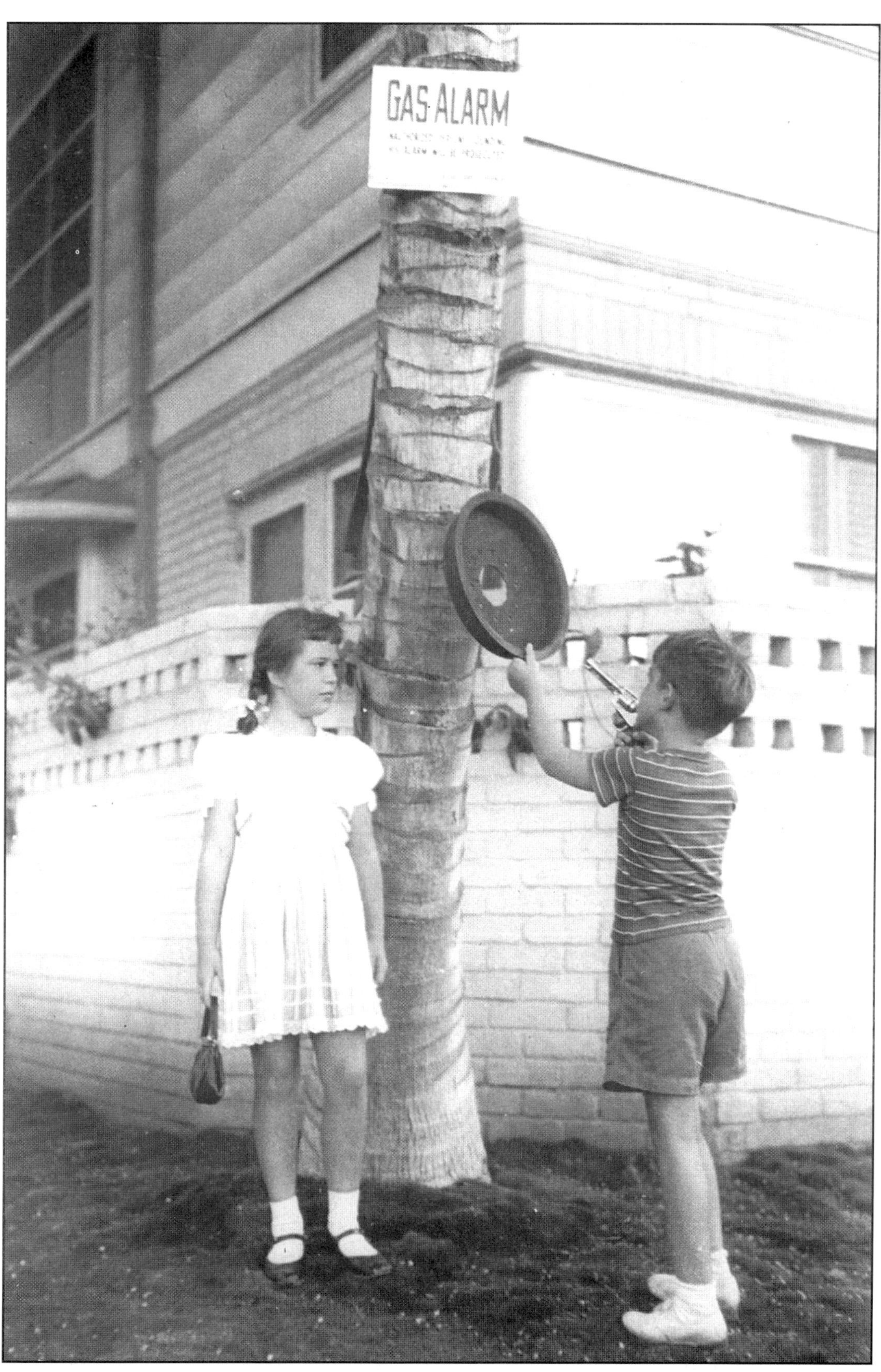

Berton and I tried out the local gas alarm, he with a six-shooter. Primitive, but it worked. Signs warned that persons sounding alarm will be prosecuted.

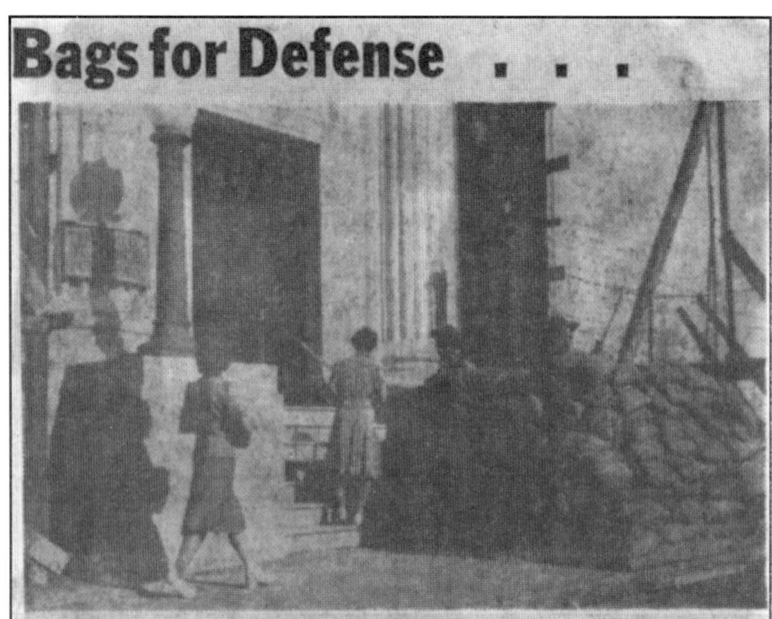

Bags for Defense . . .

BAGS AND BAYONETS—Alert guards stand watch with rifles and fixed bayonets behind a barricade of sandbags in front of the main building of the Mutual Telephone Co. on Alakea St. This defense scene is typical of scores to be found throughout the city.

This was one of many photos Mother took that ended up in print.

Honolulu Star-Bulletin, 2 January 1942

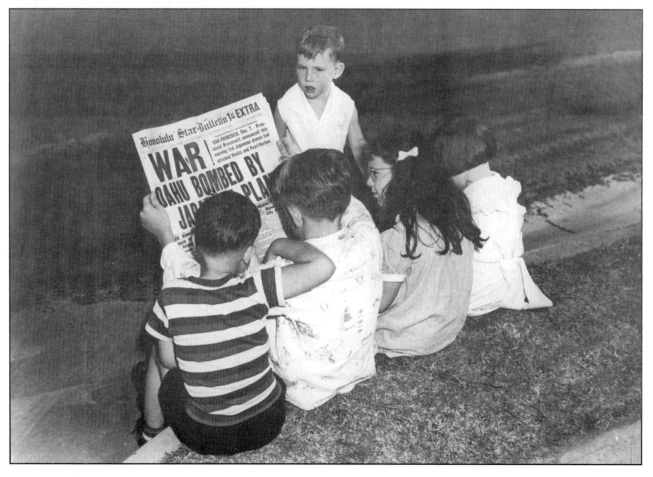

Berton, *left,* and me (glasses and bow ribbon) with friends reading the *Honolulu Star-Bulletin* the day after Pearl Harbor.

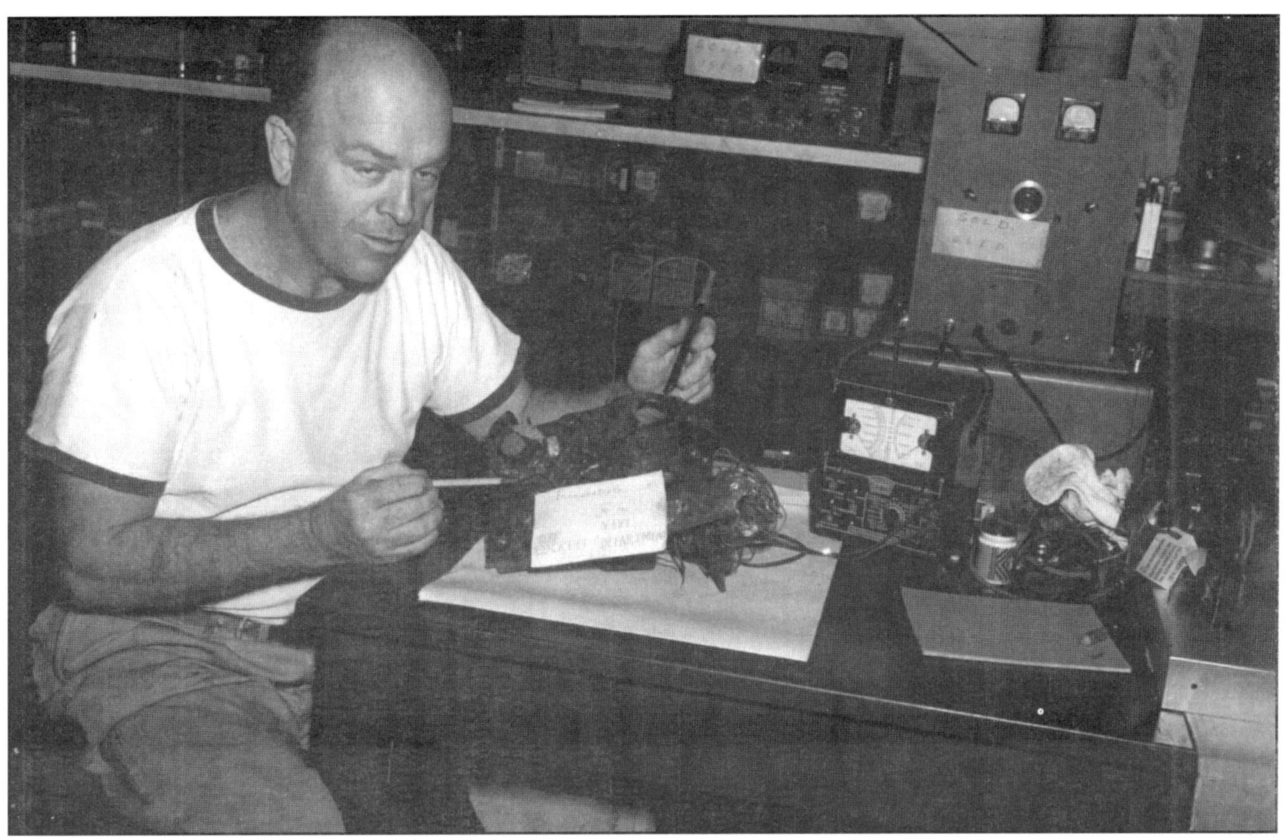

Technician examining captured Japanese radio transmitter found in the hills on Oahu and turned over to the navy.

The Western Union telegraph office in downtown Honolulu. The never-ending line began 8 December letting folks back home know "I'm OK."

Air raid! Running for cover sometime on 7 December in downtown Honolulu.

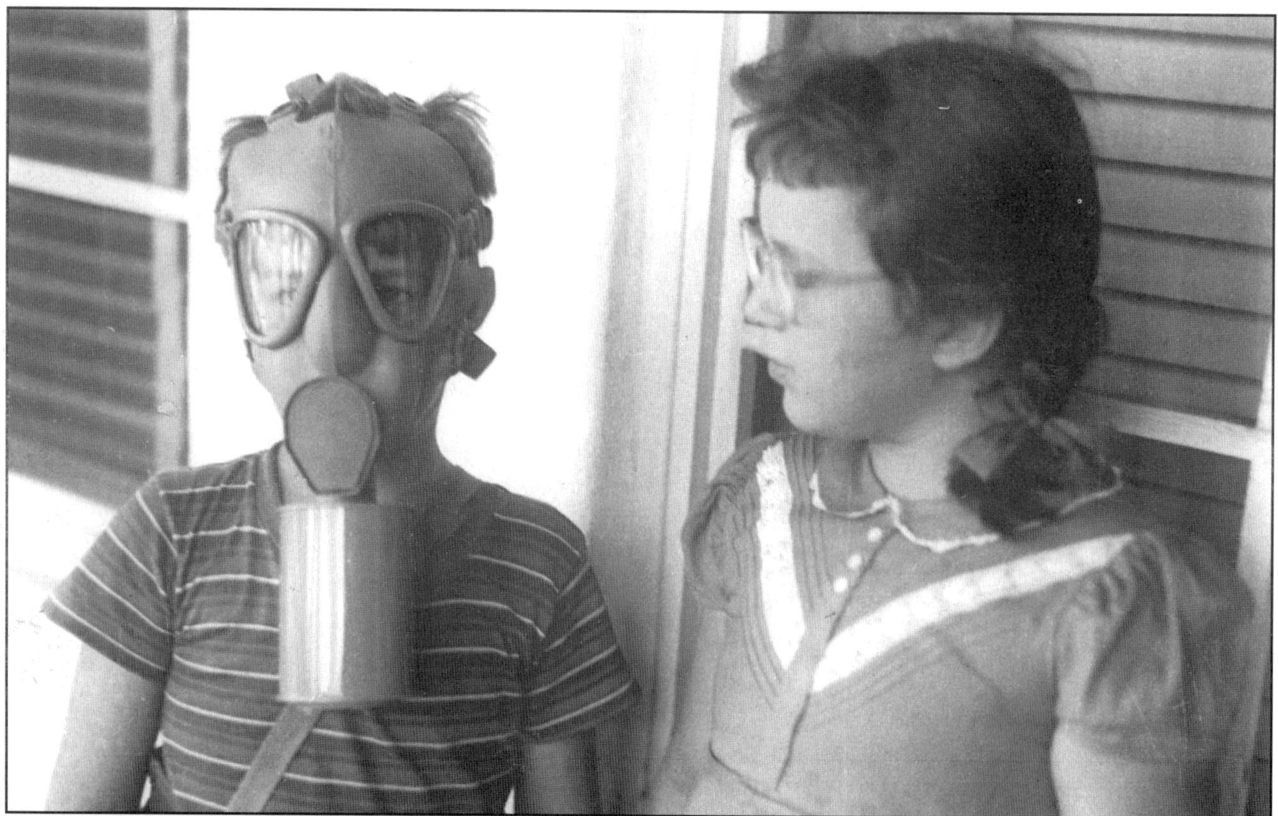

The government issued everyone a gas mask. The smaller kids' masks were called "bunny masks" and were issued after adults got theirs. Berton tried on his.

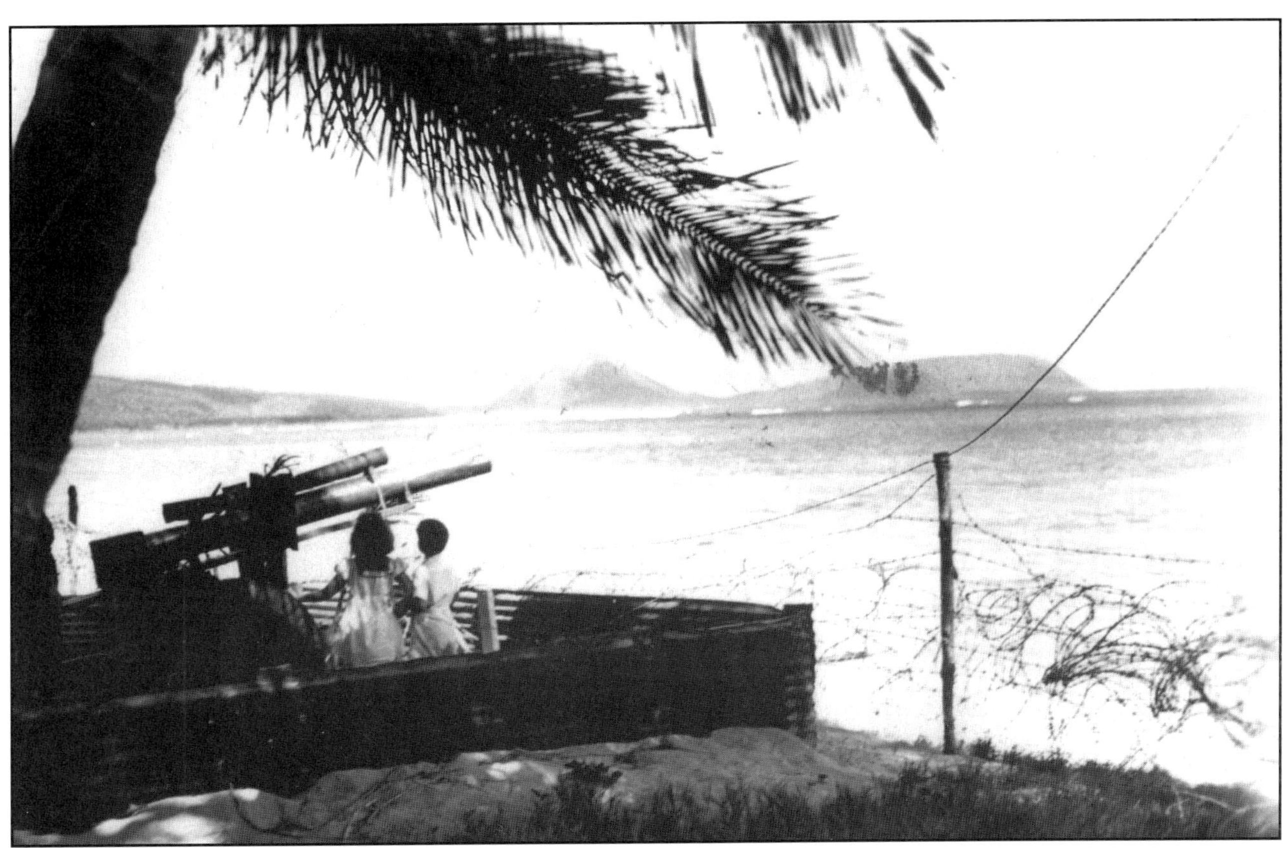

Berton and I always accompanied our mother as she moved about taking pictures. Here we found a lightly defended gun emplacement and barbed wire along the Oahu coast line.

Watching ships coming in and out of Pearl Harbor became a favorite pastime.

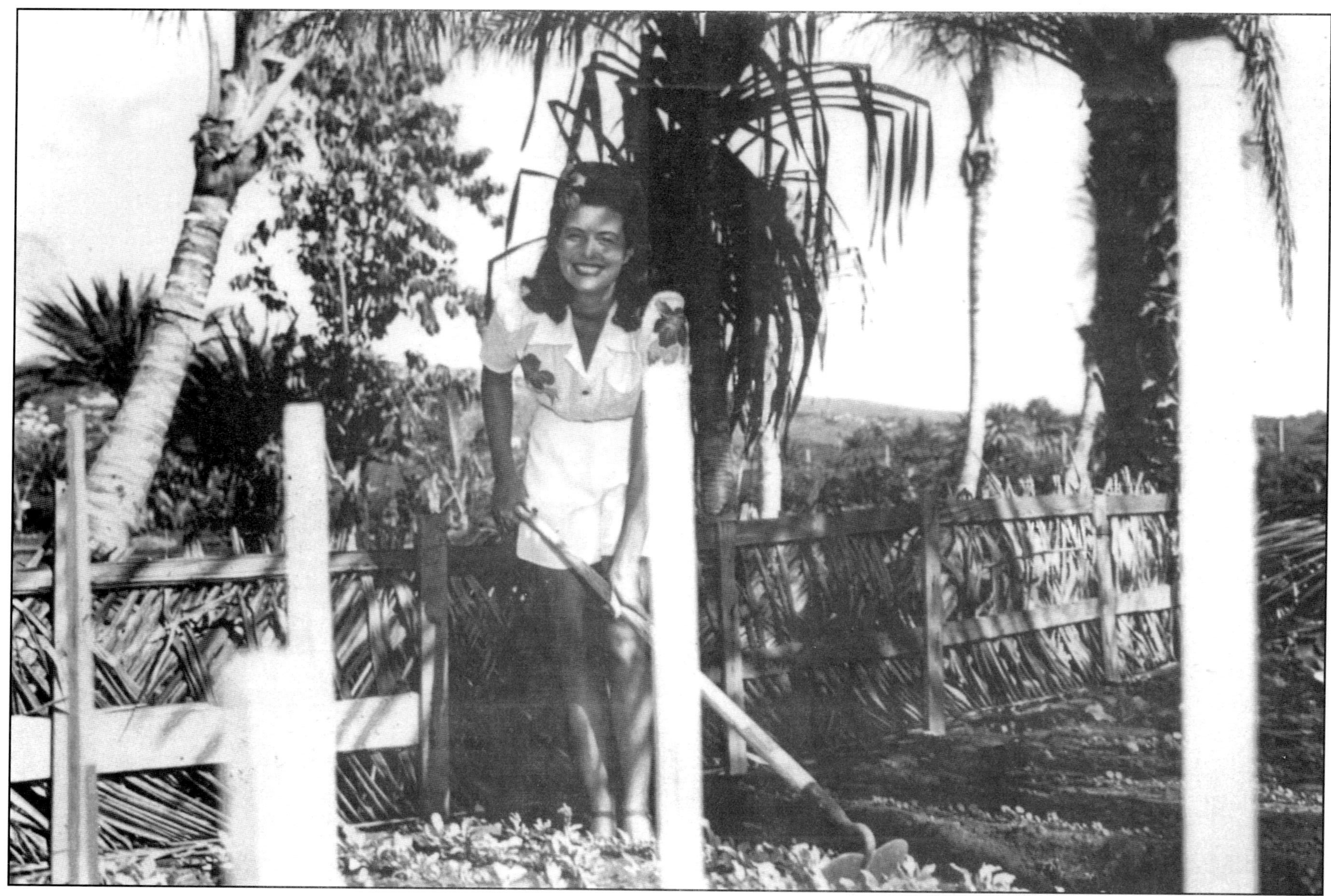

Hawaii resident Pat Smart joined college students, society ladies, and others in growing Victory gardens. Besides, the Islands experienced food shortages and the gardens helped out.

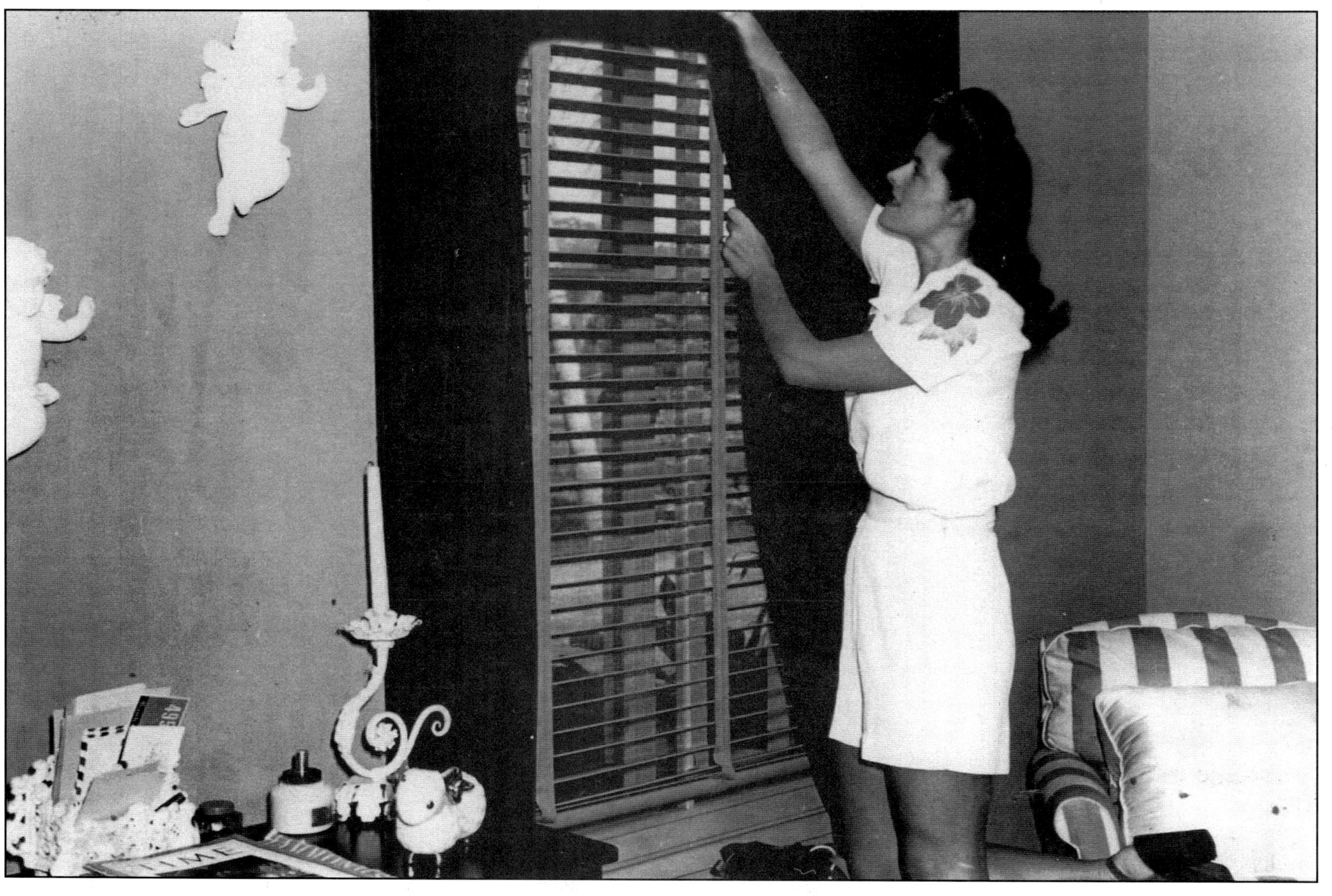

Pat Smart showed us how to hang blackout curtains at the windows, a must for security. The slightest light peeking through was a violation which could lead the occupant into martial-law court.

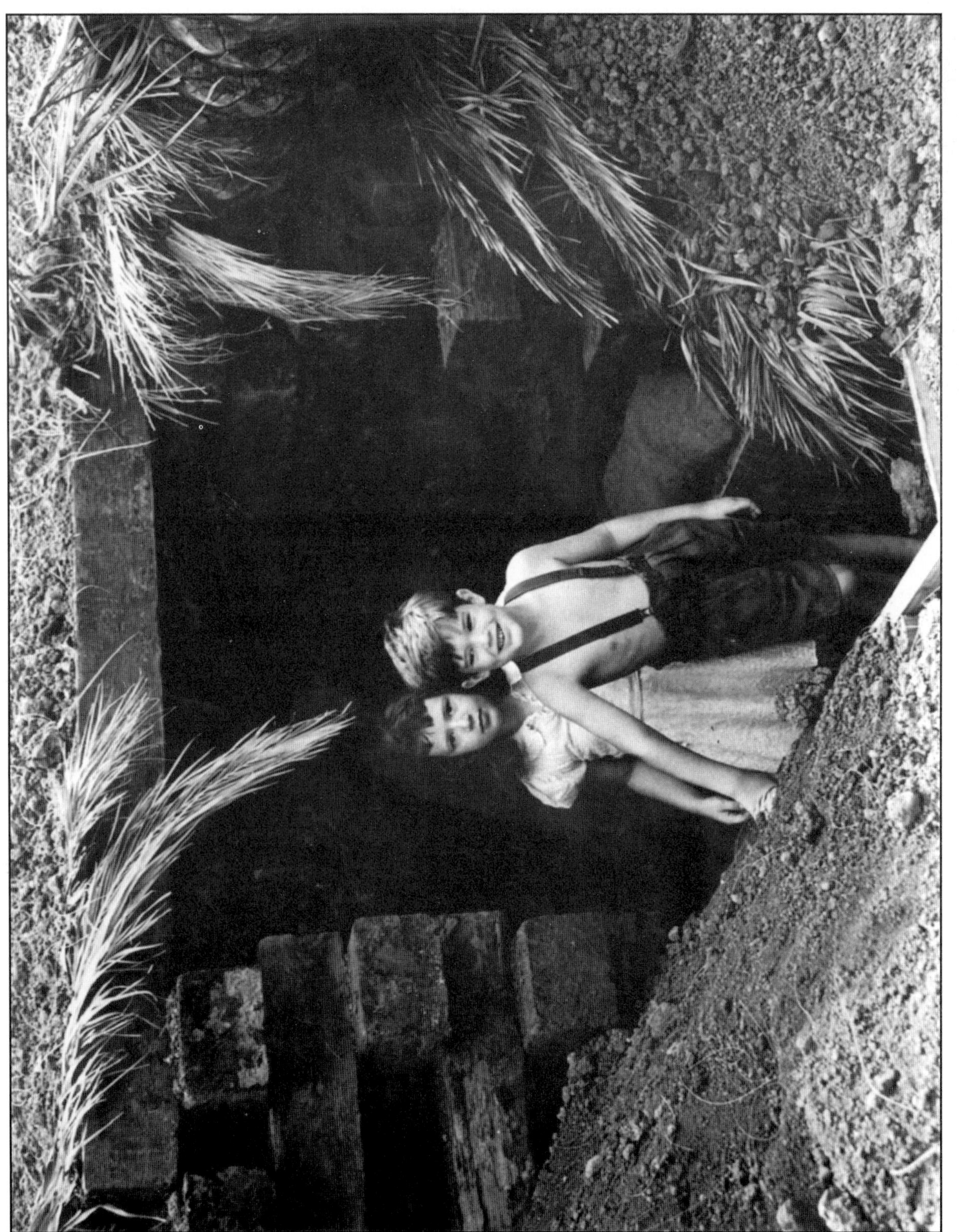

A neighborhood bomb shelter near Waikiki became one of our favorite places to play. I always wore dresses in those days regardless of what I was doing. I wore swim trunks to swim in, but all little girls wore dresses.

We played with "the gang" in an air raid trench in a vacant lot behind the elegant Gump's specialty store in Honolulu.

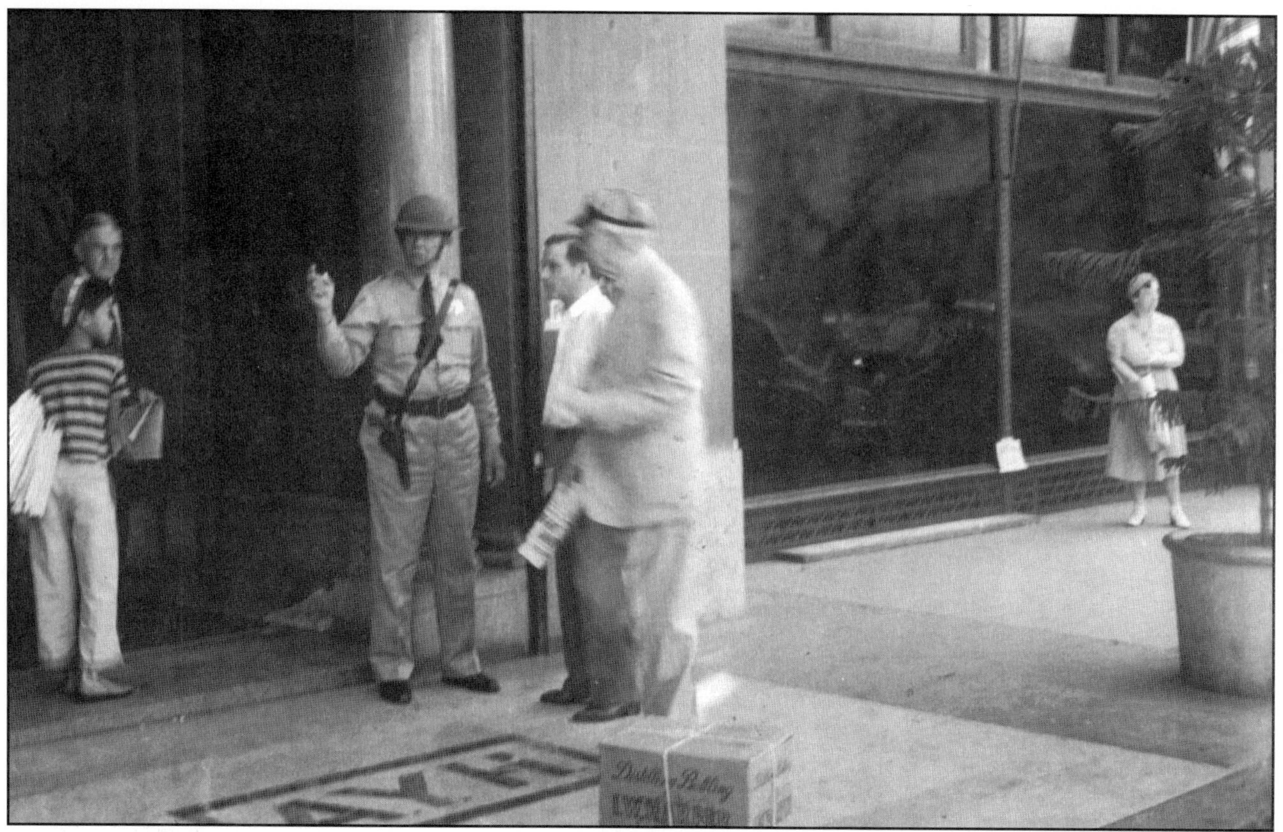

Guard and newsboy watched the entrance to the *Honolulu Star-Bulletin* office.

Growing Victory gardens became community affairs.

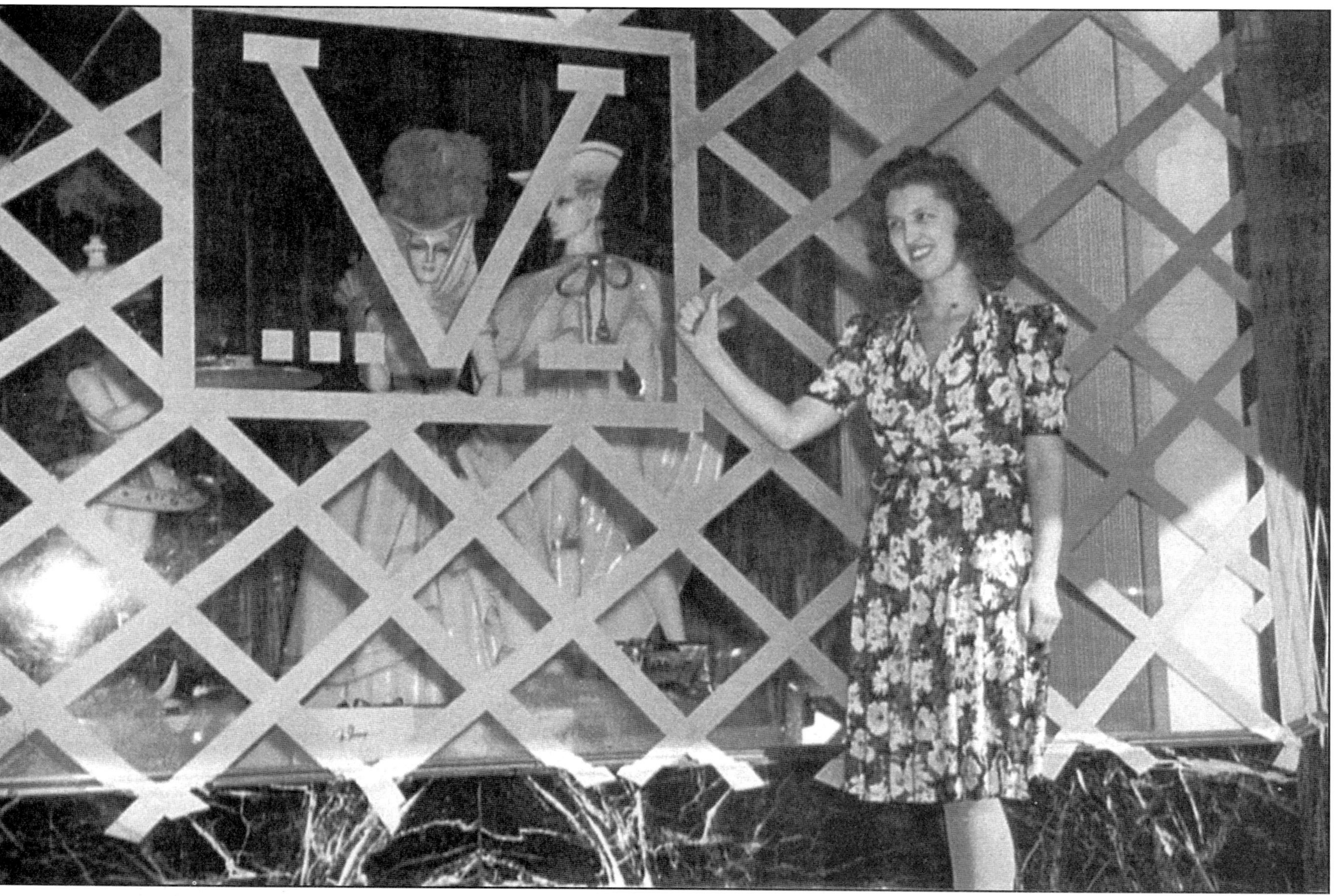

Clerk at McInerney's women's shop gave "thumbs up" to window design taped to reduce glass shattering in case of attack.

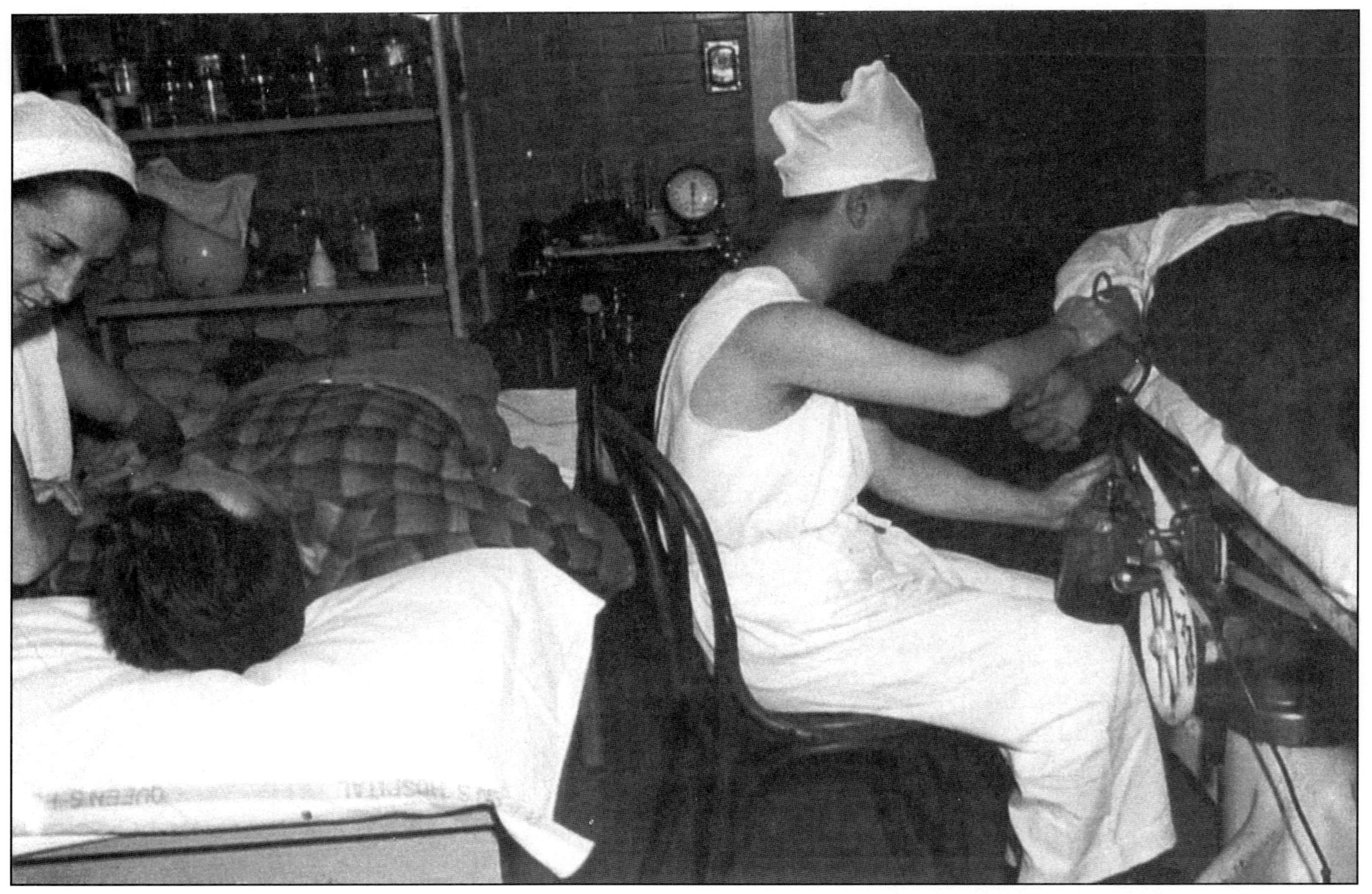

Blood donors immediately began giving blood at local hospitals. This picture was taken on 8 December.

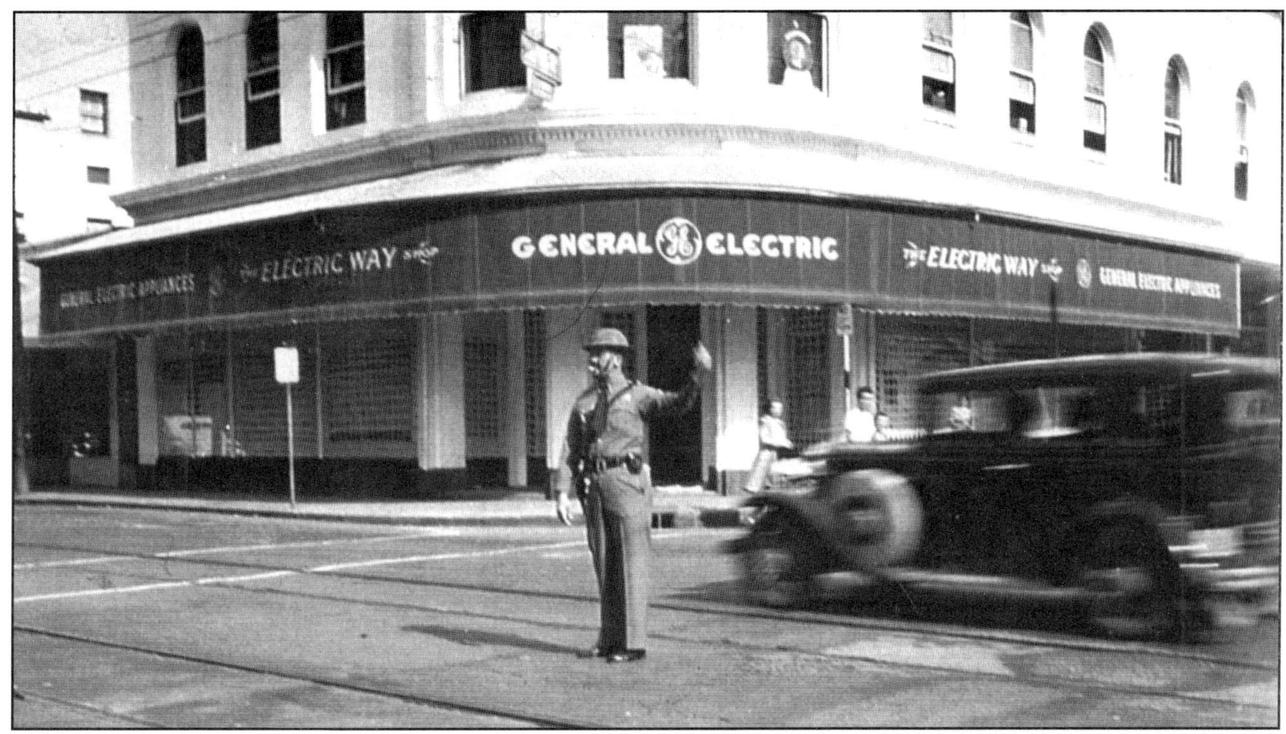

Under martial law, Hawaiian policemen stood in the middle of intersections. There was not much traffic to direct because of gasoline shortages and other travel restrictions. This officer was local Hawaiian Chinese Ah Num Ho, also shown below. Note heavily taped store windows to reduce damage from shattering glass.

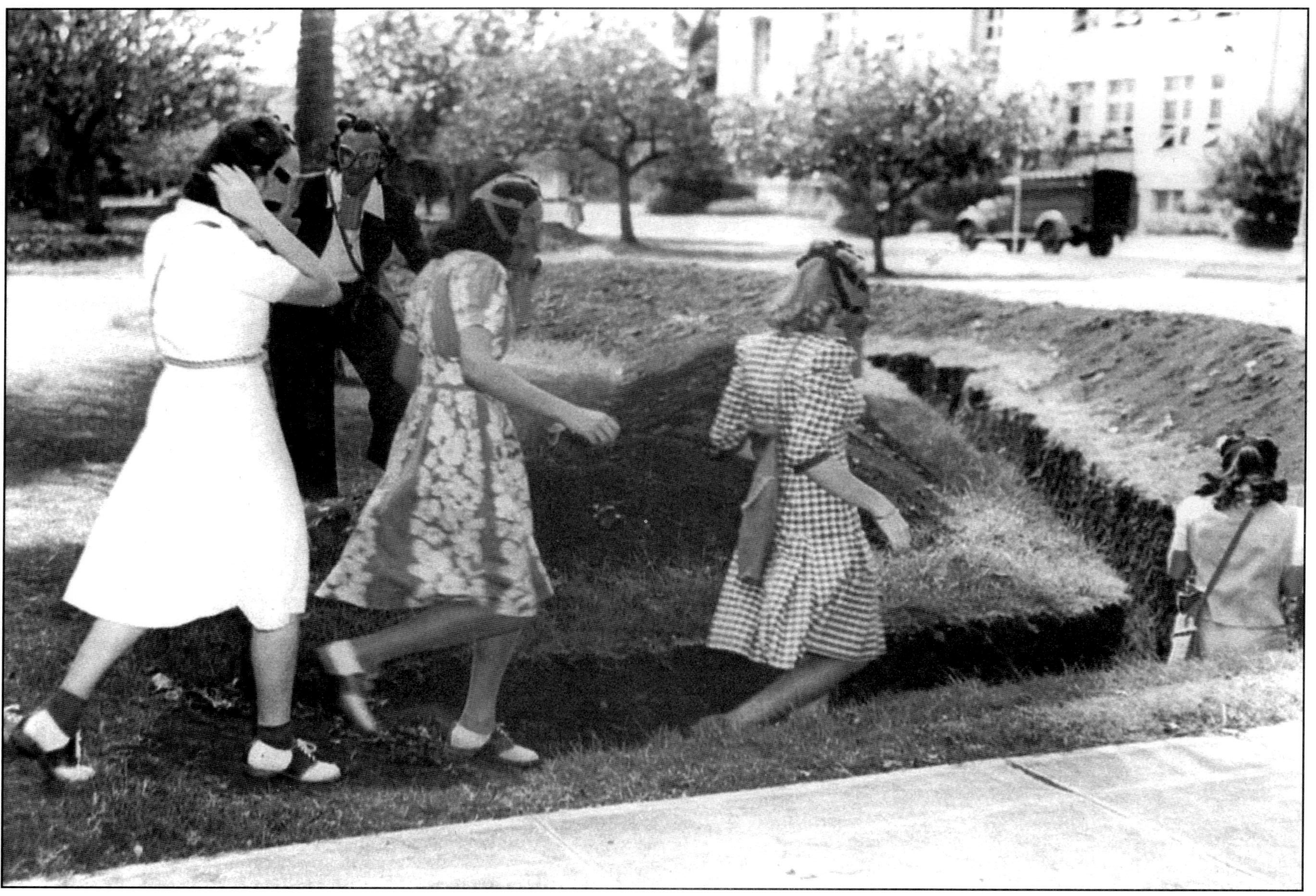

During air raid drills at the University of Hawaii, female students wearing gas masks filed into slit trenches dug on university grounds, in vacant lots, and in city parks.

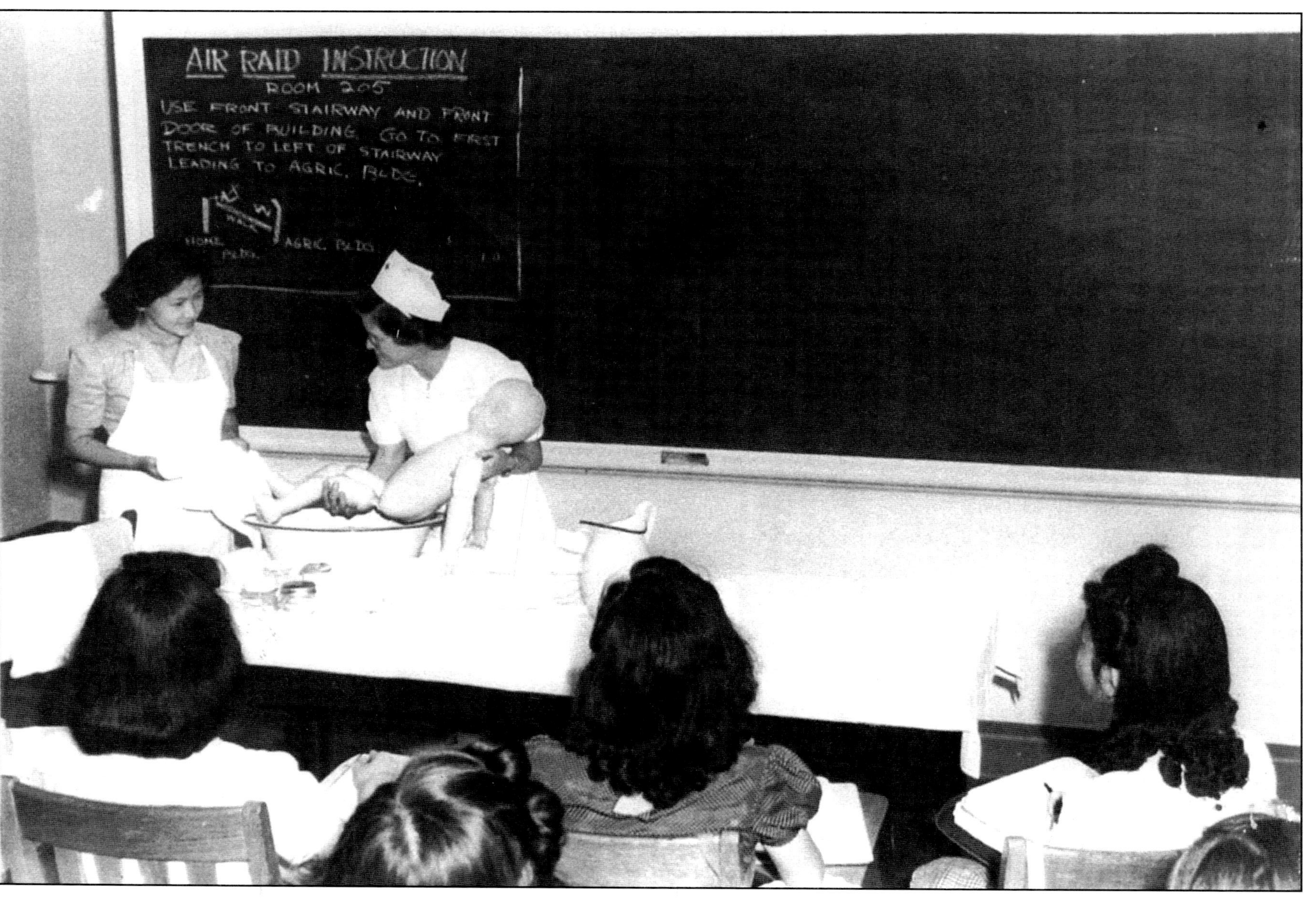

Crash courses in nursing and first aid began right after the attack. Here nurse uses doll during training.

Hawaiian-Japanese Boy Scout volunteers aided with civilian defense work.

Blind Hawaiian-Chinese newsstand operator and father of nine was also a Civilian Defense volunteer. Note "CD" armband.

Chapter 2

"Where is the American Navy?": Pacific Fleet Operations, December 1941–June 1942

The smoke and dust from Hawaii's devastation had just settled when the cry arose all over the world, "'Where is the American Navy?'" Tokyo radio jeered, and a Japanese English-language propaganda broadcast said it had been demolished. All Japan believed it.[1]

The American navy would recover quickly and begin taking the war to the enemy, if only piecemeal while buying time. Shortly after the attack, fleet commander Admiral Husband E. Kimmel and his staff devised the following offensive-defensive naval strategy, as recorded by naval historian Samuel Eliot Morison.[2]

- Employ three search-strike carrier groups, of which two will be constantly at sea and the third replenishing at Pearl, to intercept enemy raids and support any menaced base.
- Organize battleships and destroyer types in escort groups for coast-to-island convoy operations. Base the battleships at San Francisco to relieve congestion at Pearl. Pearl-based cruiser and destroyer escort groups will relieve them at a mid-ocean meeting point.
- Strip the West Coast of all but local defense forces, which may be used as coastal convoy escorts.
- Employ submarines offensively in Japanese waters, and off Wake and Midway Islands.
- Organize a thorough offshore search with army bombers and navy patrol planes.
- Keep Australia-bound shipping to the minimum for which escorts are available.
- Encourage and assist the army to build up land-based pursuit and bomber aircraft strength on Oahu as rapidly as possible, and to establish a proper anti-aircraft defense of Pearl. A vast augmentation of ship and shore radar installations will be vitally necessary.

Nimitz

The plan essentially began without Kimmel. President Franklin D. Roosevelt, on the advice of Secretary of the Navy Frank Knox, relieved Kimmel on 17 December, temporarily replacing him with Vice Admiral William S. Pye, previously commander of the Battle Force stationed at Pearl. On New Year's Eve, Admiral Chester W. Nimitz arrived in Hawaii to relieve Pye as Commander in Chief Pacific (CINCPAC), wearing civilian clothes. He looked about him and said, "This is a terrible sight." A barge of oil-soaked corpses had just passed by his launch. At fleet headquarters he introduced himself to the duty officer, "My name is Nimitz." Kimmel, the purged commander, met Nimitz there.[3]

Nimitz, who had preferred a command at sea, reluctantly accepted the post. He brought only his flag secretary and retained Kimmel's staff, telling them they had his confidence. "These initial acts of Nimitz were typical of the man whose knowledge of human nature and whose humility had made him the most accessible, considerate and beloved of fleet commanders," Morison wrote. He had an immense capacity for work, an equal talent at obtaining the best work from others, an almost impeccable judgment of men, and a genius for making prompt, firm decisions. Chester Nimitz was one of those rare men who grow as their responsibilities increase...."[4] The coming years would bear that out.

As 1942 dawned, the U.S. naval situation in the Hawaiian Islands and Central Pacific was strictly defensive, nervously unpredictable, and hopefully tenuous at best. The Japanese captured U.S. outposts on Guam and Wake Island on 10 and 23 December. Kimmel's relief expedition to Wake turned back to Pearl on receiving word. The Philippines were in jeopardy. Nimitz and Lieutenant General Delos C. Emmons, who had replaced the dismissed General Walter C. Short as area army commander, set out to shore up a defensive perimeter and examine opportunities to strike back in some manner.

One night, lying in the dark with the door and windows open I could hear some of the grownups talking about "Wake falling." Those were curious words as a "wake," in my limited understanding, was water left behind a boat, or a wave created by a surfboard or even a body. Why would a falling wake cause such gloom? The adults were speaking low, listening to the radio all covered up, and then again I heard my mother cry intoning that we were all going to be "taken over." She evidently felt there was reason to believe the ship Dad was on had either been sunk or somehow captured. I believe he was on a hurriedly put together staff of the Cruiser Task Force as aide to Admiral "Poco" Smith. I have no recollection of exact words or phrases heard that night, but the message was clear that we, on the island, might be more involved in the actual war. Mother, that night, was convinced Dad was killed, or captured. I was scared, and confessed to God all my sins and prayed for Him to make me good, thinking somehow my confession and promise of goodness would help end the war, or at least bring word my Dad was alive and Mother would stop crying. My prayers were heard. Within a few days someone brought news to us that Dad, along with a number of others, was okay. I just knew I made that happen. *Now it was pay-up time and I had a promise to keep! Could I?**

The United States had only three carriers operating out of Pearl, USS *Enterprise* (CV-6), USS *Lexington* (CV-2), and USS *Saratoga* (CV-3). The USS *Yorktown* (CV-5) was en route from San Diego. Heavy bombers had been dispatched to Australia and a navy patrol squadron to the Philippines. The area to be covered included the Midway-Johnston-Palmyra Islands line, and reinforcing American Samoa. For the moment Midway was safe. Japanese submarines laced the ocean from the West Coast to Hawaii, sinking merchant ships. The submarines USS *Gudgeon* (SS-211), USS *Plunger* (SS-179), USS *Pollack* (SS-180), USS *Pompano* (SS-181), and USS *Tautog* (SS-109) out of Pearl retaliated with war patrols into Japanese waters and scored a couple of victories. The fleet was stretched thin trying to meet its commitments to patrol and escort troop and supply ships.

In late January the Japanese took Rabaul on the eastern end of New Britain, converting it into their major Southwest Pacific base until neutralized in 1944. American forces moved into or reinforced Australia and island outposts Canton and Christmas Islands, New Caledonia, New Hebrides, and Fiji. The U.S. effort centered around countering the eastward expansion through the equatorial archipelagoes, thus cutting off Australia and New Zealand, not the southwesterly moves into the area of Malaya and the Netherlands East Indies. "It appeared to the high command that the time had come to break up Japanese plans for an eastward development, before the enemy could assemble forces too formidable for the meager, and hence doubly precious, American fleet to oppose," wrote wartime historians Walter Karig and Welbourn Kelley. "January 9 was the day upon which Admiral Nimitz told Vice Admiral [William F.] Halsey what he had to do—sail up the muzzle of the gun pointed at the American-Australian life line and blast that threat away." He told Halsey to raid the southern Marshalls and northern Gilberts, block harbors with wreckage of his combatants, destroy his aircraft and tenders, fuel tanks, power and radio stations, storehouses, and radio apparatus. "It was a large order."[5]

The February Carrier Raids

The war's first U.S. carrier raids took place on 1 February 1942 against Kwajalein, Maloelap, and Wotje in the Marshall Islands, the base of origin for the Japanese Wake Island attack force. Halsey led Task Force 8 in *Enterprise* in that strike. Simultaneously, Rear Admiral Frank Jack Fletcher's Task Force 17 in *Yorktown* struck Makin, Mili, and Jaluit in the Gilbert Islands. "At last 'Bill' Halsey was in

* Within days, Robbins was transferred temporarily to the USS *Tangier* (AV-8) for the abortive relief of Wake Island before eventually joining the staff of Commander Cruiser Task Force on USS *Chicago* (CA-29). So harried was the navy's personnel system in reassigning officers and men to temporary and then permanent duty stations that it was hard to determine who were the reporting seniors. On 21 January 1942, after his brief stint on the *Tangier*, that ship's commander wrote Robbins on the *Chicago*: "Not knowing who your commanding officer is at present, I am forwarding this to you with the request that you present it to be made a part of your next fitness report." He enclosed information for use in Robbins' performance evaluation. It would have to catch up with the records later. [C. A. F. Sprague to Berton A. Robbins, Jr., 21 January 1942. Authors' collection]

the money. He had chafed at conducting fruitless covering patrols and longed for aggressive action. His assignment to conduct a raid deep into the Japanese Mandates* was a guarantee that it would be carried out with the utmost energy and skill. This was by all means the most hazardous operation yet undertaken by the Pacific Fleet."[6]

As the task forces departed Samoa on 25 January for the first attacks northward, Karig and Kelley wrote that[7]

> few among the thousands of officers and men in that armada of 21 ships had ever heard a gun fired in anger. The pilots and gunners of the carriers' broods had never seen tracers stitch a flaming seam across their wings. The husky but untried football team of State Normal was going into its first game to stop the undefeated champions....Abreast but invisible from each other, the two forces [Halsey/Fletcher] slid over the International Date Line and flung themselves in tomorrow, but there was no festive initiation of novices into the Order of the Realm of the Golden Dragon. Another sort of initiation awaited them less than five degrees ahead.

After the planes headed for the Marshalls, "no man there, in the air or aboard ship, knew what to expect. More was known about Tokyo itself than of the South Sea Islands. The pilots had only photostatic enlargements of clippings from old charts to help them identify their targets, which is why Roi Island was not recognized in the misty dawn by the 37 planes intent upon surprise and destruction. Twelve minutes' warning was thus accorded the Japanese, before the flight identified the target...in the face of anti-aircraft fire and rising Japanese fighters." The first American bomb to be dropped on Japanese territory came from Commander Hallsted Hopping, who was killed a few seconds later by AA fire.[8]

The strikes on Kwajalein and Wotje were marginally successful militarily, but tremendously boosted the spirits of sailors and home front alike. The expeditions became a living laboratory through which lessons learned were converted into smarter and more efficient methods of future fighting. "Here, in not-too-crude beginning, the United States Navy had countered, not with a defensive arrangement but with an offensive combination which utilized the best in aerial and surface combat power," a wartime study stated. "It was an amalgam from which were to be molded fleets...." But on 6 February 1942, "the navy still seemed far from such attainment. It lacked ships, and planes, and men. The planes it had were not wholly adequate, either too slow or highly unmaneuverable, and they lacked self-sealing gasoline tanks, armor for the men, and the full firing-power they could carry. The attacks on the ships by Japanese aircraft had demonstrated American shooting to be woefully below necessary standards, the bitter fruit of years of economy."[9]

Halsey "had all the luck there was," Morison wrote. "Some kind angel was guarding them from subs and air bombers....Haul out with Halsey!" became the watchword. "It would not be fair to judge this raid by the meager material results....The over-optimistic accounts of damage inflicted on the enemy were a help to low morale, and the audacity of Halsey in striking into the heart of the Mandates gave his country its first naval hero of the war."[10] Fletcher's force destroyed the few military targets in the Gilberts.†

Halsey's *Enterprise* aircraft raided Wake on 24 February following a 30-minute bombardment by two cruisers and two destroyers. His bold 4 March raid on Marcus Island, less than one thousand miles southeast of Tokyo, caught the occupants sleeping. It was yet another planned diversion attempting to pull Japanese forces backward in defense of their island possessions. Neither of these "shows of force" was successful in that regard. Again the fleet learned. The ratio of fighters to other aircraft assigned to a carrier was too low. The number of pilots exceeding the

* After World War I, the Marshall, Caroline, and Mariana Islands (less Guam) were mandated to Japanese administration.

† U.S. losses in the Marshalls raid: one carrier bomber, four scouts, one fighter in takeoff, six officers and five enlisted killed, two officers and two enlisted wounded; 33 planes damaged. Japanese aircraft were faster or if comparable in speed more maneuverable. The Americans were better fliers; they shot down 10 enemy. The Gilberts force lost eight planes in atmospheric turmoil "that rendered radio almost useless and buffeted the aircraft as a kitten plays with a twist of paper." [Walter Karig and Welbourn Kelley, *Battle Report: Pearl Harbor to Coral Sea* (New York: Rinehart and Co., Inc., 1944), 266]

number of planes was too short and created overwork. Technical faults in the ships' gunnery, equipment, and weapons systems kept popping up.

Japan continued well into 1942 holding the overwhelming upper hand in the Pacific, highlighted by their late February victory in the Java Sea, the greatest naval battle since Jutland in 1916, without losing a ship. There an Allied surface force of American, British, Australian, and Dutch warships lost 5 cruisers, 13 destroyers, the aircraft transport USS *Langley* (AV-3, the first U.S. carrier), and an oiler. The cruiser USS *Houston* (CA-30), President Roosevelt's favorite, went down. The Japanese southward march rolled along, occupying or gaining footholds in Hong Kong, the East Indies, Singapore, New Guinea, and the Northern Solomons.

Sleep nearly always came slowly to me, and darkness brought anxiety and sometimes outright fear. I would lie in bed wide awake remembering not the nightmares but the fear of those nightmares and waking so frightened I would shake. Years later I wondered if there was a correlation between the nightmares and my very unconventional childhood and very unconventional, high strung mother left alone so much even before the war began. Mother cried a lot at night and somehow I felt my brother and I were at fault. She missed Dad terribly, and they were devoted to one another almost to an extreme the rest of their lives; however, I felt Mother to be the controlling partner in that relationship as she always tried to be with us.

The Doolittle Raid on Tokyo

The war's most dramatic carrier strike was the 19 April Doolittle raid on Tokyo, a feat of dazzling proportions considering the obstacles, risks, limited training, and narrow objectives. Army Air Forces Lieutenant Colonel James H. Doolittle commanded a flight of 16 B-25 *Mitchell* medium bombers flying from the USS *Hornet* (CV-8) for bombing runs on Tokyo (with 13 aircraft), Kobe, Nagoya, and Osaka (with three). The *Enterprise*'s Task Force 16 under Halsey's command escorted the *Hornet* group. Secrecy of the plan was such that the *Hornet* commanding officer, Captain Marc A. Mitscher, learned of it only 18 days before, and the targets were not announced until at sea. Cooperation between the army and navy could not have been better.

The first problem to be overcome was how the B-25s would be placed on board. Their non-folding wingspan meant they had to remain on the flight deck, with *Hornet*'s planes being stored on the hangar deck below. Her only defense was the ship's guns until rendezvousing with TF 16 on 13 April. The flight crews had only a month's training but never practiced taking off from a carrier. "The carrier plane pilots, eager to substitute for the army aviators in the strike, played poker with them assiduously in every spare hour, each navy flyer hoping to run up an enormous credit before D-day, which he would generously discharge in return for being allowed to fly a B-25!"[11]

The second problem was where to launch the bombers. Their final destination was the Chinese airfield of Chuchow, 1,093 nautical miles from Tokyo. Armed with four 500-pound bombs and carrying a maximum of 1,141 gallons of fuel, each had to take off within 500 miles of the Japanese coast. Doolittle preceded the flight and dropped incendiary bombs as beacons and to light fires. Early on the 19th, a Japanese patrol boat spotted *Hornet*'s scouts. Surprise had been lost, but the ship was still 650 miles away. It was doubtful whether the B-25s could make China. Halsey decided to launch in daylight 623 miles from land and 668 miles from the heart of Tokyo. "The wind and sea were so strong that morning," recalled Admiral Halsey, "that green water was breaking over the carriers' ramps. Jimmy led his squadron off. When his plane buzzed down the *Hornet*'s deck at 0725, there wasn't a man topside in the task force who didn't help sweat him into the air."[12]

The final plane was airborne at 0824. Ironically, Tokyo had just completed exercising at an air raid drill when the B-25s roared overhead at rooftop level at noon, rising quickly to avoid any blast from their bombs. Consequently most of the citizens and interned Americans thought the attack was the end of the mock attack and never realized Tokyo was actually bombed, reducing any psychological impact on the population, but aiding in the aircraft's safe exit. Authorities were unprepared. They had anticipated that shorter-range carrier planes would be used in any such raid, and that the carriers would launch closer to land. Thus, the B-25s had little opposition, and no alert sounded for 20 minutes. Assigned targets were military, chemical, steel, gas, and munitions plants, but some of the wrong buildings were hit.

"Japanese officialdom was hard put to...explain how such an attack could possibly have taken place, suffered considerable loss of face," but little information was divulged. No plane was lost over Japan. One was impounded in Vladivostok, Soviet Union. Its crew was interned but later escaped. The other 15 planes reached China until fuel exhausted. Five men died on landing, three were executed, one died in prison, but 71 of the 80 crewmen survived. "No event in the war prior to the Battle of Midway gave the American people so much satisfaction as the news that Tokyo had been bombed," one historian noted. Roosevelt said the planes came from Shangri-La, the mysterious Tibetan city. The raid prompted Japanese officials to overextend their forces that led to the Midway operation. "In my opinion," wrote Admiral Halsey, "their flight was one of the most courageous deeds in all military history."[13]

The Battle of the Coral Sea

By April 1942, the Japanese decided to improve their positions in the Solomons and New Guinea, where the principal objective was Port Moresby on its southern side facing Australia. The plan was to sail a force from Truk and Rabaul consisting of the carriers HIJMS *Shokaku* and HIJMS *Zuikaku* with 2 heavy cruisers, 6 destroyers, and 11 transports. Supporting forces included the light carrier HIJMS *Shoho*. On the 17th, Nimitz's intelligence learned of the movement, correctly believing the target was Port Moresby. He dispatched TF 17 under Rear Admiral Fletcher in *Yorktown*, and TF 11 under Rear Admiral Aubrey Fitch in *Lexington*, to rendezvous west of the New Hebrides and patrol the Coral Sea. Fletcher was in tactical command.

On 1 May the two task forces joined. Fletcher diverted to Tulagi in the Solomons and on the fourth attacked the recent landings there. At the cost of three aircraft, he inflicted only minor damage on the invaders. "Admiral Nimitz later showed his disappointment when he said that very little was accomplished considering the amount of ammunition expended."[14]

Fletcher then rendezvoused with Fitch's and Royal Navy Rear Admiral John C. Crace's groups, and the Port Moresby invasion force steamed toward the objective.

On 6 May the Japanese carriers and escorts under Vice Admiral Takeo Takagi rounded the east end of San Cristobal Island, turned west, and entered the Coral Sea. Their mission was to engage and destroy enemy forces attempting to interfere with the landings. The battle would rage over the Solomon Sea and northern Coral Sea. Neither side was aware of what the other was doing. Fletcher had no long-range patrol planes, and Takagi chose not to use any. Early on the seventh, Japanese patrol planes spotted the oiler USS *Neosho* (AO-23) and destroyer USS *Sims* (DD-409). Takagi ordered an air strike, believing them to be a carrier and cruiser. He sunk *Sims* immediately, and caused *Neosho* to be scuttled on the 11th. A *Yorktown* scout sent a mis-coded message about spotting Japanese carriers, triggering a strike launch. Once it was discovered that the force was only cruisers and destroyers, the raid was aborted. "Then Lady Luck, the true goddess of war, took a hand." Returning to *Yorktown*, the aircraft spotted the Port Moresby group steaming southward in the Solomon Sea. In 10 minutes they sunk the *Shoho*, and the cry "Scratch one flattop!" shrieked over the U.S. radio network. That evening, the *Yorktown* beat back an attack, including destroying six Japanese planes trying to land on her, and 21 of the 27 attackers.[15]

Pre-dawn patrols on 8 May found both sides' carriers, and both launched strike aircraft, 121 Japanese and 122 American. The numbers and ship types of the opposing task forces were also similar. But where they were operating was a stark contrast. The Americans were in the placid, bright, and sunny Coral Sea, the Japanese in overcast and rain squalls. The U.S. bombers badly damaged *Shokaku* and *Zuikaku*, sending them into a month-long repair period at Truk where they missed the Battle of Midway. *Lexington* was hit badly and despite heroic damage control had to be scuttled later that day. *Yorktown* was severely damaged. Takagi called off the Port Moresby invasion and returned to his bases. Nimitz, knowing that half his Pacific carriers were out of action, ordered Fletcher to Hawaii.

Coral Sea was history's first naval battle where none of the ships either saw or fired on each other. The entire battle was fought by carrier aircraft. It set the tone for the carrier battles that followed through Leyte Gulf in October 1944. Tactically it was a standoff. The Japanese sank more ships, but lost 43 of their aircraft to only 33 American aircraft. Strategically, however, Fletcher's luck had stopped the enemy advance into southern New Guinea (their first setback) and with it, the immediate threat of an invasion of Australia.

We did our part to help the fleet. Until classes resumed on Oahu, several kids living nearby joined us in forming a club, and erecting a clubhouse in back of our building made of old sheets, a blanket, and grass mats. We soon spent most free hours defending the club and members from enemy raiders. The "raiders" were imaginary but in our minds we were prepared for the worst. Why not? We lived in a tense little world where this was commonplace conversation and all around us was evidence of impending invasion. Not your everyday Dick, Jane, and Spot childhood. Our biggest fights were over who would be the leader. There was only one other boy, who wore glasses, and whose mother constantly reminded us we couldn't hit him or let him get hurt. Two sisters, one older than me by two years and a bully, and one between Berton and me and a cry baby. Somehow we all managed to get along enough of the time to make each day a wonderful adventure. We devised exciting games involving bomb shelters and trenches, scrunching down behind sandbags, spying on whoever was close by.

We collected bottles and cans from alleys and empty lots and took them to the local liquor store for money or bottles of Nesbitt's orange drink. We made friends with the manager of the movie theater a couple of blocks away, and he would occasionally let us in free after the show started. We found however, that the EXIT sign way down front was just as good an entrance. I'm sure this kind man knew of our illegal trespassing but felt sorry for us poor urchins. Can't remember how many times we saw Song of the Islands, *with Betty Grable and Victor Mature.*

The Battle of Midway

In June 1942, the coral island of Midway, located 1,136 miles west of Pearl Harbor at the end of the Hawaiian Archipelago, was a U.S. Navy refueling station and naval air base. Its forward strategic position was highly valuable to the Japanese as a springboard to the potential capture of Hawaii and further advances toward the U.S. West Coast. Such action, if successful, would seriously endanger U.S. and Allied interests in prosecuting an offensive against Japan and holding Australia and New Zealand. In planning the invasion of Midway, Combined Fleet commander in chief Admiral Isoruku Yamamoto, realizing a substantial advantage in surface ships, also sought to coax the Pearl Harbor-based fleet into a decisive, knockout showdown. With such victories, Yamamoto believed America could be forced to accept a negotiated end to the war. As final plans for the attack proceeded, Yamamoto added a simultaneous diversionary invasion of Attu and Kiska in the U.S. Aleutian Islands. He chose a target date of 4 June for a naval air attack on Midway, and 6 June for the invasions. The available forces were:

Japan
8 carriers, 11 battleships, 18 cruisers, 65 destroyers

United States
3 carriers, no battleships,* 8 cruisers, 15 destroyers

Honolulu in May was abuzz with an "undercurrent of unrest" that "something might happen" soon of enormous military impact. Authorities alerted Hawaii's 7th Air Force and moved aircraft to Midway,† called to night guard duty on 1 June the Defense Volunteers, a recently organized citizen paramilitary

* U.S. battleships had been removed to the West Coast earlier in the year.

† Captain Cecil Faulkner and his B-17 crew left Hickam Field for Midway to search for the Japanese and were among those who bombed the Striking Force on the fourth. On 5 June, six other crews flew out to relieve them, including Captain James T. "Butch" Brady. Each crew carried a volunteer maintenance man from the flight line. Sergeant Fred S. Crane was on board Brady's plane and spent the next several days on the island. He installed a new engine in plane damaged by a bird and repaired aircraft damaged in the battle. [James G. Carroll, *Sopac Holiday* (Self-published, 1986), 3; Interview with Fred S. Crane, 13 October 2000]

group, who wore uniforms to their regular jobs during the day, and urged women and children living downtown to evacuate elsewhere. Once the clash began, authorities in Hawaii did not officially inform the population but advised that evacuations were necessary because of imminent air action. When the navy announced the news on 4 June, the people waited for an invasion.[16]

Yamamoto divided his surface forces into four main groups: the First Mobile Force, Carrier Striking Force (Vice Admiral Chuichi Nagumo in carrier HIJMS *Akagi*)*, with its 261 aircraft, which would attack Midway prior to the invasion; the Midway Occupation Force (Vice Admiral Nobutake Kondo in cruiser HIJMS *Atago*) of transports, which would invade Midway; the First Fleet, Main Body (Yamamoto in battleship HIJMS *Yamato*) of supporting battleships and cruisers; and the Northern Area Force (Vice Admiral Kikuji Kakuta) with the light carriers HIJMS *Ryujo* and HIJMS *Junyo*, which would invade the Aleutians. Additionally, Yamamoto deployed an Advance Expeditionary Force of 16 submarines to the Hawaiian Islands. The units began sailing for Midway by late May.

Meanwhile, through deceptive misinformation, U.S. naval intelligence on Oahu, using the MAGIC decryption device, had decoded Japanese fleet radio messages indicating the primary forces were steaming toward Midway. Nimitz assembled two task forces to meet the threat. Under Rear Admiral Raymond A. Spruance, TF 16 left Pearl on 28 May headed north with *Enterprise* and *Hornet*. After miraculously quick repairs to *Yorktown* (damaged at Coral Sea), Fletcher's TF 17 followed but in a different northwestward direction. The two joined some 350 miles northeast of Midway on 2 June, with Fletcher in tactical command. In a series of continuing good fortune, the American carriers sortied from Pearl just before four Japanese submarines arrived in the area. Thus the Japanese were unaware the carriers were gone, and never knew the locations or dispositions of the American groups until the battle commenced. Twenty-five U.S. subs under Rear Admiral Robert H. English then moved into position around Midway.† Japanese patrol aircraft arriving at French Frigate Shoals, between Hawaii and Midway, where they planned to refuel from submarines, found only Americans and turned back. Another attempt to reconnoiter the American whereabouts failed.

The Japanese plan was first to launch air strikes against Midway defenses, then follow with the invasion transports. The Main Body, with transports but no carriers, would remain in the rear until needed. On 3 June land-based planes from Midway found the Main Body. In movements preliminary to the battle, B-17 bombers out of Midway bombed the transports but inflicted no damage. PBY *Catalina* patrol planes followed this with a night attack with identical results. At the same time, Kakuta's force bombed Dutch Harbor in the Aleutians.

After midnight on the fourth, acting on scout plane reports, Nimitz advised TFs 16 and 17 of the Main Body position, about 574 miles from Midway, course and speed. Around dawn a *Catalina* sighted two carriers and their escorts: "Many planes heading Midway from 320 degrees distance 150 miles!" Nagumo had dispatched the first waves of 108 fighters, bombers, and torpedo planes. The battle had begun. Although hitting some island buildings, gun emplacements, and other installations, and destroying 17 of the 26 U.S. fighters that rose to stop them, the raid was inconsequential. On returning to his carrier, its leader requested another run.

At 0715, still unaware of any U.S. carriers in the area, Nagumo agreed. Since not anticipating any surface action, he decided to recover all returning Midway strike aircraft and ordered both his reserve aircraft and the returning force to be rearmed with bombs for another land attack. This proved to be one of the costliest errors of the Pacific War. As the replenishing began, Nagumo learned from a lone scout plane that the U.S. carriers had been sighted.

* Nagumo's Striking Force had attacked Pearl Harbor with four of the carriers now on the Midway expedition: *Akagi, Kaga, Soryu,* and *Hiryu.*

† Besides the four Japanese and three U.S. carriers, the American forces included 234 carrier aircraft and cruiser-launched float planes, plus 110 army and navy fighters, bombers, and patrol planes on Midway.

At about 0800, Fletcher, himself knowing the Japanese were in the vicinity, exercised the initiative. He dispatched a wave of torpedo and dive bombing planes from *Enterprise*, *Hornet*, and *Yorktown* to find the carriers. They arrived overhead about 0930. A Japanese combat air patrol of fighters and heavy surface anti-aircraft fire annihilated the carrier-launched attackers, who inflicted no damage themselves. From Midway, B-26s and more B-17s joined in the loosely coordinated attack and neither caused nor suffered damage. Of the 41 carrier planes, only six survived.

While his aircraft were in transition being refueled and armed for land attacks, the four flight decks were littered with gasoline, ordnance, and stacked-up planes. Although totally unsuccessful in hitting their targets, the U.S. wave created two significant openings in Nagumo's defense. His combat air patrol was "on the deck" warding off the first wave of low-flying torpedo planes and dive bombers, and his anti-aircraft steaming formations had been disrupted.

At about 1030, the second wave of SBD Douglas *Dauntless* dive bombers arrived from *Enterprise* and *Yorktown* during the confusion. Within five minutes the *Enterprise* planes hit and fatally damaged *Kaga* and *Akagi*, and *Yorktown* pilots wrecked *Soryu*. At 1100, the fourth carrier, *Hiryu*, counterstruck at *Yorktown*, disabling the U.S. ship before she was put out of action by another *Hiryu* attack. In return, at 1700 *Enterprise Dauntlesses* mortally damaged *Hiryu*. On the fifth, Japanese destroyers scuttled both *Akagi* and *Hiryu* (*Kaga* and *Soryu* were on the bottom). On the sixth, a Japanese submarine torpedo laid to rest the struggling *Yorktown* and also sank the destroyer USS *Hammann* (DD-412).* The same day, dive bombers from *Enterprise* and *Hornet* sank the heavy cruiser HIJMS *Mikuma* and damaged two destroyers. The battle was over.

U.S. Aircraft in the Battle of Midway

USS *Yorktown* (CV-5)
  Fighting Squadron 5 (VF-5)
    25 Grumman F4F *Wildcat* fighters
  Bombing Squadron 5 (VB-5)
    18 Douglas SBD-3 *Dauntless* dive bombers
  Scouting Squadron 5 (VS-5)
    19 *Dauntlesses*
  Torpedo Squadron 5 (VT-5)
    13 Douglas TBD-1 *Devastator* torpedo planes
USS *Enterprise* (CV-6)
  VF-6
    27 *Wildcats*
  VB-6
    19 SBD-2 and SBD-3 *Dauntlesses*
  VS-6
    19 SBD-2 and SBD-3 *Dauntlesses*
  VT-6
    14 *Devastators*
USS *Hornet* (CV-8)
  VF-8
    27 *Wildcats*
  VS-8
    18 SBD-1, SBD-2, SBD-3 *Dauntlesses*
  VB-8
    19 SBD-2 and SBD-3 *Dauntlesses*
  VT-8
    15 *Devastators*

The bloodied Nagumo had lost all four carriers, two-thirds of the Combined Fleet's heavy carriers, and retired westward. Spruance, who had been given force command, did not pursue and also retired out of range of the Main Body which was fast approaching Midway and hoping to engage. Failing to make contact, Yamamoto then canceled the Midway invasion and left the area. Spruance followed but failed to find the battered Striking Force or Main Body, and departed for Pearl.

Midway was the turning point of the Pacific War and one of the most decisive battles in history. Like Coral Sea, it was fought entirely by aircraft with no surface ship-to-ship engagements. The threat of a Japanese invasion of Hawaii and the West Coast was relieved, and the setback postponed (never resumed) reduced ventures into the South and Southwest Pacific. Japanese expansion essentially had been

* Rear Admiral Fletcher transferred his flag from *Yorktown* to the cruiser USS *Astoria* (CA-34) and his tactical command to Spruance. Lieutenant Commander Berton A. Robbins, Jr., served aboard *Astoria* at Midway and USS *Chicago* (CA-29) at Coral Sea as a staff member of Rear Admiral William W. Smith's Cruiser Task Force. Spruance, a surface warfare officer and not an aviator, directed the final days at Midway and is generally considered *the* "hero" of Midway. He surely was one of the foremost fighting and thinking flag officers in U.S. naval history. Fletcher lost only his carrier flagship and none of his genius or luster and shares in the Midway glory.

stopped. Several key factors worked in the U.S. favor: the effective use of MAGIC/ULTRA intelligence information, superior carrier warfare tactics and leadership, fearless courage and leadership of U.S. naval aviators, and—above all—extremely good luck.

Japanese losses were 4 carriers, 1 cruiser, 322 aircraft, 3,500 lives (including 100 pilots). United States losses were 1 carrier, 1 destroyer, 150 aircraft, and 307 lives.

With the report of victory "Hawaii breathed a deep sigh of relief...[it was] the beginning of Hawaii's change from an outpost of defense to a staging area for offense." In the months after Midway, "tension gave way to a steady routine of living and working. Sometimes the war touched homes with sadness and sometimes it brought fear, but at other times it made life pleasantly hectic and brought exhilaration. There was excitement in exchanging the latest rumor, in complaining long and loudly about inconveniences, and in writing letters to Mainland friends about flashlights that would not work, passes and identification card that were lost, and bomb shelters that caved in." Six months after Midway the army declared the Islands safe from invasion, but fears of air raids and commando raids continued until the end of the war.[17]

We were, as most kids are, resilient and our routines became normal occurrences filled with adventure and curiosity. What would today bring? We were truly "make-it-happen" types with active imaginations. Our mother suffered from loneliness and angst over Dad, how to deal with us and still do a professional job, finding enough nourishing food for our growing bodies, and somewhere in there I'm sure she worried about our education, or lack of it, or perhaps we were learning things too far in advance of our age group. Day-to-day existence took more effort than adult counterparts' on the Mainland, and with all the rules and regulations imposed on all of us living under wartime conditions, parenting must have been exhausting.

As the days grew longer we kids seemed to have more freedom outside with longer hours on the beach and staying later in our club house with the Cease sisters. Saturday nights were always special because of the Hit Parade *broadcasting the top 10 favorite songs of the week. There was always great excitement leading up to the number one song complete with drum roll and finally announcement. Even though we usually knew what it would be, there was a feeling of having won the answer if we called out ahead of time the correct name. Then we would sing the song at the top of our lungs, wishing the show to go on and on until we were tired enough to go to bed. Our favorite for many weeks was* Chattanooga Choo Choo, *because we could make the* choo choo *sound in the beginning and the end, and it had such opportunity for improvisation and playing different parts. Also, no one needed a lot of talent to belt out this one. Our rendition of* Old Black Magic *was probably enough to make Johnny Mercer cry, and* Mairzy Doats *made Mother groan. Even the adults at the Comstock would often join us in this wonderful once-a-week happening, and this made Saturday night very special.*

Wilmingtonians at Midway

Wilmington and New Hanover County, North Carolina, is proud of its three native-son decorated heroes at Midway. Two were bonafide, the other not. The two were pilots of *Dauntless* dive bombers of Scouting (Squadron) Six from the *Enterprise*, Lieutenant (Junior Grade) Clarence Earl Dickinson and Ensign Carl David Peiffer. Each is credited with helping to sink the *Kaga*. Each received the Navy Cross for his actions, as did all naval pilots participating in the battle, Peiffer posthumously. Dickinson, earlier credited with sinking a Japanese submarine on the surface on 10 December 1941, the first Japanese vessel to be sunk after Pearl Harbor, ditched his plane on return to *Enterprise* and was rescued. Peiffer suffered fuel exhaustion and ditched, but was never found. In 1944 a destroyer escort was named for him, the USS *Peiffer* (DE-588), and in 1945 a small commercial airfield in his home county which was open for a few years.

Lieutenant Colonel Brooke E. Allen, U.S. Army Air Forces, a B-17 pilot, helped lead the B-17 attack from Midway on 4 June. As second in command of the bomber flight, he led it back safely after the flight leader was forced to return early. Allen received the Distinguished Service Cross, the army's equivalent to the Navy Cross, but in retrospect did not deserve it. None of his bombing group's bombs hit any Japanese target. When America needed heroes, he came along at the right time. Allen saw later combat action and eventually in his career was promoted to general.*

U.S. Aircraft Carriers in the Pacific
December 1941–June 1942

7 December—On station (not in Pearl Harbor): *Enterprise, Lexington*; en route from California: *Saratoga*
1 January—On station: *Enterprise, Lexington, Saratoga*; en route from California: *Yorktown*
12 January—*Enterprise, Lexington, Yorktown*; *Saratoga* damaged, en route Bremerton, Washington, for repairs
13 April—*Enterprise, Lexington, Yorktown, Hornet*
7-8 May—Battle of the Coral Sea: *Lexington, Yorktown; Lexington* sinks on 8 May, *Yorktown* damaged, repaired in Pearl; on station: *Enterprise, Hornet*
3-6 June—Battle of Midway: *Enterprise, Hornet, Yorktown; Yorktown* sinks on 7 June; *Saratoga* arrives Hawaii
10 June—*Enterprise, Hornet, Saratoga;* USS *Wasp* (CV-7) arrives in Pacific, proceeds to Pearl
15 June—*Saratoga* (Task Force 11), *Enterprise* (TF 16), *Hornet* (TF 17), *Wasp* (TF 18)

U.S. and Japanese Carrier Task Forces
December 1941–June 1942

The composition of U.S. and Japanese carrier (CV) task forces, including battleships (BB), heavy cruisers (CA), light cruisers (CL), and destroyers (DD) during the same period were:[18]

United States, 1941				
Raids	1 CV	3-4 CA/CL	5-9 DD	(Note 1)
United States, 1942				
Raids	1-2	4-6	5-10	(2)
Coral Sea	2	7	12	(3)
United States, Midway				
TF 16	2	6	11	(4)
TF 17	1	2	6	(4)

(Note 1) Attempted relief of Wake Island, then raided Gilberts
(2) Raids on Marshalls and Gilberts were by one-carrier TFs; raid on Papua had two CVs

* Dickinson also participated in the Marshalls raid. He wrote a 1942 book titled *The Flying Guns: The Cockpit Record of a Naval Pilot from Pearl Harbor through Midway*. The county library still has the original copy it received at the time. It is the naval equivalent to the better-known marine-written *Flying Leathernecks*, about which a wartime movie was made. Both Dickinson and Allen visited Wilmington in 1942 after returning from combat, made speeches, and helped sell war bonds.

Allen's nomination for the Midway award likely was based on several factors: erroneous after-action reports of damage inflicted by the B-17s, the navy's reticence to divulge the extent of its involvement after breaking the Japanese code, by default allowing the army air forces to claim undeserved public credit for the victory, and the country's thirst for heroes in a war that had been going against it.

(3) Two separate TFs operating in cooperation
(4) Two TFs operated in cooperation

Japan, 1941				
Pearl Harbor	6 CV	5 BB/CA/CL	9 DD	
Wake Island	2	2	2	(5)
Rabaul	4	4	7	(6)
Japan, 1942				
Coral Sea	2	4	6	(7)
Midway	4	5	12	(8)
Aleutians	2	2	4	(9)

(5) Included one division of Pearl Harbor Strike Force (First Air Fleet)
(6) Included two divisions of PHSF
(7) The reunited First Air Fleet
(8) Excludes Midway invasion force with its one light carrier (CVL)
(9) Excludes Aleutians invasion force and battle fleet with its one CVL

U.S.-Allied Pacific Naval and Related Action
December 1941–June 1942

7 December	Japanese carrier forces attack U.S. forces at Pearl Harbor and other Hawaiian installations
10 December	U.S. forces surrender on Guam.
23 December	U.S. forces surrender on Wake Island
11 January	Carrier *Saratoga* severely damaged by submarine near Hawaii, returns to Bremerton, Washington, for repairs
23 January	Marines arrive to reinforce Samoa
24 January	Java Sea surface action; Battle of Makassar Strait
1 February	U.S. carrier raids under Admiral Halsey on Marshall Islands, and Admiral Fletcher on Gilbert Islands
20 February	U.S. carrier attacks attempted on Rabaul, New Britain
24 February	U.S. carrier raid under Halsey on Wake
27–29 February	Battles of the Java Sea and Sunda Strait; cruiser *Houston* and carrier *Langley* lost
4 March	U.S. carrier raid under Halsey on Marcus Island
10 March	U.S. carrier raid on Salamaua and Lae, Papua, from *Lexington* and *Yorktown*
12 March	U.S. advance forces (Americal Division) arrive at Noumea, New Caledonia, to build base
14 March	U.S. Army troops begin arriving in Australia in substantial numbers
17 March	U.S. General Douglas MacArthur arrives in Australia to take command of Southwest Pacific area
30 March	Joint Chiefs of Staff divides Pacific into two commands: Pacific Ocean Area under Nimitz in Hawaii, and Southwest Pacific Area (includes New Guinea, Australia, Bismarck Islands, Solomon Islands) under MacArthur in Australia
9 April	U.S forces surrender in Bataan, Philippines
19 April	U.S. B-25 raid on Tokyo under Lieutenant Colonel Doolittle from carrier *Hornet*; *Enterprise* accompanies

4 May	U.S. carrier raid under Admiral Fletcher (in *Yorktown*) on Tulagi, Solomon Islands
6 May	U.S. forces surrender on Corregidor, Philippines
7–8 May	Battle of the Coral Sea; *Lexington*, destroyer *Sims*, oiler *Neosho* lost
18 May	U.S./Filipino troops in Panay surrender, ending formal resistance in Philippines
31 May	U.S. battleships USS *Colorado* (BB-45) and USS *Maryland* (BB-46), in San Francisco since early 1942, depart for Hawaii
3–6 June	Battle of Midway; *Yorktown* and destroyer *Hammann* lost
6–7 June	Japanese occupy islands of Kiska and Attu in Aleutians (Alaska)
14 June	U.S. 1st Marine Division begins arriving in New Zealand
15 June	U.S. and Australian fleets reorganize: Task Force 1 (battle line of battleships) at San Francisco; TF 8 (cruisers and destroyers) in Aleutians, TF 11 *(Saratoga* group); TF 16 (*Enterprise* group), TF 17 (*Hornet* group) all at Pearl; TF 18 (*Wasp* group) temporarily at San Diego; TF 44 (cruisers and destroyers) in Australian waters

"Butch" vs. the *Kates* or *Bettys*[19]

Naval historian Samuel Eliot Morison recounted an interesting sidelight in the first fight between carrier aircraft at sea as the *Lexington* task force headed for a strike on Rabaul on February 21, 1942. It was "conducted in great part right over the task force, in full view of the *Lexington* and the other ships, amid scenes of wildest enthusiasm—everybody topside waving and yelling encouragement to the pilots. 'I even had to remind some members of my staff that this was not a football game,' said [Vice] Admiral [Wilson, Jr.] Brown. The action went on intermittently from 1620 to after 1800, as two waves of nine planes each attacked; and it is believed that few escaped. Lieutenant Edward H. ("Butch") O'Hare especially distinguished himself by shooting down five *Kates* [Nakajima B5N2 torpedo-bombers] one of which attempted to crash *Lexington* in its fall. Only two of our planes and one pilot (Ensign J. Woodrow Wilson) were lost. This air action made 'Lady Lex' the proudest carrier in the United States Navy, and enhanced the morale of all carrier plane pilots in the fleet." Surprise lost, Brown called off the attack on Rabaul. He was later awarded the Medal of Honor and was killed in action. (His Medal of Honor citation indicates the five aircraft were twin-engined, not single like the *Kates*. Therefore, they could have been Mitsubishi G4M1 *Bettys*.) The city of Chicago, Illinois, named its airport in Butch's honor.

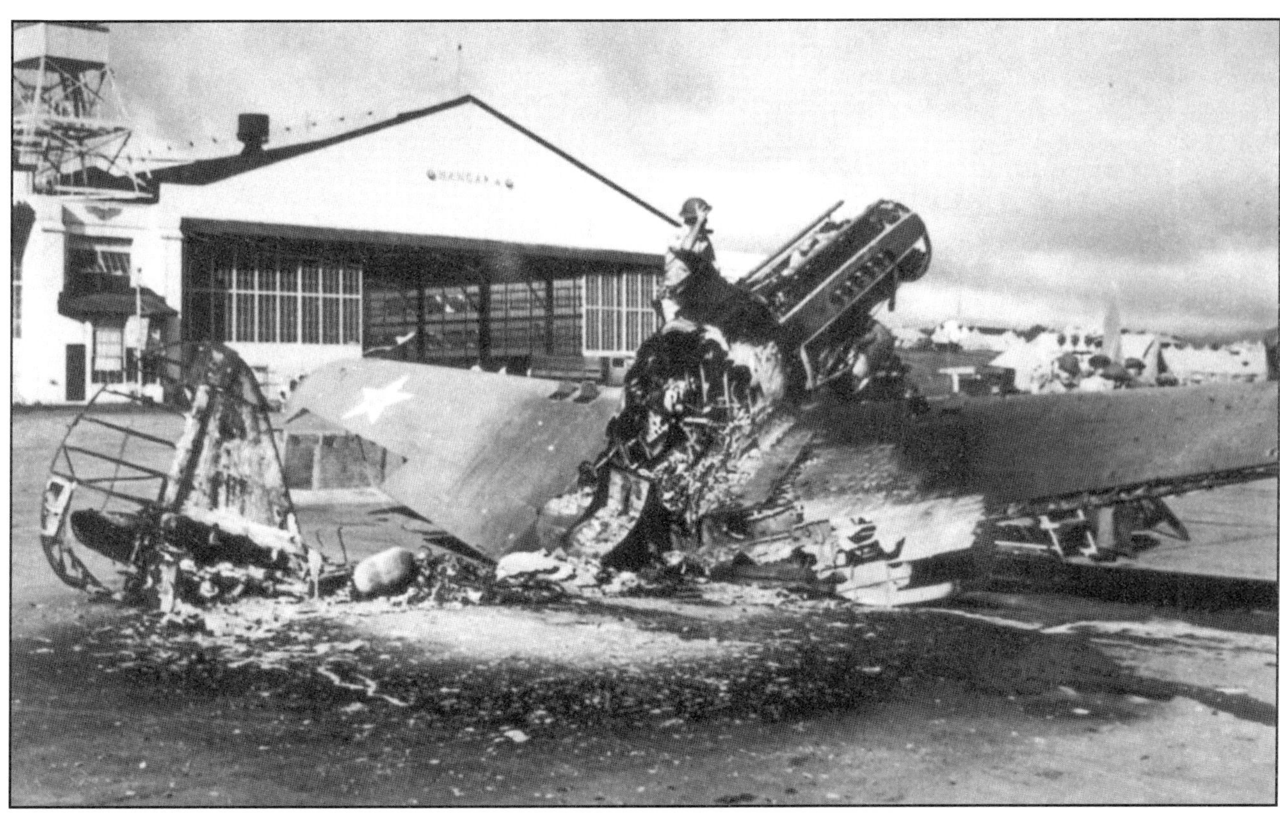

Burned wreckage of U.S. army air forces' P-40 near Hangar 4 at Wheeler Field. Note long blast tubes on the plane's nose machine guns.

Naval Historical Center

Destroyed U.S. aircraft, including P-40s, at Wheeler Field.

Naval Historical Center

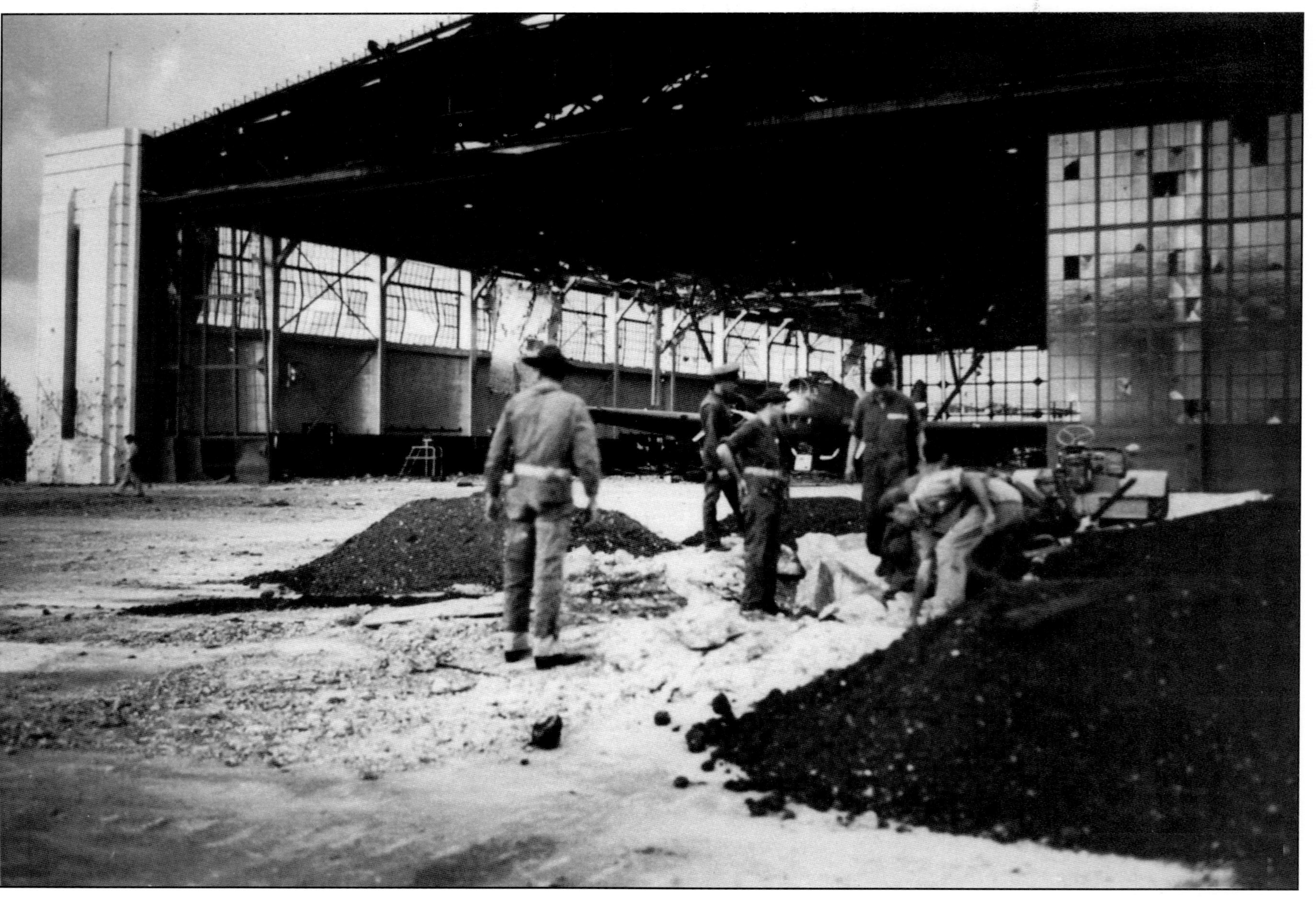

Bomb damage to hangars 11-13 and 15-17 at Hickam Field. Note bomb crater in foreground and damaged B-18 bomber in hangar.

Naval Historical Center

Wreckage of downed Japanese *Zero* fighter in residential area of Honolulu.

Naval Historical Center

Wrecked B-17 *Flying Fortress* bomber at Hickam Field.

Naval Historical Center

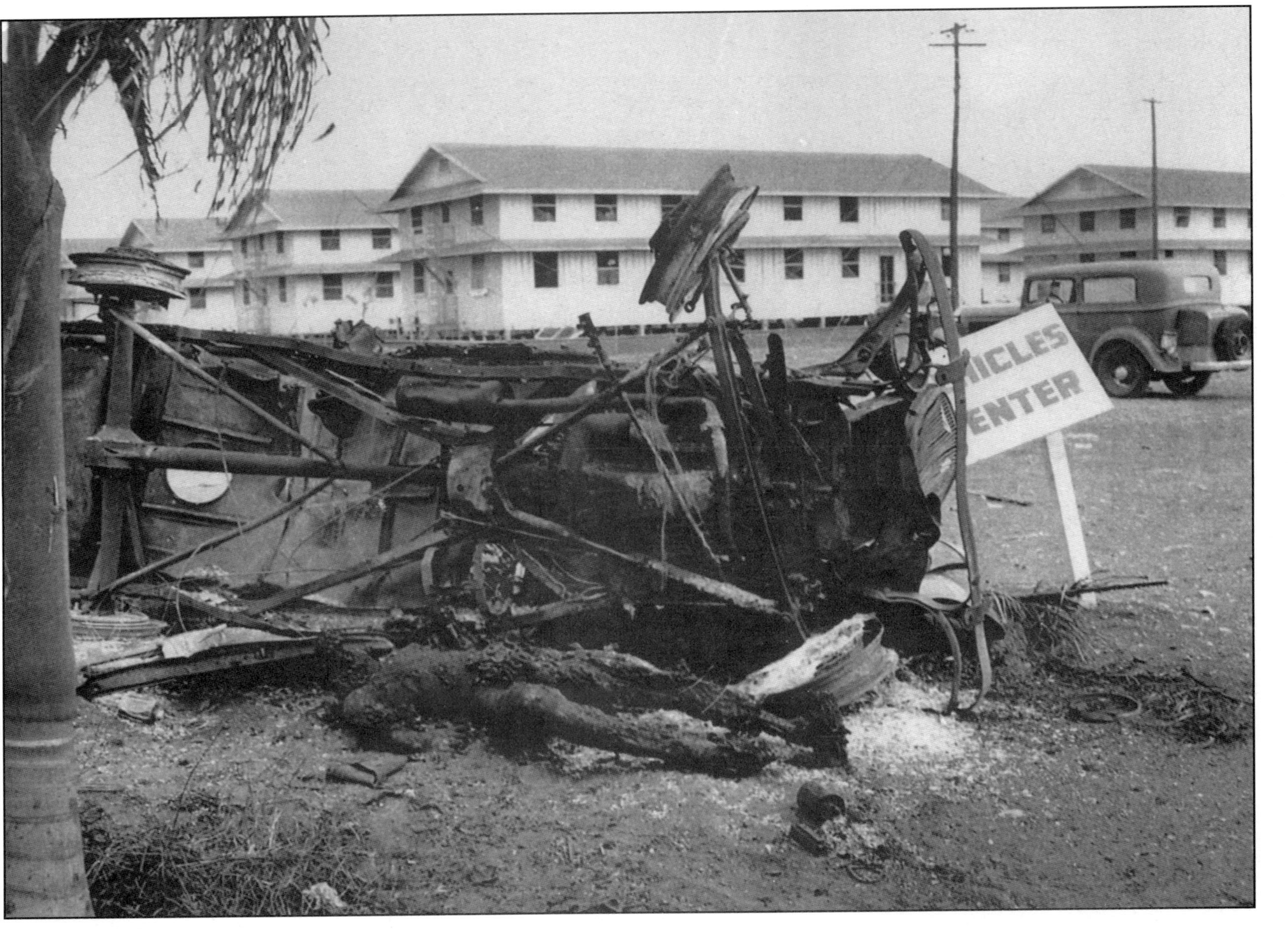

Wreckage of vehicle with charred body of occupant on U.S. military base.

Naval Historical Center

Army pilots Lieutenants Kenneth Taylor and George Welch shot down this Japanese dive bomber near Wheeler Field.

Naval Historical Center

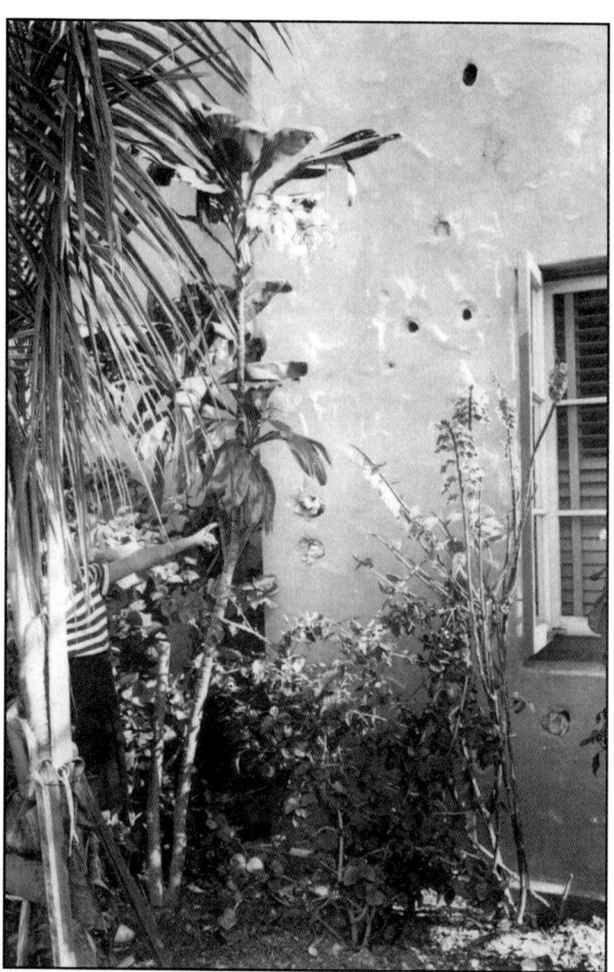

Bullet and shrapnel holes caused by aircraft and anti-aircraft fire pock this residential building, a block from where we lived at the Comstock Apartments Hotel, less than two blocks from the Royal Hawaiian Hotel.

This is one of Mother's most famous and recognizable post-attack photographs that has been widely reprinted. It shows a bullet-riddled passenger car (even the tires) with three dead occupants. Sometimes we didn't know if Japanese planes caused damage like this, or our own anti-aircraft fire.

This was once a truck on which unfortunately landed an errant bomb or shell.

Wrecked houses in the vicinity of Pearl City near Pearl Harbor. Berton and I are on the porch.

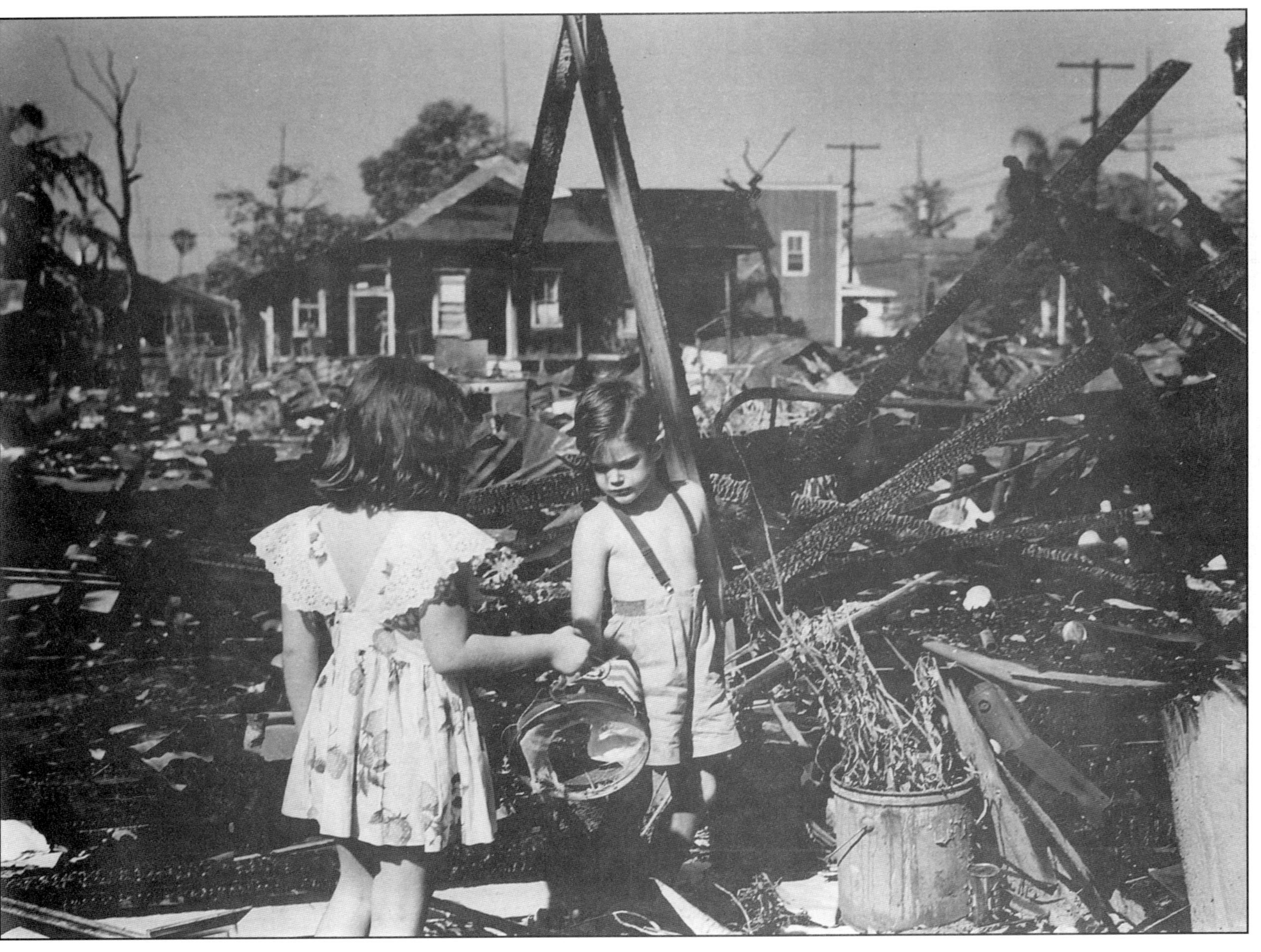

Here we are looking through the debris of damaged houses. It definitely was no scavenger hunt.

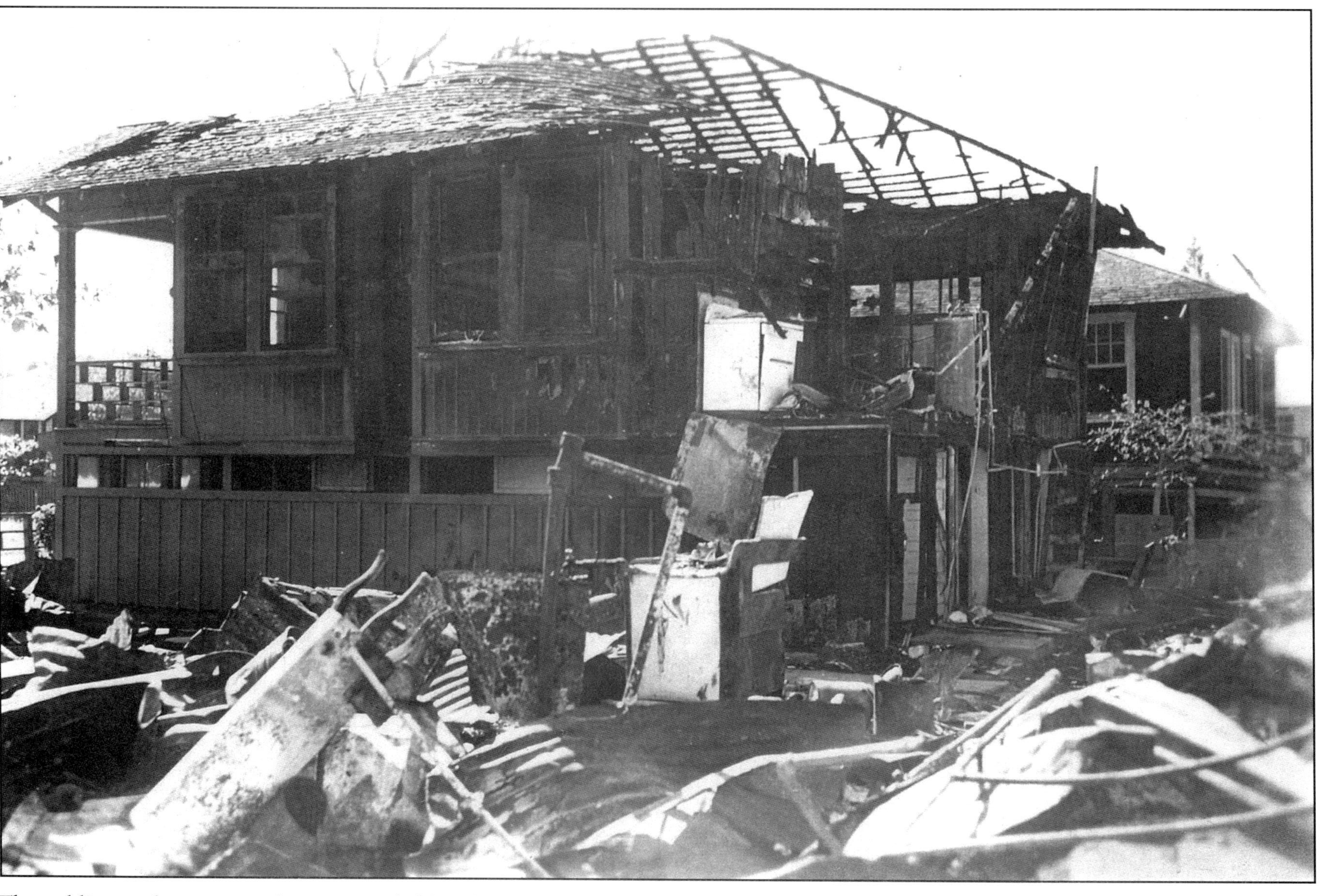

The public may be unaware that unintended bombing occurred in some residential and business areas as well as military bases. Also, many of our own anti-aircraft shells that missed hitting planes fell into these areas and caused significant damage.

Chapter 3

"Destroyed to Pieces": Ship Salvage Operations

> When the repaired U.S. battleships went back into action it is possible that they were not recognized by the enemy as the ships the Japanese had so often boasted that they had "destroyed to pieces." They went back with new contours and sometimes completely new silhouettes, but always they went back better than new.[1]

The fleet required these ships, and the damage to ships at Pearl Harbor had to be repaired. Restoring the battleships to their original condition was out of the question. The obvious solution was to rehabilitate them using recent design and equipment improvements. With their modernization, the fleet was enhanced by added armor, firepower, and operating efficiency. Had the Japanese not attacked Hawaii, and had the United States eventually gone to war with its existing Pacific Fleet, one wonders how well and how long the archaic battle wagons and other damaged ships would have performed.

Of the almost 100 ships that occupied berths at Pearl on 7 December, only 19 were sunk or damaged. All of these ships except three engaged the Japanese either soon or down the road—fitting revenge for the dastardly act. The battleship USS *Arizona* (BB-39) was left to rest where she sunk and not salvaged. The battleship USS *Oklahoma* (BB-37), which capsized and lay with its superstructure in the mud, was righted in an astounding feat of salvage engineering. Later it was decided to scrap her. The target ship USS *Utah* (AG-16), a former battleship, lay out of the main stream and was not salvaged.

The Pearl Harbor Navy Yard, commanded by Rear Admiral William R. Furlong, conducted the ship salvage operations. The officer charged with devising, coordinating, and executing the salvage plan was Captain Homer N. Wallin of the navy's Construction Corps. Later decorated with the Navy Distinguished Service Medal, Wallin was largely responsible for the success of what was probably the largest and most dramatic such undertaking in naval history. At the time he was the senior Battle Force Engineer in Hawaii.* "This energetic specialist knew the complicated insides of many of the sunken vessels as well as some doctors knew their patients."[2] Salvage included not only literally raising ships from the dead and making minor permanent repairs and sending ships back into service, but also temporary repairs to many who sailed for the West Coast for permanent repairs and modernization.

Speed was of the Essence

The threat of further Japanese attacks on Hawaii and the U.S. Pacific Fleet dictated a salvage schedule driven by speed. The easiest to repair were accomplished first, while the more difficult were carefully planned and equipment gathered for their labor. By 22 December, the battleship USS *Pennsylvania* (BB-38), damaged in dry dock, was repaired, and the battleship USS *Maryland* (BB-46) was seaworthy. The navy yard, aided by the *Maryland*'s crew, had repaired her afloat, thus saving drydock space for ships with greater problems. She was ready for action before New Year's Day, if ordered. The battleship USS *Tennessee* (BB-43), wedged between the sunken USS *West Virginia* (BB-48) and its Ford Island berth, but not seriously hit, posed a formidable

* Wallin, a 1917 Naval Academy graduate, did postgraduate work at the Massachusetts Institute of Technology in naval architecture and had tours of duty in navy yards and Washington, D.C., in the Bureau of Ships. Following his post-Pearl duty as fleet salvage officer, he commanded three naval shipyards and was promoted to rear admiral. He retired in 1955. His book (1968) on the salvage operations is the most complete account.

problem. Under full steam she did not budge. By 20 December she was ready to move after fuel had been pumped from her bunkers to lighten the ship. That week, the cruiser USS *Helena* (CL-50), heavily damaged by a torpedo but credited with bagging several Japanese planes, sailed for the Mare Island, California, Shipyard.

From the Mainland came shipments of salvage equipment, including pumps, lumber shorings, torches, and steel cables for winches to be used in righting capsized ships. All were unavailable in the Hawaiian market, as was the specialized manpower needed. Hundreds of experts and unskilled laborers hurried to Oahu by ship to find work and aid in the operations. The task was slow, muddy, slimy, tedious, and perilous. Experienced men soon found women in water-resistant white coveralls working beside them on the ships' grimy, barnacled outjuttings. Officials trained acetylene torch cutters on the job to slice away at the twisted sections which obstructed pumping and raising.

Wallin, who apportioned his time to priority projects requiring his services, realized that ample supplies and skilled workers were not at hand. In serious short supply were lumber, fastenings, electric welders, carpenters, civilian mechanics, and engineers. A major salvage task was the removal from disabled ships of as much anti-aircraft weapon systems and ammunition as possible to reinforce defenses around the navy yard, fleet moorings, and air stations. Of great value were range finders, small arms, gun directors, and ordnance instruments. Divers did much of this work. The proper handling of personal property and classified material was carefully assured.

Removing human bodies from flooded compartments in the damaged ships was a psychological problem to working parties soon overcome with a bit of ingenuity. The scheme was that 2-3 feet of water was left in each compartment so the bodies could be floated into canvas bags, the bags tightly tied, lifted out, and transported to the nearby naval hospital for identification and subsequent burial.

"The cleaning of compartments of unwatered ships was a beggarly job," Wallin wrote. "Trained men for the fleet were in short supply; even recruits were in great demand." Most of the several hundred cleaners came from nearby vessels or the receiving station where men were awaiting permanent assignment. Each cleaner had a tank suit and knee-high rubber boots. Suits quickly became oil soaked and were turned in for clean ones. Men entering improperly ventilated spaces wore gas masks. The cleaning routine was first to remove wreckage, ammunition, debris, stores, and usable items, then apply a high pressure fresh-water hose.[3] During the complex salvage operations four men were killed. Two died beneath the surface in the *Arizona* wreckage after acetylene torches ignited gases, and two were overcome by hydrogen sulphide gas on the USS *Nevada* (BB-36).

Wallin described the *Nevada* deaths to historian Paul Stillwell.[4]

> As the unwatering schedule continued, a number of people felt ill effects from the apparent prevalence of gas which seemed to fill the ship. The very dangerous toxic properties of this gas were discovered on 7 February....Lieutenant James S. Clarkson was in the pumped-out trunk forward of the steering engine room and removed the cap from the air test fitting on the door to determine the water pressure within. The water which entered the trunk from the steering engine room released a large volume of toxic gas and Lieutenant Clarkson was overcome and collapsed. Other persons entered the trunk to rescue him, with the result that eventually six or more persons were overcome. The final result was that Lieutenant Clarkson and Chief Machinist Mate Peter C. DeVries died as a result of gas poisoning. Thereafter, a very careful investigation was made of the gas situation, and it was determined that the gas was generated by reason of the polluted and stagnated harbor water being under pressure in closed compartments, thus forming hydrogen sulphide which is given off in large volumes in lethal concentrations when the water is released from pressure. Immediately, precautionary steps were taken to provide additional ventilation, mostly suction blowers. Also, persons were prohibited from entering compartments without respiratory equipment

> if the compartments were found to contain dangerous concentrations of gas. There were no more persons overcome by gas on board the *Nevada*...."

Salvaging the USS *California* (BB-44)

Her crew affectionately called the *California*, launched in 1919, "The Prune Barge" for the product produced in the state. The commanding officer was Captain Joel W. Bunkley. She suffered primarily from two huge gaping torpedo holes between frames 46-60 and 95-100 on the port side. A 250-kilogram bomb passing through the main deck and exploding on the armored second deck did considerable damage, killing a number of sailors, but did not affect stability. The whole quarterdeck and forecastle were under water. Experts figured it would take four years to salvage ships like *California* that were electric-driven (*Nevada* had reciprocating engines). The first concern was unloading all guns except from turret four which was below water.

She was well designed and tough, staying afloat for three days before finally settling partially under water with a list to port by 5-1/2 degrees. On 7 December at 1000, *California* was temporarily abandoned when a surface oil fire from *Arizona* crept over the ship, interfering with damage control and probably facilitating her sinking. She drydocked without a patch.

When salvage began, some 50 bodies remained. Workers removed the ship and flag-conning towers and mainmast, and from barges constructed a wooden cofferdam around quarterdeck and forecastle areas in 30-foot sections from 4-8 inches in thickness. Each cofferdam section was made watertight at the deck coaming, braced against fixed objects, and fitted for sandbags to overcome the wood's positive buoyancy. Workers set up electric deep-well pumps. Divers and the Pacific Bridge Company did most of the work. Once the inside water level was below that outside, they checked water leakage with oakum enclosed in canvas, and divers below decks plugged overboard vents and other ports. Lowering the water level stayed in sequence with removal of bodies, oil and stores, preservation of equipment, and cleaning compartments.

On 24 March 1942 the ship floated nearly on an even keel with a 40-foot draft. After the cofferdams were knocked off she entered dry dock #2 on 9 April where permanent repairs were made to most of the damage. Under her own power she departed from Pearl on 10 October for Puget Sound, Washington, Navy Yard where she received the designation "newly-modernized old battleship (OBB)."

The *West Virginia*

The "Weevie," launched in 1921, was more severely damaged than *Nevada* or *California*, enduring seven port-side torpedo hits, at least three below the armor belt. While the ship listed 20–30 degrees it is possible that one or more entered through holes made by previous torpedoes. The series of gashes were 120 feet long and 12–15 feet high. One bomb hit had collapsed the main, second, and third decks together 10 feet below the original third deck. "Inside it looked as if a giant had crumpled the ship and then lighted a torch to the remains...."[5] Her own and *Arizona*'s spreading oil fires were not extinguished for 30 hours and caused considerable additional damage. *West Virginia* likely would have capsized if it had not been jammed against *Tennessee* moored on her starboard side. Some of her officers and crew remained attached but most were transferred to other ships.

Three men trapped inside kept a calendar and lived until at least 23 December, surviving off emergency rations at a fresh water battle station in an unflooded area. Workers found 62 bodies in all. Several others in flooded areas had crawled on top of overhead steam pipes to take advantage of air pockets as long as they lasted. The total number who died was 105, including the commanding officer, Captain Mervyn S. Bennion.

Engineers built a series of cofferdams 50 feet deep bolted to the hull to form one large outer wall, then installed underwater concrete patches of cement that hardens under water from above the waterline to below the turn of the bilge. Civilian technicians and ship's crew combined to pump out, clean, and raise the ship. ("The common workmen of the navy yard blenched at the indescribable filth and grisly human remains in her wrecked and soaked interior.")[6] Highly successful, the patches eventually required small dynamite charges to loosen them. On 17 May *West Virginia* refloated, and because the anticipated repair time was long, the ship docked in dry dock #1. Damaged ships returning from combat had priority on the larger #2.

West Virginia steamed under her own power to Bremerton, Washington, where she was transformed into practically a new ship. This included a welded rather than riveted hull, doubly thick deck and turret armor, new ventilation system, improved watertight integrity, additional anti-aircraft armament of 40mm quads, doubling of 5"38 guns to 16, and torpedo "blisters" on each side. She rejoined the fleet in mid-1944.

The *Oklahoma*

Oklahoma had rolled over following at least five torpedo hits, trapping hundreds of men, and "lying like a great whale almost totally submerged."[7] Immediately after the all-clear, men on a passing boat heard faint tapping from within the hull and used acetylene torches to cut their way to the men inside. For fear of fires and asphyxiating the survivors, mechanical cutters and compressed air hammers proved safer but slower. Navy Yard master leadingman Julio DeCastro headed the rescue team. One rescue crew penetrated 150 feet into the hull freeing sailors. They saved 13 men some 24 hours after the attack, and by the end of Tuesday 32 had found their way to freedom. All told, 415 of the 1,354 crewmen perished.

In the most arduous and most spectacular salvage task, *Oklahoma* was righted from its capsized position by a series of winches and cables. Its salvage for potential future use uncertain, planning proceeded cautiously and slowly. The preparatory work took a year to complete. *Oklahoma* had to be cleared from the harbor, but would she sail again? From a scale model designed to orient divers to what they could expect from an upside-down interior, divers sealed the torpedo openings and open vents for air to enter and water to flow out. Decomposed organic matter from bodies, clothing, and provisions created a deadly gas requiring workers to don gas masks. Thus the 29,000-ton ship was given a positive buoyancy of 18,800 tons. With restoration of buoyancy, the attempt to pull the ship over to an upright position began.

To distribute strain across the hull bottom, workers erected 21 triangular frames 40-feet high (the "bents"). Six heavy steel cables led from the steel cap of the apex of each bent to padeyes welded into the starboard side. Also from each cap two steel cables led to a 16-sheave button tackle whose pendant was geared at a ratio of 8,000-to-1 to 21 5-horsepower electric winches planted in a concrete foundation on Ford Island which would operate in unison. Some machinery and about one-third of the ammunition was extracted but none of the 14-inch projectiles. Propeller blades were removed. Wallin stated he believed *Oklahoma* would roll (which he desired) instead of slide, but the bow rested in soupy mud which permitted sliding. Workmen placed two thousand tons of coral soil around the bow to prevent this. The righting process began in March 1943, and all purchases were equalized for an even pull. In one hundred hours the hull had been pulled over 90 degrees. Bents and cables were removed, and the topside cables then rolled her over completely.

Once the ship was nearly upright, divers investigated her port side damage. Masts and most superstructure were broken off on contact with the harbor bottom. She floated on 3 November 1943 with a mean draft of about 46 feet and a starboard list of only 26 minutes. Wallin was pleased the ship behaved as tested with the models. *Oklahoma* entered dry dock #2, but the navy chose not to spend more money to refurbish the ship. On 1 September 1944 she was decommissioned and sold to a wrecking company as scrap for $46,000 in December 1946. While being towed to the West Coast in May 1947, she sank during a storm.

The USS *Shaw* (DD-373)

In floating dry dock #2 on the south side of the harbor channel, *Shaw* was likely the bystander target of attempts to halt the *Nevada*, one of two ships to get underway during the attack, steaming toward the harbor entrance in a "gallant dash for freedom."* At 0930, perhaps aiming for *Nevada*, a

* With skillful leadership, the wounded *Nevada* ran aground on Hospital Point and was abandoned rather than block the channel with a dying ship. Called the "Cheer-Up Ship," she survived an atomic blast test at Bikini, and was sunk as a gunfire target ship off Oahu in 1948.

bomber dropped a single bomb into the *Shaw*'s forward magazine. It detonated, blowing apart the entire bow as far aft as frame 65, causing a white-hot fireball of flames directed upward because of the confines of the dry dock. When the dry dock sank, the ship's forward section went down with it. From frame 60 aft, the ship remained afloat.

"Exploding shells trailed multicolored smoke and streaks of fire flashed and sizzled across the sky in all directions. The largest blast yet, exceeding even the *Arizona*'s mighty explosion, sank the dry dock. It was seen by witnesses for miles around, momentarily blanking out the pillars of smoke from ships, from the oil still burning on the harbor waters and from storage tanks and hangars at Hickam Field."[8] It is amazing how the rest of the ship was not destroyed, and that Lieutenant Berton A. Robbins, Jr., who was on the drydock going aboard, was uninjured.*

The second ship named *Shaw* was launched at the Philadelphia Navy Yard on 28 October 1935. She arrived in Hawaiian waters in February 1941 and entered Pearl Harbor Navy Yard YFD-2 for repairs in November. She took two more bombs through the forward machine gun platform and port wing of the bridge. Fires spread quickly, and by 0925 the order was given to abandon ship. Efforts to flood the dock were unsuccessful. The ship originally was reported as a total loss but the machinery was in good condition. Electrician's Mate William Leckemby jumped overboard to swim to shore 150 feet away and saw the explosion once ashore. Men like Leckemby who had lost their ships reported to the receiving station and were issued new clothes, got a good meal and shower, and were assigned new ships.

She received temporary repairs by January 1942 including an entirely new false bow section, just enough to make her seaworthy. The bridge area was scrapped and a temporary mast and ship control station installed. On 9 February the ship departed for San Francisco for further repairs and modernization. "She was the first severely damaged vessel to put to sea and there was great jubilation at Pearl Harbor to see her leave under her own power...."[9] The YFD-2 was also repaired and put back into service in early 1942. By 31 August, *Shaw* was back at Pearl ready for action. Until late October, she escorted convoys between Hawaii and the West Coast. One ship she accompanied was the troop ship which took Patricia O'Meara Robbins and her children, Carroll and Berton, to California.

Besides extensive escort duty in 1943, *Shaw* provided gunfire support for the 25 December assault on Cape Gloucester, New Britain. She was badly damaged by Japanese aircraft and retired to San Francisco again for permanent repairs on 1 May 1944. By June she was back on the line supporting the Marianas Campaign, and later the 9 January 1945 invasion at Lingayen Gulf. Here Commander Robbins, captain of the destroyer USS *Leutze* (DD-481), was able to see his old ship for the first time since Pearl.

Following further action in the Philippines campaign, shortly after VJ-Day, *Shaw* was decommissioned on 2 October 1945 and scrapped in July 1946. She earned 11 battle stars.

Six months after Pearl Harbor Wallin said, "The salvage work thus far completed at Pearl Harbor has been successful well beyond the most optimistic anticipations. The work has been carried on as a cooperative endeavor to which many persons have contributed their support, their ideas, and their effort....I am pleased...to express the conviction that this important work had throughout been directed and controlled by the One Mind which governs all things well."[10] Later he added, "There was a meeting of the minds in all the jobs in which the Salvage Division was engaged. There was never a lack of confidence. Instead, there was a feeling of assurance....one mind which governs all things well."[11]

The untiring efforts of Wallin, his staff, and the navy yard workers paid high dividends as the fleet pushed back the enemy. The destroyers USS *Cassin* (DD-372) and USS *Downes* (DD-375) received seven and four battle stars respectively. Among the prize battleships, *Nevada* was a flagship in the

* Ironically, *Shaw*'s commanding officer was a Lieutenant Commander W. G. Jones. Robbins, the executive officer, had reported aboard only the day before from the USS *Tucker* (DD-374), also at Pearl, on which he had served 10 months. Jones, at home during the attack, reportedly hid under his bed.

Normandy D-Day invasion and returned to the Pacific to fight at Iwo Jima and Okinawa. *California* steamed back to Pearl on 5 May 1944 in time to fight in the Marianas Campaign, eventually earning seven battle stars. *West Virginia, Maryland, California, Tennessee*, and *Pennsylvania* "crossed the enemy's 'T'" at the Battle of Leyte Gulf (Surigao Strait), the final blow to the Japanese Combined Fleet on 25 October 1944. (*California* "pumped over sixty 15,000-pound projectiles into a Japanese battleship of the *Fuso* class.")[12] The battle wagons then participated in the Okinawa invasion where they were slightly damaged by kamikaze attacks. *West Virginia* proudly sailed into Japan with the occupation force on 27 August 1945 and was alongside USS *Missouri* (BB-63) at the official surrender signing ceremony in Tokyo Bay on 2 September.

I have no recollection of how either Berton or I celebrated our sixth and eighth birthdays in spring of 1942, but Easter made an impression. Again, the resilience and acceptance of the young in times of strain and changes can be food for the soul. We made a big thing over Easter in our family as both a religious observance of great importance and a fun time for children and being with relatives. Easter meant a pretty new dress and hat to wear to church, a decorated basket filled with special decorated candy eggs and usually one with our own name on it, and a chicken, rabbit, or duck softie to cuddle. It meant a great family feast, egg hunts for the kids, and nearly everyone behaving; adults too. But Easter 1942 was the best Mother could do, and remembering the little I do of that time so long ago, I recall only the joy of celebrating the event with the best make-do possible. Our family of three invited several of "the girls" from Diamond Head for dinner. We actually set the table with whatever rented dishes we had, pretending it was china, silver, crystal. Berton and I wore the clothes we also wore to the weddings we were in, and somewhere Mother found some real balloons she partially blew up and centered on grass with a few real hard boiled eggs saved for breakfast the next day.

If there was candy I've forgotten, and if there were any stuffed toys I have also forgotten, but the day was festive because we were with friends, each having brought a contribution to share, dressed in our best (but getting very tight) clothes, with more friends, all women, stopping in and bringing something for the occasion. How very strange to realize that during those years cigarettes were a valued commodity and a most welcome gift. Often rationed or unavailable, cigarettes were more cherished than a box of chocolates. Mother, always a smoker until her asthma became chronic, made the ultimate sacrifice that Easter by putting on the table a plate with a grouping of cigarettes to share. That was her sacrifice, a true act of love.

Seaman Henderson of the *California*[13]

Lawrence Homer Henderson, of Hampstead, North Carolina, near Wilmington, was a Seaman 1st Class in the 2nd Division on the USS *California* (BB-44). *California* was Vice Admiral William S. Pye's Battle Force flagship. Henderson manned his battle station in the high turret forward during the attack. A torpedo knocked out power, forcing them to pass the ammunition by hand. The order to abandon ship came down about 0930 and he swam through the fiery oil to Ford Island. With oil-soaked clothes and no fresh ones, he was ordered back aboard after the oil fire on water had gone by the ship. Without power, crewmen fought the shipboard fires with buckets dipped from the fantail.

Some of those killed were asphyxiated from burning paint fumes. He took wounded to Ford Island, ran out of stretchers, and improvised with mess tables. He watched as three planes from a carrier tried to land on Ford Island and were shot down. He stayed on the ship the next couple of days standing watch on the 5"/25 caliber guns, which had to be fully operated by hand. He slept in the barracks at fleet landing, went by boat each night to his watch shift on board *California*. The ship had posted sentries bow and stern. One night their boat heading toward ship was hailed and guards fired into the boat. No one was injured. It was that kind of world—everyone with a weapon was trigger happy.

Cranes lifted off the ship's 5"/25 guns still above water. They were barged to West Loch and Hickam and turned into anti-aircraft batteries. He and other crewmen were posted in West Loch sugar cane fields where they built gun emplacements, filled sandbags, and scraped charred paint off gun barrels. They stood Condition III watches (four hours on, eight off) on the guns. One night a pack of dogs entered the field chasing a bitch in heat. His gun crew hailed them, "halt, who's there?" but the noise continued. They had only a Lewis machine gun but no sidearms and fired. The next morning they found a bunch of dead dogs. This was their lone alert. They did test fire the 5"/25 guns although there was plenty of ammunition from the West Loch depot. A rigged air compressor salvaged from the ship supplied power to the guns to ram the rammers. They were granted no liberty there, issued no new clothes, and had to wash what they were wearing when they got off watch. They ate at the ammunition depot.

The crew received 3x5 postcards to send home to families. All they were allowed to do was check off either "I am wounded," "I am sick," or "I am well." He checked "well" and mailed it home. The ship carrying his mail to the West Coast was sunk and the mail lost. The men took daily musters in the cane fields, but apparently none ever got back to the naval headquarters in Washington, and personnel still on duty on the ship didn't know where they were. So, the navy notified his parents, A. R. and Ethyl Henderson of Hampstead, by telegram (he still has it) that he was missing in action. Others in his group experienced the same situation. Reports simply were not sent or received as they should. In late March 1942 Henderson was reassigned to sea duty and participated in the invasions of the Marshalls, Marianas, and Peleliu.

Baker Jeffords of the *West Virginia*[14]

Taylor Marion Jeffords, Jr., a 1939 graduate of New Hanover High School in Wilmington, North Carolina, was a Baker 3rd Class on the USS *West Virginia* (BB-48) at Pearl Harbor. When the crew abandoned ship, he assisted his best buddy Baker Johnny Twedt, who could not swim, in reaching Ford Island. Jeffords remained there for three days making sandwiches and helping arm naval aircraft. With the island's fresh water main broken, their drinking water came from the swimming pool, and had to be boiled. Wounded filled the Bloch recreation area gym.

At the Ford Island receiving station, the feeding lines were so long a man would get a meal and then go stand at the end of the line for the next one. He baked goods for the men and helped cook in a makeshift kitchen arrangement but with a modern bake shop. As reservists began to report for duty, he helped train them. Soon the navy built 10 mess halls around the Ten-Ten dock area (called "boys town") to feed shipyard workers who came from the Mainland. He made many pies during his assignment there. "The navy was paying me like I was a defense worker." He was paid for this duty in addition to his regular navy pay, and had to get a new social security card (which he still has) to cover it. After a while that part of Pearl "got to be like McHale's navy around there."

Because liquor was rationed, he made imitation bourbon that tasted like paint thinner. Friends flew in bourbon from states for him which he bought for $5 and sold in "boys town" for $30. He also made money re-selling beer. "The whole navy was doing that." His bakers also made raisin jack from sugar cane. "That bunch would do most anything." They never scrubbed the bake shop ("a McHale's navy attitude"). Rather than clean it they would have shipyard workers come in and spray paint it before inspections, and gave them butter in return.

A chief petty officer he knew named Dutch Newbar ran the Bloch enlisted recreation area. One day Newbar received a phone call from Admiral Nimitz's office asking for a case of beer. Dutch said okay, come on down and get it. Nimitz's car showed up for the beer and Dutch accompanied it back to Nimitz's office. Newbar asked Nimitz why he didn't call the officers mess for the beer, and he replied that he was the admiral and would call wherever he wanted. The admiral asked Newbar to have a cup of coffee before leaving, but he declined. He wanted to leave. Nimitz insisted, and Newbar drank a cup quickly. Later he said his whole mouth was on fire from the hot coffee.

Jeffords owned a 1940 Ford convertible while stationed at Pearl. The "tires were so thin every time you would run over a sandspur you'd get a flat." Got into Honolulu often on liberty. Beretania Street off of Kapiolani Park was always loaded with servicemen, bars, and cat (whore) houses. He joined the Elks Lodge and there hit it off with Walter Dillingham who owned the Hawaii Pineapple Corporation (Del Monte). Jeffords and his *West Virginia* shipmates hung out at Woo Fats Chinese bar: you signed the log on entering and got a free drink. "Everything was so much more advanced than Wilmington." After the attack he stayed in Pearl for nine months. The Red Cross sent for him to come home because his mother was dying. "By the time I got home my mother was well. It took so long to get there." He later saw sea duty on a seaplane tender and two carriers, where he was advanced to chief commissaryman.

Aerial view of destroyer *Shaw* in floating dry dock, *on right*, and Ford Island Naval Air Station. North is to the left of the photograph.

Naval Historical Center

Shaw in sunken floating dry dock YFD-2, 8 December 1941. Looking east. *Background,* Battleship Row.

Naval Historical Center

Shaw leaving Pearl Harbor in February 1942 headed for California for repairs. Navigation (conning) station is two-thirds of the way aft of the jury-rigged bow.

Naval Historical Center

Shaw at Mare Island, California, Navy Yard in mid-February 1942 just after arrival for repairs. Note jury-rigged bow, foremast, and navigating (conning) station (the structure just aft of the single remaining gun).

Naval Historical Center

Smoking *Shaw* in sunken drydock YFD-2. Stern (with hull number 373) shows in right of photo. Bow pointed southwest.

Naval Historical Center

Shaw showing exploded forward area of bridge (bow was toward left of photograph). Shack and vent funnels are on the floating dry dock, which also sunk.

Naval Historical Center

Looking westward toward YFD-2 at *Shaw* burning from first bomb hits, prior to magazine explosion, 7 December 1941.

Naval Historical Center

In one of the war's most definitive and famous images, *Shaw*'s forward magazine explodes from 250-kilogram bomb hit. Debris scattered one-half mile and showered down on Lieutenant Berton A. Robbins, Jr., who was on the dry dock attempting to board the ship at the time. Looking southwest from Ford Island. This is the second-most famous image of the attack after that of the sunken, burning battleship USS *Arizona* (BB-39). USS *Nevada* (BB-36) is seen on right of photo headed for grounding.

Naval Historical Center

After the explosion, Dad went aboard *Shaw* to do his duty. Before leaving the ship a day or so later he took the ship's ensign, which had been raised on the fantail during the attack, and brought it home. Mother and Dad eventually gave it to the Naval Academy where it is on exhibit in their museum.

The floating dry dock (behind crane) where *Shaw* was berthed, as it appeared in December 1975.

Authors' Collection

Pumping out water after installation of cofferdam during salvage operations on the battleship USS *California* (BB-34). Among her crew was Hampstead, North Carolina, native Lawrence Homer Henderson.

Naval Historical Center

Removal of one of the 14-inch main guns from *California*. Note lack of safety precautions: no life jacket on man riding the rig.

Naval Historical Center

California just after dry-docking. Note mud on propeller shafts and struts. 9 April 1942.

Naval Historical Center

Torpedo hole in port side of *California* after she had been raised and dry-docked. Note armor belt above hole. 1942.

Naval Historical Center

The raised *California* shows its cofferdam on port bow area. 30 March 1942.

Naval Historical Center

Principal salvage officers discussing raising of *California*. On left end is chief ship fitter and master diver J. M. Ephland. Captain Homer N. Wallin, chief salvage officer, is in center with opened blueprints. 1942.

Naval Historical Center

Battleship USS *Oklahoma* (BB-37) lies capsized after attack with half of its propeller visible.

Naval Historical Center

System of 21 motors, winches, and rigs provide steady pull to right the capsized *Oklahoma*. Looking northwest toward Ford Island.

Naval Historical Center

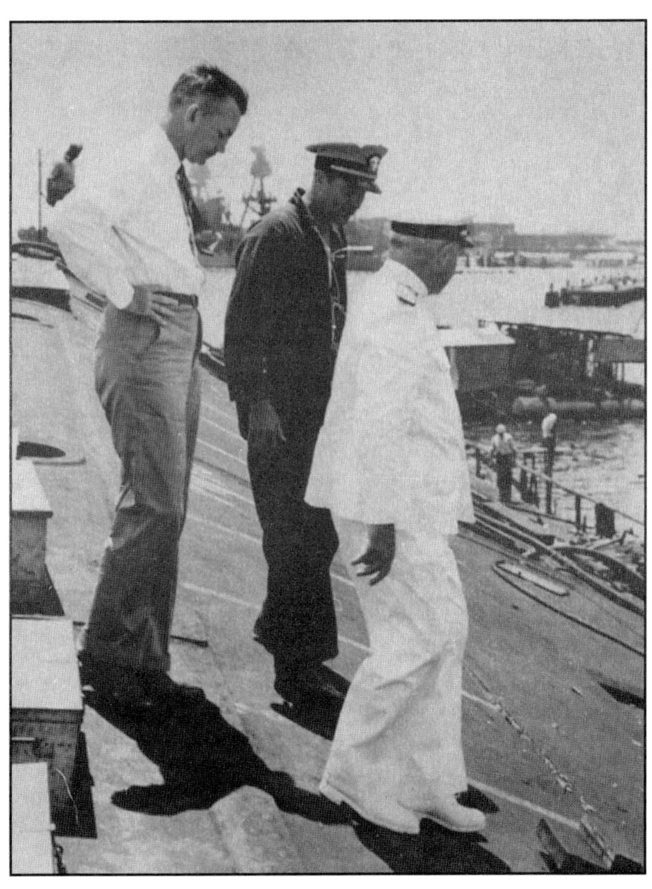

Undersecretary of the Navy James Forrestal, *left*, and Rear Admiral W. R. Furlong, *right*, on the upturned hull of *Oklahoma*, 6 September 1942.

Naval Historical Center

Pearl Harbor chief salvage officer Captain Homer N. Wallin, *left*, with commanding officer of USS *West Virginia* (BB-48), Lieutenant Commander W. White. 1942.

Naval Historical Center

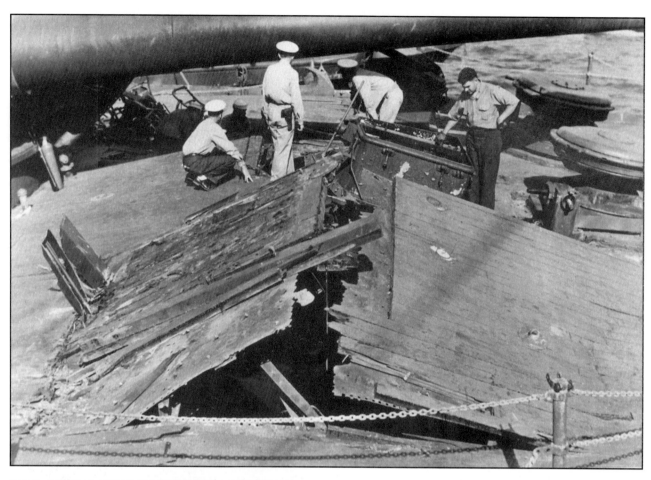

Bomb rupture of bow of battleship USS *Nevada* (BB-36). From deck of USS *Rail* (AM-26) alongside.

Naval Historical Center

After photographing the oil- and mud-smeared interior of capsized *Oklahoma*, Photographer's Mate 3rd Class T. E. Collins rests. He entered the ship through #4 air lock, where pressure was raised to 10 pounds per square inch. An oxygen mask had to be worn at all times. Note tank suit, mask, boots, and gloves worn by all who entered the sunken ships. 18 January 1943.

Naval Historical Center

Divers standing in front of decompression chamber during salvage operations at Pearl Harbor Navy Yard.

Naval Historical Center

Battleship *West Virginia* en route to Mainland west coast for permanent repairs after being salvaged and temporarily repaired. 20 April 1943.

Naval Historical Center

USS *Arizona* (BB-39) lies in the mud off Ford Island in Battleship Row.

Naval Historical Center

Wilmingtonian Taylor Marion Jeffords' ship, the *West Virginia,* burning on 7 December. Looking westward, *right*, USS *Tennessee* (BB-43) is inboard next to Ford Island.

Naval Historical Center

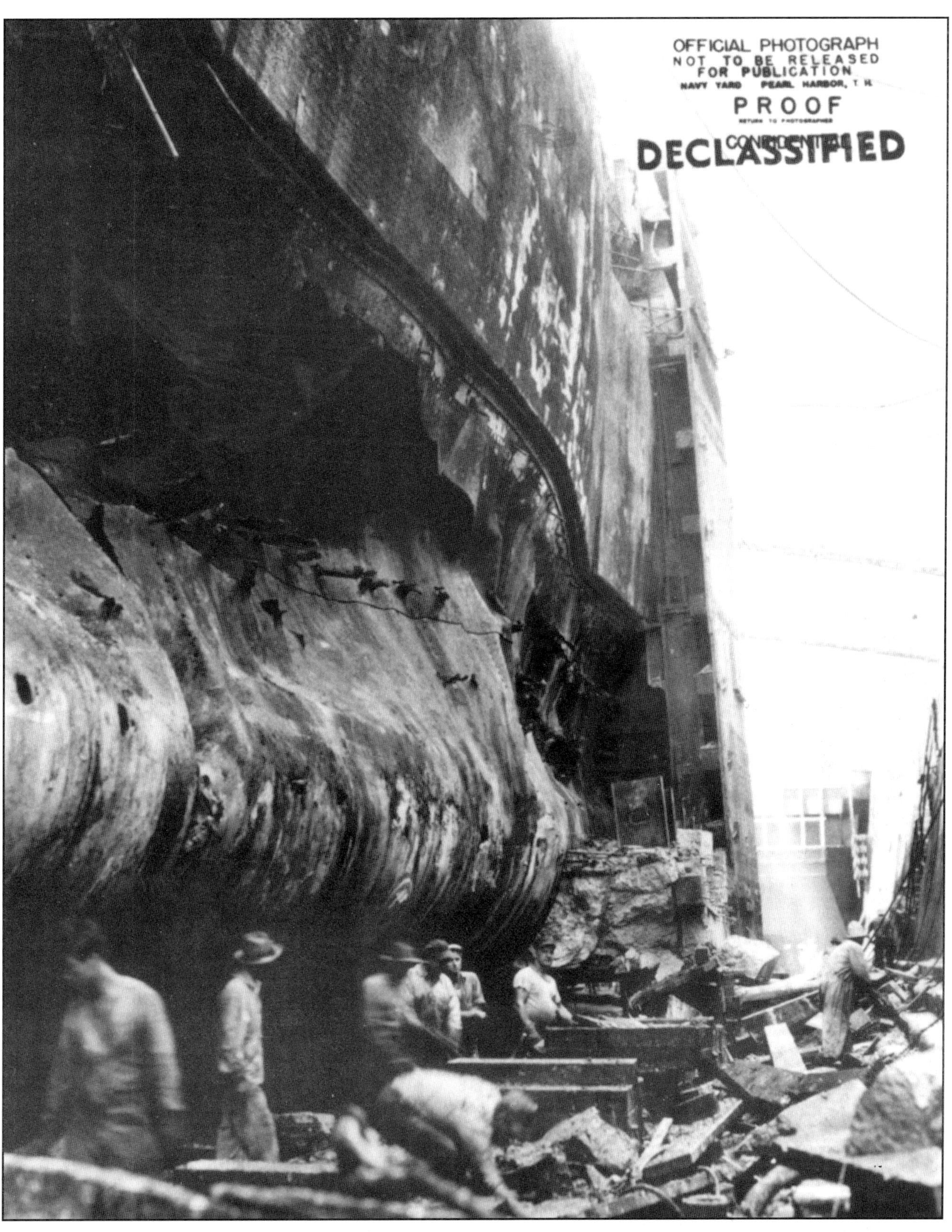

West Virginia in dry dock undergoing repairs. Note holes made by torpedoes. June 1942.

Naval Historical Center

Chapter 4

"To Carry on the American Way of Life": Oahu Settles Down

> After the first week of war Honolulu looked the same. Diamond Head, the clouds above the Tantalus, the light showers turning the upper valleys purple, the welcoming green foliage, Aloha Tower and the big pineapple-shaped water tank high above the cannery. Walk down Bishop Street to see change the war has made in Hawaii's daily life and habits. Gone are the lei sellers who used to line the docks holding out fragrant armloads of brilliant ilima, pikake, and ginger flowers to the delight of the tourist and kamaaina alike.[1]

War ended Honololu's most colorful industry. The lei makers now made camouflage nets to hide the army's gun emplacements. Blake Clark wrote in 1943, "In place of the lei sellers, you would see women in the grey uniforms of the Motor Corps stepping into banana wagons; men in khaki, rifles in hand, on guard in front of the newspaper buildings, radio stations, and power plants; nuns, robed and hooded, wearing their gas masks suspended beside their rosaries; children carrying their special "bunny masks" as they go to the trench-equipped schools." And Waikiki was barricaded with barbed wire.[2]

Berton and I befriended three old Hawaiian ladies who made leis and sat in front of a beauty parlor right around the corner from our apartment. Mother would sleep well into the morning after often staying up quite late studying chemistry, optics, or just reading, and was a self-declared "night owl." We were not allowed to wake her. So we would get up, dress, eat breakfast and go around the corner and talk "pidgin English" with the ladies. They not only taught us how to make leis, but encouraged us to help sell them. More new-found friends.

They asked us to call them "Aunties." This soon became a part of our routine, and many times we would take a sandwich and sit there for hours stringing the very fragrant flowers with exotic names, learning just which point to insert the wire with thread for stringing. They had a few regular customers, but one of the questions in my mind years later was: with no tourists, and most of the military gone to sea or remaining close to their bases, who *bought the leis? There were times Mother would pay them to watch us while she worked, which seemed to suit us all. We learned native traditions and history through their stories, and sometimes they would sing quietly and move their hands describing the words to their songs. They often smiled toothless smiles and never got mad at us. One of them had a son who was a beach boy who would come by and get money from his mother. He would take customers out on his canoe, or give surfboard lessons. Business must have been slow, as he would sometimes take us across the street to the beach in front of the Royal Hawaiian Hotel where his equipment was parked and try to teach us about surf and waves. I think he was the one who taught us how to walk on coral without getting hurt, and how to look for eel. I flunked that course by stepping on the wrong place and getting a bite on my heel by an eel, fortunately not poisonous. Both Berton and I learned to body surf and ride waves, which meant we had to go out a good distance. The "boys" were probably as childish as we were, but never let us get into dangerous situations.*

Then there were the men in uniform who brought a profound change, hundreds of thousands of them from throughout America who "scrambled eagerly for that much publicized charm and relaxation that tired millionaires enjoyed so much in Hawaii before the war. It wasn't to be found," a Hawaiian wrote, "or there wasn't enough to go around, and there were bitter complaints. We did our best to carry on the American way of life, not in the face of the enemy...but against the demands of our defenders."[3] Or, as a 1950 University of Hawaii essay posed it,[4]

> The...servicemen and defense workers arrived in Hawaii expecting soft moonlight, waving palms, sunny beaches, and beautiful girls. The moonlight and palms were there, but the beaches were crowded with humanity and strung with barbed wire. As for the girls—there was one to each hundred men, or one to a thousand, according to which story you heard. Hawaiian hospitality was so overtaxed that thousands of men thought it was a myth. Islanders did entertain friends, sons of friends, friends of friends, and even chance acquaintances....But many men stayed in the Islands for months without making any civilian contacts, so they griped and moped, or downed their woes with drink. They called Oahu "The Rock" and said that if they never saw "Ha-way-yah" again it would be too soon.

In spite of their quick transition to war, and relative isolation from Mainland America, worker morale in 1942 remained high. With work directly related to their own defense, they felt their role in the battle action. When the raiders returned from the attacks on the Marshalls and Gilberts, defense workers lining the harbor cheered the new heroes. "And when the pall-covered stretches bearing the dead were carried in, the workers stood, hats in hand, silently dedicating themselves to match their own sacrifice with soldiers' sacrifice....They keep silent on the subject of their work, but they take a very personal pride in delivering ahead of schedule, and in performing industrial miracles."[5] Confidence, too, was apparent.

The Uniforms

"If every girl in the Islands had taken a serviceman to bed with her each night," a Hawaiian noted, "there would not have been nearly enough nights and certainly not enough beds to go around." Anything for the war effort...:[6]

> We did what we could, but not enough to dispense with the long lines of men standing before the houses of prostitutes who came from the Mainland to help those local girls who felt their patriotic duty inclined that way. In between times, the servicemen demanded honky-tonk amusement and honky-tonks sprang up overnight to supply it. The rest of us picked up the soldiers and sailors in our cars and took them as far as our limited gasoline rations would allow. We brought a few of them home, where our wives—whose maids had gone to be photographer's models or cashiers in the aforementioned honky-tonks—cooked and served all the meals they could prepare in time spared from canteen or Red Cross service.

The first troops began arriving in numbers in April 1942. By June, the 7 December garrison of 43,000 had increased to 135,000. The Naval District's 5,800 sailors ballooned to 20,000 by the end of 1942. Three categories of service personnel came to Hawaii: those who stayed island-bound for most of the war, those who passed through on training, and those who glimpsed the waving palms from offshore. The army had four prewar posts in Honolulu: Forts Ruger, DeRussy, Shafter, and Armstrong, and the larger Schofield Barracks in mid-island. Tent camps with Schofield as the hub spread over Oahu. Practically every square mile was changed physically. The army took over parks, schools, plantation fields, and vacant lots for barracks, supply depots, and offices. They dredged channels, drained swamps, reclaimed land, and cut tunnels into mountains for storage. The air force extended airfield runways and carved out new ones. The Coast Guard assumed security responsibilty for the Honolulu waterfront.

As envisioned, Hawaii quickly became both principal staging and training ground for the anticipated westward assaults. Fortunately the Hawaiian terrain and climate matched in many respects the coral and jungle environments the troops would experience in the Southwest and Central Pacific. Soon the sound of maneuvering soldiers and marines and their practice gunfire echoed throughout the Islands. Hawaiians ran into every type of fighting man in the Pacific and the women who backed them up as nurses and USO and Red Cross gals. Hawaii had its own three army infantry divisions, the 7th, 24th, and 25th. A regiment of the 7th honored Queen

Liliuokalani ("The Queen's Own Regiment") and was charged with the Islands' defense.*

As 1942 progressed, the downtown traffic seemed to become more and more crowded, and bus transportation could be an all-day exercise. The traffic was from an influx of military personnel coming in from the Mainland in a constant stream which strained not only public transportation but availability of goods, a seat in the drug store, and caused even longer lines for most everything. It had to be.

Social Life

Waikiki Beach normally accommodated three hundred bathers. Thirty-thousand sought space. Lodging for servicemen was virtually nonexistent. Honolulu had only six adequate hotels, and the navy comandeered one of the largest, the Royal Hawaiian, for its officers and men.† The result was soldiers and sailors on liberty had extremely few options even if they had ovenight passes. Blackout and curfew regulations practically eliminated night life. Honolulu's infrastructure and natural beauty suffered for lack of maintenance personnel and resources. Service industry personnel and salesgirls became careless, and bus drivers rude. Some Islanders and Mainland promoters exploited servicemen and defense workers to "get rich quick."

Military pilots had access to a Kalakaua Avenue mansion, and submariners the Royal Hawaiian, the famous "Pink Palace." Soldiers and sailors could utilize The Breakers on Waikiki, leased as a rest stop, while the Haleiwa Hotel catered to a "brassier" officer patronage. Enlisted personnel were given free lodging at these places, and officers paid a nominal sum. The army converted Fort DeRussey, with its swimming pools, ballroom, barracks, and dining hall, into a vast recreation complex. Residents went out of their way to invite service personnel into their homes for meals and overnight stays. With the blackout restrictions, the latter was naturally assumed. There would be no way to get anywhere in the dark. Millionaire socialite Doris Duke donated her mansion to staff officers. Services sponsored and conducted their own shows, sports events, libraries, radio stations, and newspapers, with frequent appearances by sports and entertainment stars. By the end of 1942, the USO (United Service Organizations) had extended its Oahu operations to five islands with 80 professional employees, 400 camp show entertainers, and 2,000 volunteers in 51 clubs and units.

Harriett Weaver was renting a large house on Diamond Head with a number of single young women who were friends from well-connected families in Los Angeles. Mother had known her slightly in L.A., but had known Harriett's brother Sylvester "Pat" Weaver better through a connection with my uncle Carroll. Pat Weaver went on to become a big advertising executive with Young & Rubicam and at NBC Television, as did my uncle, and later had his own very successful ad agency in New York. He also had the distinction of being the father of Sigeurney Weaver, an actress of some note. Harriett was always a very outgoing being and had great organizational skills. She saw a need for relaxed social outlets for returning soldiers and sailors and young officers, as well as for those on their way out to fight, and her brainchild "Stars and Bars" was begun.

The emphasis of "Stars and Bars" was on relaxed group activities such as dining and just talking together in pleasant, clean and informal surroundings. No pressures for either the young men or women, and nothing expected in return. These gatherings were evidently successful as they continued throughout the war with chapters up and down both coasts on the Mainland, and years later in most major cities in the United States and overseas where there were military personnel. I remember years later as a young adult living in Alexandria, Virginia, a suburb of Washington, D.C., being invited to some of the gatherings at the downtown

* Ultimately, 12 army and 3 Marine divisions (2d, 4th, and 5th) of more than a million men trained on Oahu, Hawaii, Kauai, and Maui, and staged for virtually every major Pacific campaign from Guadalcanal through Okinawa and the Philippines. The Queen's regiment served with the 25th on Guadalcanal and in the Philippines, and the 24th on New Guinea. Kauai named the 27th Division, bloodied in the Central Pacific, as their "savior" and "adopted" division.

† The navy leased the Royal Hawaiian for $17,500 a month. Its gardens remained, but the luxurious Coconut Grove cocktail bar became a soda fountain, and cots were crowded into suites. One-hundred thousand men averaged a 10-day stay, officers paying only $1 a day and enlisted men nothing.

Hilton Hotel, fairly new at the time. I never went. Perhaps my long ago memories as a child interfered, but I was on the receiving end of the newsletter she edited until after I married. Harriett did her part for the war effort very successfully, and I'm certain she gave some hours of relaxation and pleasure to many young men when they needed it most. The last time I saw an announcement for a gathering of hers was in Los Angeles in the '60s. I think Harriett helped "fight" in every war we were a part of since 1941.

"Everything possible was done to try to encourage servicemen to stay away from the gambling places, bars and other tawdry Loreleis and Hotel Street and similar byways of the city's red light district. Vice and racketeering was at times so bad that unscrupulous hucksters attempted to sell gold stars to mothers, hinting that their sons were dead."[7] Ah, Hotel Street. It quickly became the most famous thoroughfare of the Pacific War, with perhaps Rover Street in close pursuit. Along one mile of Hotel and its intersection streets was a milieu of cheap attractions to whet the fun-seaking spirits of young men with money to spend and nowhere else to go. "The owner of one entertainment gallery boasted that it was among the largest in the world, with more than 100 employees. While its swing band competed with the guns of the shooting gallery, the customers played pinball machines, drank Cokes, or had their pictures taken. Tattoo shops etched anchors, American eagles, and pretty girls on 200 to 300 sailors, and 100 or so soldiers and defense workers a day."[8] Beer and hard liquor were easy to get, regardless of a man's age. Mainland-made souvenirs of Hawaii went for three times their worth. Girls in hula skirts (being native Hawaiian didn't matter) posed in any fashion with servicemen in front of dull and rigid black-and-white palm tree backdrops.

Along with longer days of light came longer visiting hours, shopping, and later dinner for some of us. A favorite treat was eating a hamburger and drinking a milkshake at the outside snack bar at the Outrigger Canoe Club. These must have been days when Mother was really tired as this was hardly her idea of nutrition; actually it suited us just fine. She would let us play in the water with the beach boys until nearly dusk, and then we would sit on those tall stools at the counter watching as "a little more chocolate" was added to the whirring milkshake machine. It wasn't real chocolate, but something akin to Bosco, but who cares? What she didn't know was how many of these wonderful snackbar treats we would get free for "helping" keep the beach clean picking up trash, and folding chairs, putting wet towels and mats in a pile, and assisting "the boys" drag surfboards, canoes and other gear up onto the beach. All the boards would be thrust into the sand on-end, and the outriggers would be positioned facing seaward. We were never allowed to go out in the canoes. The boys took good care of us.

Until they were shut down in 1944, legal houses of prostitution flourished as never before. Honolulu police registered 20 houses with 250 girls, and an unknown unregistered number also existed. Fifteen houses were located in the small area bounded by Hotel, River, Nuuanu, and Kukui Streets. Civilians and servicemen stood forever in long lines waiting for the opportunity. Out of an estimated gross annual income of $10–15 million, the madames averaged about $150,000 and the girls $25,000. Men headed for the unkown of combat lived as if there were only today, or as much as wartime conditions and little time would allow.

Living Without, or With What You Brought

Salvage and defense workers joined military personnel in adding to the huge influx of people entering the Islands. Feeding all civilians became a mounting problem until late in 1942. Congress appopiated $35 million for mostly staples food stocks. At first the imports of canned goods, toiletries, paper products, and other household items trickled in. Imports from the Mainland gradually increased, including a shipment of 2,500 empty Coca-Cola bottles and a year's supply of sardines. Local food production slowed, mainly because most truck farmers were Japanese who didn't know whether they would be deported and failed to plant crops. Fresh fruit and sugar was plentiful. A ruinous drought hit the Islands in the summer of 1942, making the lima bean the only vegetable to do well on Oahu. The locals soon tired of limas and carrots, for some reason the only vegetable regularly imported. Hog production increased because the major hog food, garbage, was in bountiful supply.

Slaughtering was regulated, however, and commercial luaus—a Hawaiian tradition—were banned and private luaus severely restricted. The staple poi was also scarce. For military wives, the Navy Yard commissary gradually improved its inventory, but for the year many items were unprocurable. "We did make our refrigerators, electric stoves, automobiles, and the other things essential to the American way of life last for the duration. We had no choice."[9]

Occasionally on our downtown trips we would go into Liberty's department store, or even Sears, Roebuck and on special trips would visit important friends of Mother's at Government House where we would be served wonderful trays of goodies. We had been invited to visit the Cook family and their numerous children for an afternoon of play. The Cooks were among the oldest families in the Islands (they discovered them) and owned "everything." We just knew they had to be rich because their children wore all white, which meant to us, that each child must have had their own laundress. After spending the afternoon doing not much of anything but shyly testing one another, and sitting around, my brother and I changed our minds about all the laundry people and just figured they never got dirty. We were impressed there seemed to be so many children's attendants in evidence dutifully watching our every move and always asking if we had to use the potty. We needed no assistance, thank you. A few years later at a birthday party in Beverly Hills, I ran into much the same situation which was astonishing given my age at the time. My brother and I always had good manners, but we managed to have fun, too.

In 1942 nearly eight thousand Hawaiian shops or stores closed, succumbing primarily to lack of merchandise, government red tape, prices, and manpower. Early in the war Washington and the local military governor each set controls. Price controls to halt inflationary pressures were probably more acute in Hawaii than the Mainland. Payrolls and the accompanying spending skyrocketed. In January 1942 the military set controls on food prices and in May added all other commodities. Regulations from the federal Office of Price Administration included prices on such things as photographs with hula girls, shell leis, and standard blackout bulbs. Gradually the OPA replaced ceilings with specific price schedules.

Buses were extremely crowded during morning and evening rush hours. Streets were jammed with military and civilian vehicles, making reasonable trip lengths difficult. Office and store hours were staggered to free up movement. Inter-island travel was halted briefly on 7 December. Later airlines offered some service but ships did not resume their prewar schedules. New cars were not available and the demand for used ones was obviously heavy, particularly by war workers unable to find transportation to distant jobs. By 1943, two-year-old cars were selling at 33 percent over their original cost. Gasoline rationing was severe. Consumption dropped by 45 percent from January 1942 through April 1943, almost double that of some places on the Mainland.

We didn't always have the Ooga Ooga for transportation. The owner, a classmate of Dad's, would occasionally return for a very short period of time and reclaim it. This meant traveling by the dreaded bus if we had to go any distance such as downtown to shop or for one of Mother's many appointments. Bus travel was long, crowded, hot, and slow. Buses did not run on a reliable schedule, and seemed to always take on more passengers than safety allowed. We little kids were crushed, stepped on, and elbowed. We never got a seat as we were taught not to sit if an adult was standing. These outings were torture for all of us, but as I recall, they had to be made for such things as retrieving packages from the post office, for example. Most packages were limited in size, and when opened for content approval by either the sending or receiving end often resulted in torn and crushed boxes. Still, it was exciting to get a "care package" from the Mainland. Aunt Katherine or Aunt Mimi in L.A. tried to send underwear, socks, p.j.'s, and occasionally crayons, books, and paper dolls. There were occasions when items sent never quite made our destination, but that became an acceptable risk. This was due to outright pilferage and not censors.

The worst times on the bus was going with Mother to the Associated Press headquarters or one of the government offices downtown inhabited by tall, silent men looking straight ahead, striding purposefully down corridors with bare walls through unmarked doors into secret rooms. Not a sound, not even footsteps to warn us someone was approaching. Often Berton and I were required to sit quietly on hard wood benches along the wall for what seemed like hours without wandering around, much less taking a stretch. Even though we were usually equipped with crayons and book or some mind game, this was pure torture. No one paid attention to us, and we were too afraid of these silent people to ask about the nearest bathroom. Perhaps we felt they were beyond such a function! These infrequent trips to what was in reality offices of naval intelligence, became another case of "what am I supposed to do with them, drown them?" Having heard often enough how baby girls born in China were sometimes drowned at birth since girls were considered inferior and of no value by some classes, I was always thankful to have been spared such a fate in spite of Mother's impatience with dragging us around.

But restaurants, initially hard hit trying to stay open during blackout restrictions with no tourist customers, boomed with business from the newcomers. Other businesses that flourished were banks, dry cleaners, and laundries. The only measurable glut of anything was the immediate appearance of second-hand furniture and automobiles for sale in December and early 1942 from families departing the Islands who believed it could not be shipped. Fearing that large sums of U.S. money would be smuggled in by saboteurs or be captured by invaders, the government printed new currency redeemable only in Hawaii, imprinted prominently with the name "HAWAII." Citizens exchanged real U.S. dollars for the "counterfeits," and some $200 million in "old money" was burned in the Nuuanu Cemetery crematorium. Private citizens were limited to no more than $200 each, and businesses $500.

Mail delivery to and from the Mainland was irregular, air mail letters sometimes taking weeks to arrive. This communications system weakness identified Hawaiians with wartime and the feeling of isolation, handicapped businesses, and caused personal and family hardships. The army took control of the Mutual Telephone Company on 9 December and had first choice on equipment and services, leaving the company to set civilian policies with what remained. Transpacific calls doubled in 1942 and rose steadily. In 1941 a housing shortage existed in Honolulu before defense workers began coming. Scarce land, high building costs, and rapidly rising rents were reasons, and it only got worse.

Another treat was going with a traveling USO show to several military bases on the island. Again, this was because Mother was to photograph entertainment as a morale booster for the boys in uniform. The show was mostly Hawaiian music and dancing, and the inevitable inclusion of uniformed men asked onto the stage to participate. There would be a lesson in hand movements, and as we saw it, wiggling the fanny, and of course a lovely wahine was available to place a lei around the neck along with a smack on the lips bringing lots of whistles and approving remarks. These shows were happy, partylike affairs, and we reveled in being the only kids there getting attention and goodies to eat. Our favorite was the "Hilo Hattie" type in all the shows, and once we even saw the real one. Hattie was outrageous, and much of her act was unfit for minors; however, what we didn't understand did us no harm. Her appeal for us must have been costumes and the constant laughter she brought from the audience and *the band behind her. These traveling shows were different from the regularly scheduled shows at the hotels where the girls wore shiny hula skirts and makeup, and a comic would be part of the act. The USO shows had "real" Hawaiians in grass skirts, and the men wore head gear, and necklaces of sharks teeth and did dangerous fire dances. All the flowers were real, and a narrator would describe the story being told by the hand movements of the dancers. Sometimes they were very sad, but mostly they were of love and happiness.*

Mother sent me to a class for kids to learn the hula. This lasted one day. Our Hawaiian friends said what I learned was all wrong, and Berton and I were taught the old traditional way which I suspect had some questionable stuff thrown in for kicks. A few years later I got to know Leilani Owens and her brother Little Butch, the children of Harry Owens, the famous bandleader of Harry Owens and His Royal Hawaiians, and creator of the song Sweet Leilani, *written for his infant daughter. That song became a huge hit and was the theme song for the tremendously popular Owens Band. Harry's wife, Edie Owens, my "Auntie Barbara" Clampett Morrison Jones, one of Mother's oldest and best friends, and our mother would occasionally spend some great times at Auntie Barbara's ranch in Hemet, California. This was a glorified ranch if ever there was one, and basically maintained for her race horses, and a getaway from Los Angeles, where she could entertain people privately in a very relaxed atmosphere. We kids loved it as there were few rules to bind us and they were reasonable. This is where I learned in amazement that Leilani, a year older than me, did NOT dance the hula, and didn't even like island music.*

Changes

Social upheaval "...touched every age group from the baby who was popped into a 'bunny' mask at the first wail of an air raid siren to the retired septuagenerian who now went back to work." The civilian population of Oahu climbed from 258,000 in 1940 to 348,000 in 1945, much of it *haole* (Caucasian, Mainland), and approximately 30,000 Negro servicemen and defense workers. Before the war Hawaii had few Negroes. The tendency had been to welcome them equally, but it didn't take long for other newcomers to spread their ideas of race relations to the detriment of Negro residents.[10]

Gwenfread Allen, writing for the University of Hawaii, continued:[11]

> Combined with easy money and general uncertainty, the unbalanced sex ratio, always present in Hawaii but tremendously intensified during the war, undermined a proper sense of values, both socially and economically. Welfare workers noted a breakdown of family solidarity, neglect of children, and a demand for more parties and a gayer life. Many Oriental girls, unaccustomed to the flattery and impulsiveness of the Mainland men, took seriously what the newcomers considered merely transient flirtations. The girls worried about broken love affairs and the silence of boys who sailed away and forgot. They worried about their reception by prospective Mainland in-laws....Island girls were sensible indeed whose heads were not turned by the attention they received. Even school girls in their earliest teens and career women crowding middle age were deluged with dates from generals and admirals down....Interracial marriages zoomed, despite army and navy efforts to apply the brakes by requiring servicemen to obtain official permission to marrying.

Mixing government boundaries, personalities, and regulations confused everyone to an extent. "Hawaii's wartime government was further complicated by personal conflicts of old feuds, annoying mistakes by top executives and inexperienced clerks, and other human frailties."[12] Resolving the distinction between military and civilian governmental jurisdictions took time and trial-and-error. The fuzzy chain of command allowed volunteers at first to work just to get it done without attention to who was their final authority. The military habit of giving "general orders" to the public through radio stations and newspapers, without sufficient official follow-up, led to misunderstandings, sometimes resulting in citizens being tried before martial-law courts for disobeying a nebulous or contradictory edict. But overall, the Territory and county governments generally performed as they did in peacetime. A larger population and unsettled family life brought on increased juvenile delinquency, adult crimes, prostitution, and drunkenness, but serious offenses did not grow abnormally.

Authorities closed bars and stopped liquor sales, except with a doctor's approval, until 23 February 1942. Under rationed sales of bottle liquor, bars reopened then for afternoons only. Every adult except for enemy aliens (Japanese) was eligible for a liquor permit for either a case of beer, three quarts of wine, or a quart of liquor per week. Hawaii ran out of alcoholic beverages in September, and authorities encouraged local production. "Bring your own bottle" was the watchword for party guests.

Of all groups, the war impacted school children the most. The army comandeered some 29 schools for office, troop, storage, and hospital space, including the exclusive private schools Punahou, which had just celebrated its one hundredth anniversary, and Kamehameha. Army and Civilian Defense authorities used schools (878 public school units such as classrooms and gymnasiums) and their teachers for draft boards, registering the population, and distributing items such as gas masks and liquor authorizations. Oahu public schools reopened in February 1942 but with fewer teachers and staff, less class time, and restricted by numerous regulations.

By late 1942 the army returned many school facilities to educational uses as its construction caught up with demands for space.

All the public schools and, I believe, parochial schools were closed to children by a general order, opening again on a limited basis sometime in February 1942. Teachers were utilized in many activities unrelated to teaching and administration. War agencies and the Armed Forces took over most of the school room spaces. I later learned that all public schools and three private schools were appropriated by various agencies. Even when classes resumed they were on a limited time schedule, and transportation was a severe problem. Mother decided we could learn just as much at home under her tutelage in spite of irregular hours, and instruction in whatever Mother was in the mood for that day and time period. In fact, I don't recall that we had "school" each day. I do remember it was often agony, this early attempt at "home schooling."

In spite of bad eyes I loved to read and helped teach my brother. I would become lost in make-believe, often becoming part of the story or rewriting it in my head to suit my fantasy of the moment. Mother would take us to the library where we selected books above our age, and select from these readings vocabulary words. This became the basis of school: reading, spelling, and vocabulary. Math was a fuzzy monster she had little patience with and which I hated. It mostly consisted of time tables, and adding and subtraction using money as a guide. This was when Mother's frustration level with me would surface and tears (mine) and loud voices (both) would signal the end of "school" for the day. We had a large map on the wall and this was the primary geography aid, particularly learning where California was in relation to the Islands, and which direction war in the Pacific was heading. It is a wonder that when we returned to regular schooling in California, we entered grades on schedule for our ages.

The University of Hawaii reopened in February with a registration decrease of 64 percent in credit courses, or only eight hundred students, by far mostly women. Authorities used much of the university assets, the only such U.S. institution operating in a war area, in the war effort. Professors worked with army censors and intelligence. Trenches zigzagged its broad green, palm-shaped campus. "Professors and girls...grab their gas masks and leap into trenches and bomb shelters when the air raid warning sounds."[13]

One morning we were told to put on haole *clothes, and not to forget the shoes, please. We had to go with Mother to the University of Hawaii all day while she took photos of campus life in wartime. We couldn't have cared less, especially having to put on real clothes and worst of all shoes. What was such a big thing about a university anyway, and* what *was it? The entire long and loud trip was given over to a lecture on behavior from Mother, and stopping every so often to tie down the flapping side of the Ooga Ooga hood. The stops slowed us down, which made Mother angry and her voice louder, and by the time we arrived, the mood was heavy with anticipated wrong-doings and snafus and a very impatient photographer. This was an important assignment, we were told, so please cooperate. We'd heard this many times and were usually well-behaved kids who tried to be helpful out of fear of what could happen to us later. For some reason, the sight of a huge water fountain in the middle of large green, well-laid-out flower beds, beautiful buildings and smiling co-eds oohing and aahing over us triggered such joy in these new, well-maintained surroundings that we celebrated by running full speed ahead, jumping into the water fountain, splashing around with abandon, fully clothed. For once our mother looked as if in total shock, and was truly speechless. Everyone else laughed, perhaps not knowing what else to do.*

We took off all but underpants so our clothes would dry, and so of course we won after all. No dresses, no shorts and shirt, no shoes. Also no beach for what seemed an eternity and lots of "homework" for me. Berton and I had no idea that our family of three was becoming known on the island—Mother for her talents and having us kids with her, and us for our totally uninhibited behavior. We were not shy kids, nor were we bratty. We were midget people with larger vocabularies than most kids our age, not afraid of adults, and accepted our unconventional lifestyle as if it were normal. We were also very self-reliant and responsible, not afraid to try most anything. Every once in a while the kid in us had to come out, and the water fountain was too inviting to pass.

We spent several days "helping" our mother out at the university, and after the water fountain incident of the first day became model kids. Being allowed to wear shorts and sandals may have contributed to our sunny dispositions. Our shorts were also our swim trunks, which we lived in most of the time. We each wore the typical Hawaiian design in primary colors of bright red and white, green and white, and blue and white, identical for each of us except for size. This way Mother could see us, and frankly, this was a smart move. The students were fun and very cooperative, as I recall. The pictorial story was based on student culture at the University of Hawaii under wartime conditions, and the changes in campus life. One very obvious change was the overwhelming population of female students compared to male students, most of whom had joined the military. Some obvious changes included students carrying the ID necklace at all times, the everpresent gas mask, air raid drills, jumping into trenches which marred the beautiful green spaces on campus, and the participation of most students in tending the huge vegretable gardens. The young women were expected to participate in volunteer work for the war effort, and I can only surmise that social activities came to a near standstill. This particular photo story was published in the August 1942 Mademoiselle *magazine (their college issue) and brought Mother great reviews from the Mainland. Berton and I were thanked for "all your help and getting it together." Life was good after all, and we were proud of our mother.*

The War Effort

On 7 December Oahu had approximately 30,000 defense workers, 8,800 working for the navy and 12,000 more for navy contractors. By 1943 the navy's total had grown to 37,000, with 25,000 at Pearl. Army employment peaked in late 1942. Hawaii's biggest employer was the army's United States Engineer Department, which spent more than $400 million on the war effort and located its offices in the Young Hotel roof garden, a favorite local night spot. New construction included pillboxes, roads, bridges, piers, recreation centers, and hospitals. A consortium of major construction firms called "The Eight Companies" handled navy projects and by 1941 was one of the world's largest construction ventures.

Relations between Hawaii and the defense workers were rocky, as this account reported.[14] "The importees came with high expectations. They found chaotic conditions, and complained about Hawaii. Many from the South brought concepts of white superiority. Islanders sometimes ignored and sometimes resented the war workers. Many lived in barracks in isolated camps; others found their own quarters in crowded residential areas; but most lived in housing projects provided by the army and the navy." The chief worker complaints dealt with undesirable roommates and habitual drinkers and gamblers. War workers developed a negative reputation. "Poor housing conditions—coupled with wartime pressures, limited community and receational facilities, martial law controls, and shifting personnel policies—erupted in complaints, slowdowns, inefficiency, excessive absenteeism, and high turnover....Many war workers came to the Islands bursting with a patriotism which later turned to cynicism." Many also came in poor mental and physical health. Homesickness intensified the difficulties.

As the war tempo increased, so did manpower problems in numbers and skills. The early wage freeze made it difficult to recruit Mainland workers. More people by percentage of population held defense jobs in Hawaii than in the rest of America, and many full-timers held supplemental jobs. An acute shortage existed in female-oriented jobs such as domestics, clerical and laundry workers, waitresses, teachers, and nurses. "Rosie the Riveter had few counterparts in civilian Hawaii....Many took positions because of the fear that those unemployed might be required to evacuate....Some women found the pace too strenuous and dropped out when the defense pressure lessened."[15] By mid-1942 upward wage revisions also opened the way for higher tips and commissions. For grass-skirted hula girls to pose with servicemen, studios paid $100 per week plus bonus and tips. They posed with as many as 150 men daily. The OPA continually struggled against free spending, no wage freeze, and the labor shortage.

Observer Stanley D. Porteus summarized the war local effort.[16]

> ...No one refused responsibility or stood aside in this crisis....No one looked for credit or acclaim. The burden was too common, the prospects of defeat too grim. Perhaps the finest thing about the Hawaiian community

in crisis was this anonimity of service....The women of the Territory did their full share of defense work. Not only did thousands of them participate by taking jobs in the OCD or volunteering for fingerprint registration and serving in countless ways, but they rallied around as vols for first aid stations, nurses' aides, hospital visitors, USO activities, etc. and made bandages....Anticipating the stream of wounded coming back here after those bloody naval battles of the South Seas, the navy called for a fuller stock of dressings, the women stayed overtime and worked like slaves. Grey Ladies gave help to men convalescing in hospitals. Even the Japanese women attended Red Cross centers, though the *haole* women were naturally to the fore since they required no organizing....There were few, if any, slackers.

Christmas 1941

A marine officer remembered Christmas Eve 1941: "There's a blackout on and only the bulky shadows of tall trees are etched obscurely against a silent sky. The same stars are there, but none light the way to goodwill among men. Here are only curses and damnation for the enemy....Out in the hallway someone just said, 'This is a hell of a Christmas.' He's right."[17]

It "was a somber day." Shopping district holiday lights were gone, "and the tinkle of bells on Salvation Army Christmas kettles was the only comforting reality in a world of camouflage, gas masks, barbed wire, and bomb shelters....The strange Yuletide dragged on, with delayed packages arriving far into January and February. For most people Christmas was a work day—a forerunner of many holidays when orders decreed business as usual."[18] Peggy Hughes Ryan wrote, "In spite of the discouraging news from the war front, [we] were determined to celebrate Christmas as much as possible in the traditional way. Few husbands would be present, because most of them had departed on operational missions. The absence of any Christmas trees posed a problem....Our thoughtful landlady supplied the need by furnishing us branches from ironwood trees...we wired to a broom handle, producing a passable Christmas tree, at least in the eyes of the little children. For the adults, I contributed our last bottle of whiskey to the communal celebration. Inevitably, the absence of the evening cocktail prompted the inventive among us to experiment with weird recipes for fermenting pineapple juice—which we had in abundance."[19]

Christmas that year was strange and at times sad. Although I did not believe in Santa Claus, I was a true believer in receiving gifts. My brother was probably at the crossover stage wanting to hold on but knowing in his heart this was all a myth. I think I probably just flat out told him the truth. This was the year for it, as no ships or planes brought goods from the Mainland to the stores. Sears, Roebuck put up a huge tree in front of their store and had it lit a few hours during each day. Someone played a sort of Hawaiian Santa, but there were no toys, or decorations to speak of. I have no real memory of what we were given as gifts. Mostly homemade things, and probably recycled stuff. It didn't seem to matter as we were all going to Diamond Head to the home of Hazel Lewis, a friend, joining several women Mother knew from Los Angeles, sharing what might have been a lonely day together. We ate roast pig. I have never forgotten that. Wearing my best "party dress," eating greasy roast pig, and running down the beach barefoot. A great life! The women sat together on a lanai *talking and having some drinks, and as dusk came, our mother began to cry. It was always scary to see a mom cry. I think we all stayed at the house on Diamond Head that night.*

"Taking all things into consideration, civilian Oahu fought a very inconvenient but privationless war, and, after the first fatal day, a bloodless one," wrote one man who lived through it. "We thought we lived dangerously, because of the constant threat, but as we know now that threat was more apparent than real....We were so much worse off than the rest of the people in America that it was hard for us not to exaggerate our plight."[20]

Remembering Kipapa's Gulch,
and Firearms at the Cat Houses

James G. Carroll, a member of a B-17 squadron originally stationed at Hickam Field, remembered expanding into Kipapa Air Base.[21]

> "At Kipapa our quarters for four were one-room shacks plopped in the middle of a pineapple field. We were spared the distraction of indoor plumbing and AEK kitchens. Here we spent our evenings in the blackout with armies of displaced spiders who wished more than to share our quarters. And we spent very long hours standing alert and flying maximum searches in our throbbing B-17s.
>
> Kipapa provided good training for precision landing techniques. The landing strip was short and up-hill, a one-way affair. The landing end was bordered by, and at right angles to, the Gulch itself, a deep canyon with a built-in downdraft and capricious cross winds....We never lost a plane to the Gulch, more than once a pilot had to fire-wall all four engines to crawl out of that Gulch for a go-around. Landing at night by the dark of the moon could get especially spooky. The Kipapa runway was also short and terminated at a main highway. Thus landing long was intolerable; no place to go other than down the highway," the landing glide a minimum-speed affair. In September 1942 the unit redeployed to Kualoa across the bay from Kaneohe on windward Oahu. "Here we were right on the thoroughly barb-wired beach. On our rare off-hours, we enjoyed its pleasures. On other occasions, the [heavy artillery] 155s in the hills thundered over our heads on target practice."

Air Mechanic Second Class Fred S. Crane was a member of Carroll's 31st Bomb Squadron of the 5th Bomb Group on 7 December.[22] An airman since July 1939, Crane had been stationed at Hickam for 2-1/2 years. His squadron was transitioning into B-17C/Ds when the attack came, and were awaiting arrival of the B-17Es that flew in during the attack. Before the attack, he had been the last man in his squadron to have leave, was on Maui for Thanksgiving, and just made it back in early December. The hurriedly constructed landing strips at Kipapa and Kuoloa were dirt. He learned to ride a friend's motorcycle on the runway. Once he was headed for Honolulu riding the bike down the runway. Someone had run across the strip with a grader, and he flipped, bruised himself, and soiled his uniform. He and buddies siphoned 100 octane gasoline from aircraft tanks into their cars.

In off-duty hours Crane visited Wahiawa near Schofield. "If you went to town you had to wear a sidearm. If you went into a whore house another man had to hold your gun when you went upstairs. You never wore a gun into a cat house." Women of Portuguese descent were the best looking. On Oahu "life was good. I had a locker at the Waikiki Tavern" and kept a swim suit there, right on the beach near the Outrigger Canoe Club and not far from Fort DeRussy. Otherwise he spent time in Catholic church activities.

Crane, now a resident of Wilmington, North Carolina, retired from the air force as a master sergeant.

Principal Oahu Military Installations, 1942
(Active on 7 December 1941 Except as Noted)

Navy
- Naval Base, Pearl Harbor
- Ford Island Naval Air Station
- Kaneohe Naval Air Station
- Submarine Base, Pearl Harbor

Pearl Harbor Navy Yard
Barber's Point Naval Air Station (April 1942)
Wahaiwa Communications Station
Naval Hospital, Pearl Harbor
Aiea Naval Hospital (November 1942)

Marine Corps
Marine Corps Air Station, Ewa

Army
Schofield Barracks
Forts DeRussy, Ruger, Shafter, Armstrong
Tripler General Hospital

Army Air Forces
Hickam Field Air Base
Bellows, Haleiwa, Wheeler Fields
Kahuka, Kipapa Air Bases (1942)
Mokuleia, Kualoa Fields (1942)

Boys of the "Frisco"

On 7 December the heavy cruiser USS *San Francisco* (CA-38), the "Frisco," was moored bow-in at the Navy Yard's Southeast Loch pier next to the large hammerhead crane. She was scheduled to move into dry dock for repairs within days. Fifty-nine years later the survivors held their annual reunion in Wilmington, North Carolina.

Rufus Stewart[23]

Signalman Third Class Rufus was on the signal bridge during the attack. His brother Harry S. Stewart was also a crew member. *San Francisco* had just unloaded ammunition and fuel prior to entering the yard. The ship's only battle damage was to a searchlight. In Honolulu, "They raised the price of drinks quite a bit. The gals of ill repute raised their prices too. Some boys thought it was their last chance, so they visited cat houses." The navy built a recreation area outside the base main gate attempting to keep the boys from going into town. From the ship he ominously looked over to the shore at the hundreds of wood caskets piled on each other. Harry sent home "the card" to their parents after the attack and checked off to say he was okay. Rufus didn't, and finally wrote them after they returned to Pearl from the first operations. "The best time of my life was in World War II."

Raymond Owsley[24]

Machinists Mate First Class Owsley had served on board for eight and one-half years. He was living in a rented house in Honolulu with his wife, Bryan, and their child. The rest of the crew lived on ship while in the yard. During the first wave attack he was at home, threw his wife and kid into the car, headed for Pearl, dropped them off at a housing area, and proceeded to his ship. He went aboard about 0830. As the second wave passed over, "we didn't have a hell of a lot to do." The ship had been stripped, including of ammunition, and was on "cold iron" (no ship's power). They received no liberty to go into town, but he did go bowling at the recreation center. "It was hustle, hustle, hustle—get things done. Every second word was 'damned Japanese.' You didn't accomplish anything by yourself. You added to what was going on." A few days later the wives went to a dependents meeting at the commissary to find out what was to be done with them. Bryan went back to San Francisco with the first group out. "We just up and left, as far as I can remember. My wife made all the arrangements with navy help" in getting out of the house. "My contribution during that period was hard work, putting things back together" on the ship.

Don Jenkins[25]

The night of 7 December was blacked out. Welders were working out on deck. A marine sentry heard something, saw a figure crawling across deck, pulled his pistol and aimed it at the image. "Don't shoot, me Filipino, me no Japanese," the yard worker yelled. Crewmen had to take gas masks the ship issued them when going on liberty and had to be back aboard before dark.

Ted Tipper[26]

The crew had only small arms during the attack with which to fight back. "I don't think we hit anything." After the attack two of their men didn't want to go back to sea, went to a sugar cane plantation railroad, placed their feet on the tracks and let the trains run over them and cut off their toes. They received bad conduct discharges. A barge called the "juice barge" scooped up surface oil in the harbor after the attack. Once the war started there were long lines at the cat houses—before the war no waiting at all.

Johnny Johnson[27]

Everyone was on liberty the night of 6 December. The streets were packed. Johnson watched the first wave from the ship's fantail. The ship was covered with redlead (paint) and open with lines entering below decks. It was obvious that the ship must be put back in order. Workers swarmed aboard finishing repairs, working 24 hours in 4–5 days to get it done. "It was impossible to get any sleep with all the jackhammers. The ship was very dark. We were not used to these blackouts. Being a young kid (18), not mentally prepared for all this, I went into a mental shock. Took about a week to comprehend what had happened. It took about 2–3 weeks before it all settled in. I had joined the navy for an adventure and was not prepared for it."

John Egan[28]

Egan, the marine sergeant of the guard, was among a detachment of two officers and 41 enlisted marines. The Black Cat Club across from the Honolulu YMCA was the crew's hangout. Men could not keep civilian clothes onboard ship, so four or five Marines kept a Hawaiian shirt in a locker at the "Y." Someone would wear it on liberty along with his marine boondockers, marine haircut, making it hard to disguise themselves as civilians. Before the war, enlisted men were not allowed in upscale places like the Waikiki hotels. "You were persona non grata. We didn't have too much contact with people off the ship." After 7 December "things opened up." He remembered the whore houses on Beretania Street. After Pearl Harbor authorities "put a clamp on the cat houses. In those days [before the attack] it was two bucks a go. After the attack there were so many customers you were limited to three minutes. They used three rooms, had one man dressing, one getting undressed, the other was making it. If it weren't for those young hookers we would have had very little contact with locals except women in bars. I am grateful to them." The girls were from the Mainland. Some were earning money to try to get to school.

The Hawaiian Japanese

Many Japanese living in Hawaii desired to show their U.S. loyalty by acting "American." Kimonos and geta disappeared, old-country wedding and funeral customs were revolutionized, and they destroyed everything Japanese at home. Later they would suffer from lacking proof or information needed for identification or employment because they had burned family records, passports, and birth certificates. Young people refused to speak Japanese, even if it was the best way to communicate with parents. "...Three of the most influential Japanese institutions—the Buddhist temples, the Shinto shrines, and the language schools—became inactive at the start of the war....Leadership in the Japanese community passed immediately to the group holding American citizenship...." Often the father was in an internment camp, the sons in the U.S. Army, the mother torn between two cultures.[29] (This was in a day before hyphenated Americans were labeled; e.g., Japanese-Americans. By coincidence, the Japanese quarter of Honolulu was the most heavily damaged and of civilians killed on 7 December, 80 percent were Japanese.)

Of Hawaii's prewar population of 400,000, some 160,000 were Japanese, the Territory's largest ethnic group. Japan recognized dual citizenship and maintained these naturalized Americans were Japanese, called "law of the blood." It directly contradicted U.S. law which did not recognize dual citizenship. Because of their general reluctance to volunteer after war began, Japanese seemed suspect. Authorities excluded them from police or guard duty, restricted area work, essential industrial jobs, censorship, air raid defense, and related civilian defense roles. Some withdrew from local politics but others did not.

In 1942 the U.S. Government interned about 120,000 Japanese West Coast residents. "The rationale for mass relocation was that common ancestry with the enemy rendered this ethnic group vulnerable to penetration by spies and saboteurs. The fact that relocation was racially determined raised legal and moral questions...."[30] Admiral Chester Nimitz persuaded Washington not to intern Japanese Hawaiians in the same manner. His rationale included that most of the Japanese were Okinawan agricultural employees and little would be gained by locking up thousands of loyal workers, and adding to the manpower shortage. Only about 1,450 Hawaiian Japanese were taken into custody. There were no guilty cases of overt acts against American laws, very few instances of open loyalty to Japan, and only occasional arrests for possessing articles forbidden to Japanese. Several hundred were released after questioning, and several thousand more were investigated and cleared without being in custody. About one-third of the interned Japanese were American citizens (born in Hawaii). The detained group had been prewar suspects and included Shinto and Buddhist priests, consular and language school officials, and leaders in the alien community. The records show that "espionage in Hawaii before the war was carried on only by the Japanese consular staff and one other person, a German. They also agree that there was no espionage after the start of the war, no sabotage, no fifth column activity of any sort."[31]

Most Oahu internees were held on the Sand Island immigration station. The government shipped many internees to the Mainland until April 1944, but federal authorities there sent back the American citizens and kept only aliens. Eventually some one thousand were voluntarily evacuated to the Mainland, almost all internees' dependents. The total of Japanese sent to the Mainland was 1,875. Nearly 1,500 returned to Hawaii, some stayed, and some repatriated to Japan.

Defense worker doing his best to learn the hula from an expert on Waikiki.

Mother, Berton, and I the day of our arrival at Pearl Harbor from California by ship, late November 1941. This was our temporary quarters at the Moana Seaside until we moved into the Comstock Apartments Hotel on Kalakaua Avenue.

Authors' collection

Mother and the kids are reunited with our dad, Lieutenant Berton A. Robbins, Jr., at Pearl Harbor. Dad was just leaving the USS *Tucker* (DD-374) to report for duty on the USS *Shaw* (DD-373). Both destroyers were homeported at Pearl, and we had not seen him for nearly a year.

Authors' collection

Easter Sunday, 1942. Rationing was tight, so our mother found colored balloons instead of candy for a centerpiece. Three eggs in the nest were real and our breakfast.

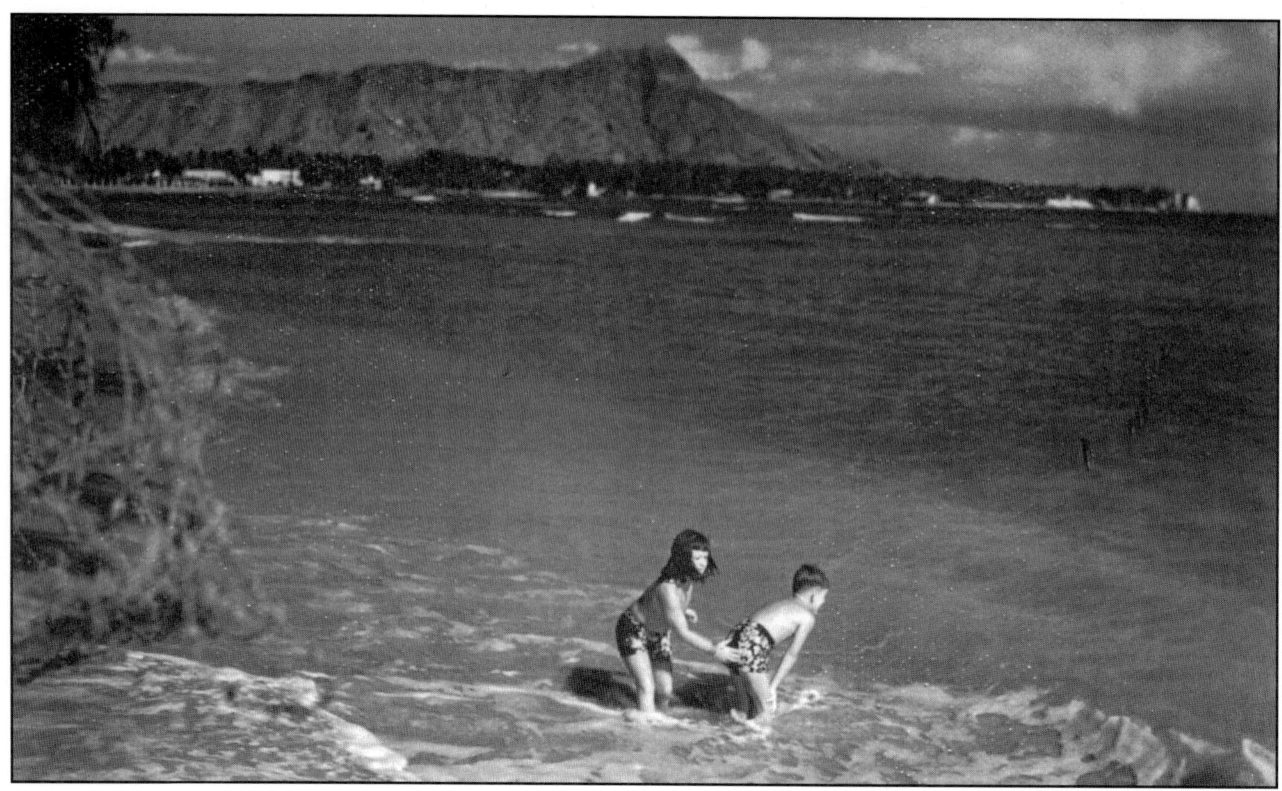

The transformation to native Hawaiian had been made. Waikiki, with Diamond Head looming, and rolls of barbed wire, *left of photo*, hurriedly put in place, became one of our playgrounds.

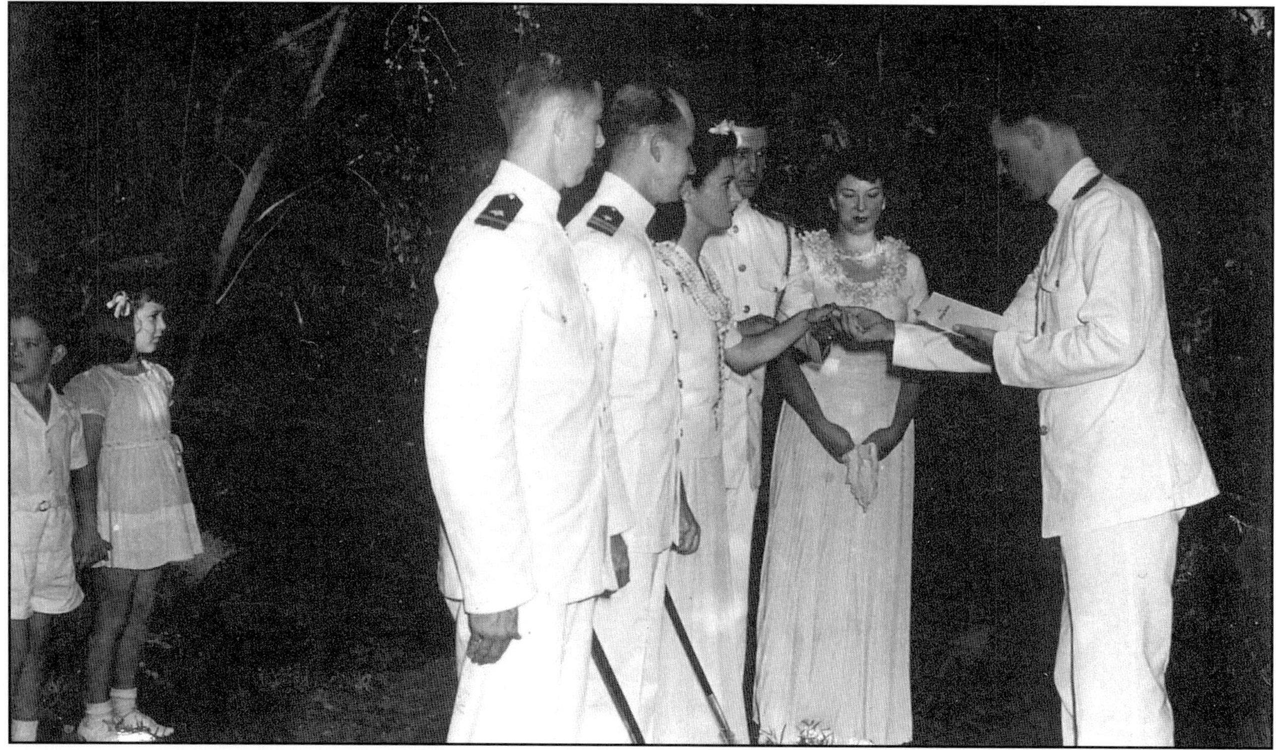

The two of us were in great demand as junior attendants in a number of naval weddings which occurred in the months following the outbreak of war.

During early 1942, an organization called "Stars and Bars" was formed in Honolulu, the brainchild of Harriett Weaver of Los Angeles. It was a smaller USO-type club atmosphere for both officers and enlisted with emphasis on group activities (dining and talking together), rather than big-band music and dancing.

Oahu became an island of lonely women and few children from the Mainland, waiting for fathers, husbands, and sweethearts to return from combat. Not all wives and dependents returned to the Mainland right away. My mother, brother, and I remained until August 1942 while she was on an extended assignment for Associated Press.

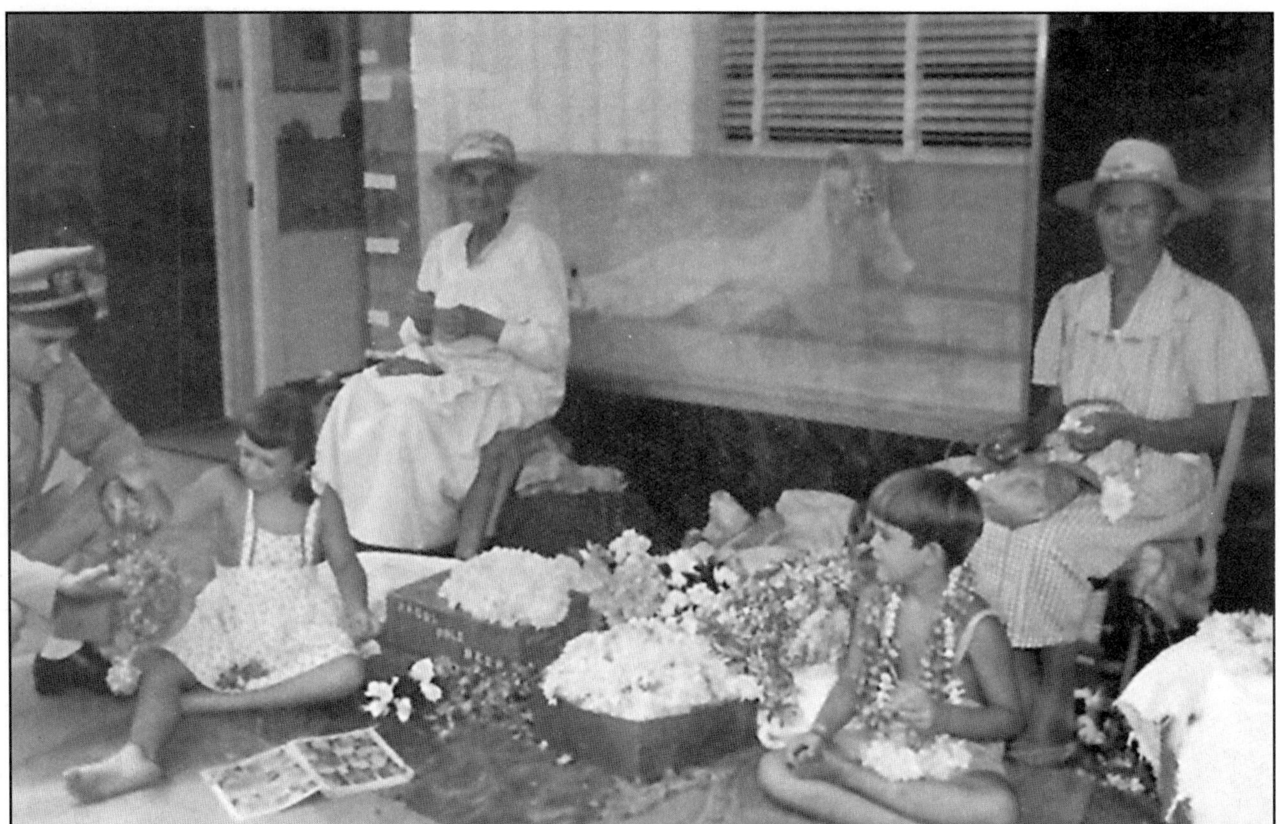

The lei makers along Waikiki became our babysitters of sorts. We loved the smell of flowers and actually brought not only a smile to passers-by but sales to the ladies. We pretended to be Hawaiian and would speak "pidgin" English.

With clothes too small, shoes too tight, wearing leis we made, in front of a store with a taped, patriotic "V" for victory, we will soon sail for California, leaving behind a nine-month adventure during one of the great moments in our nation's history.

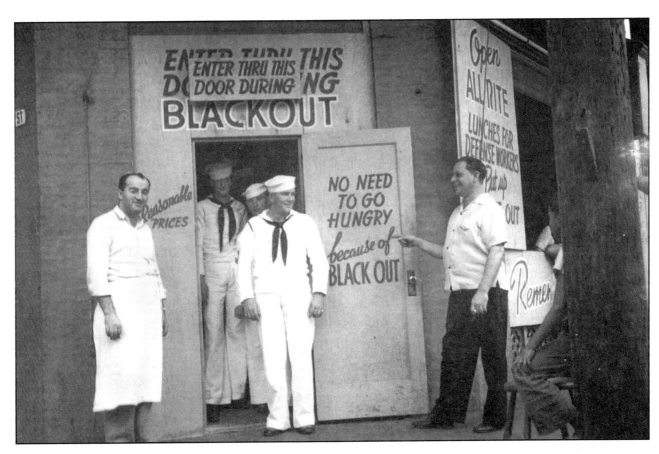

The Times Square Grill on Hotel Street in downtown Honolulu, a hangout known to every sailor in port.

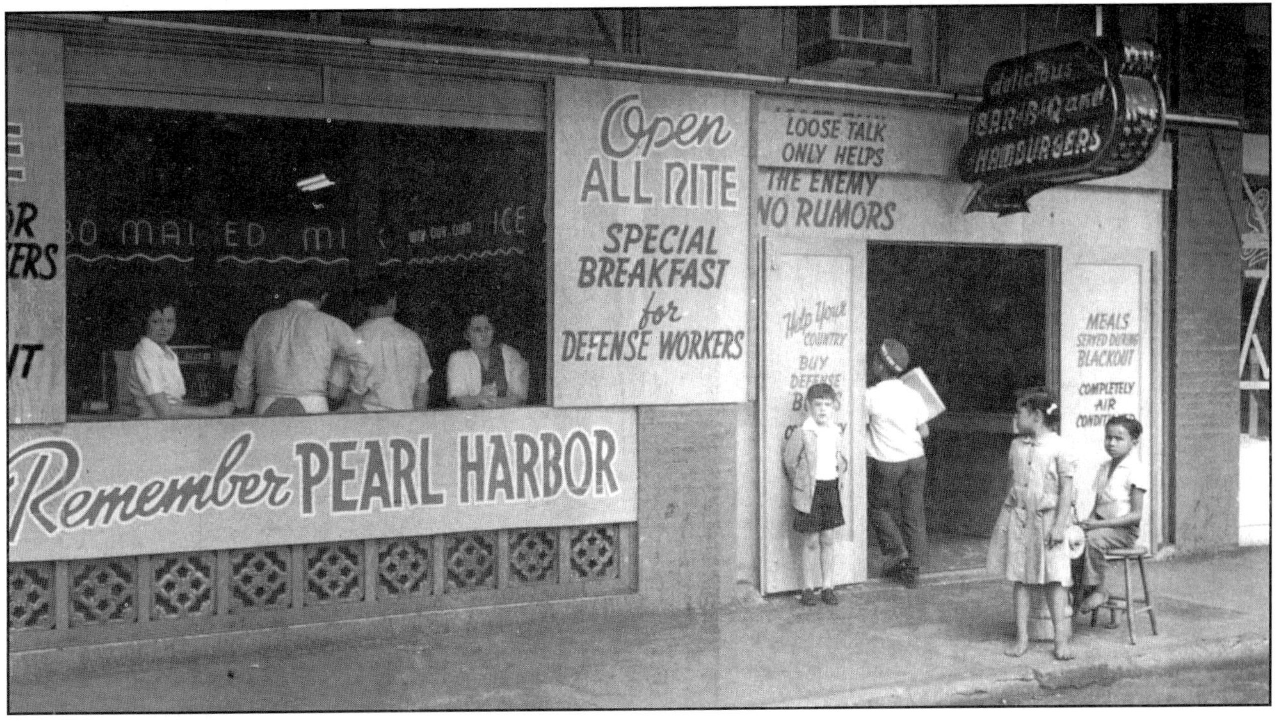

A 24-hour fast-food joint on notorious Hotel Street. Berton stood by the door but Mother wouldn't allow him to go inside.

Berton and I weren't the only ones going barefoot. The hula shows on Waikiki continued.

Mother photographed Hawaiian USO troupe that traveled around the Islands. The GIs loved to lose inhibitions and unwind a while.

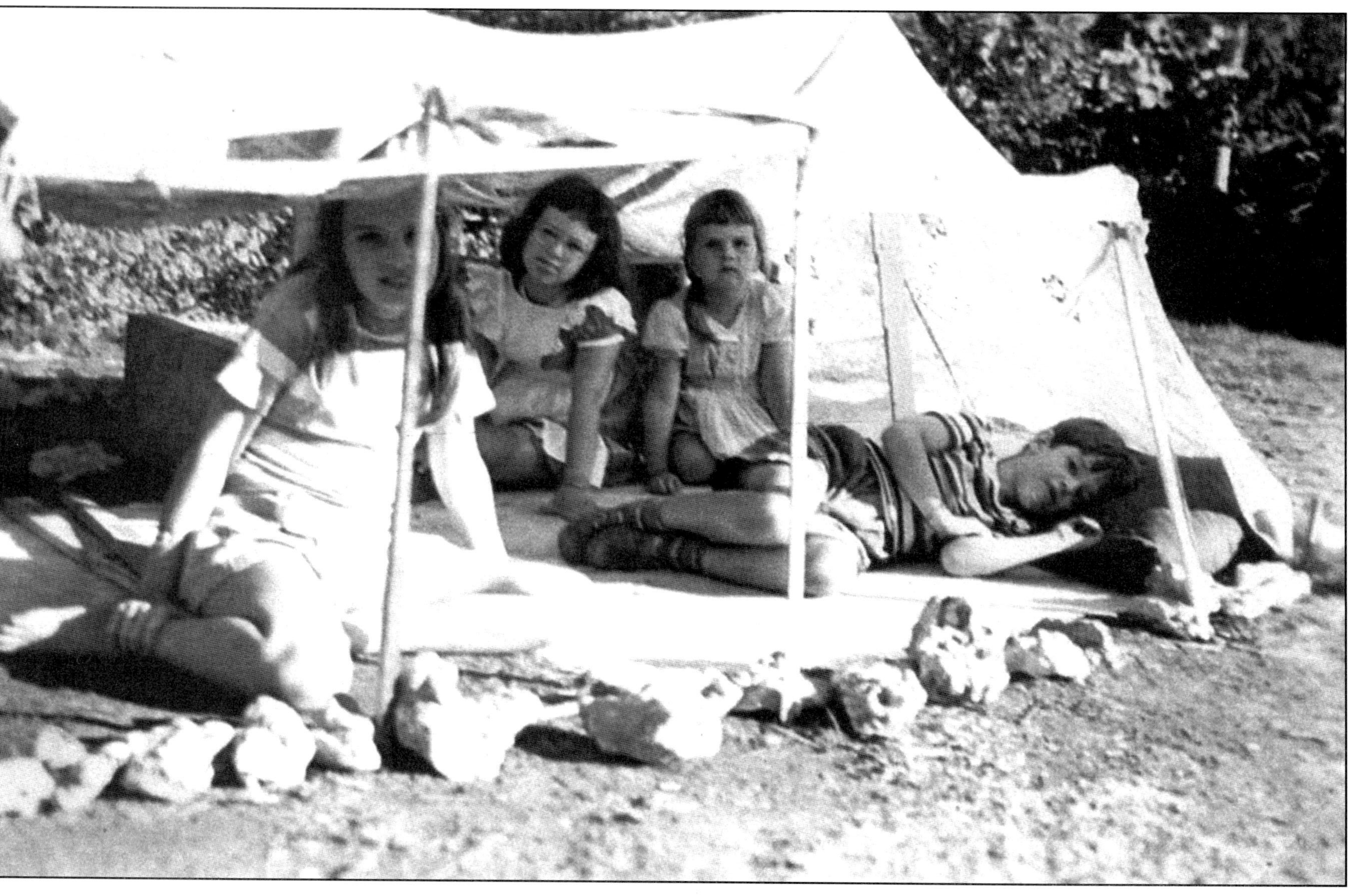

We improvised all the time for things to play with including homemade backyard encampments. Here neighbor kids Jackie and Diane Cease join us in preparing for the inevitable Japanese invasion.

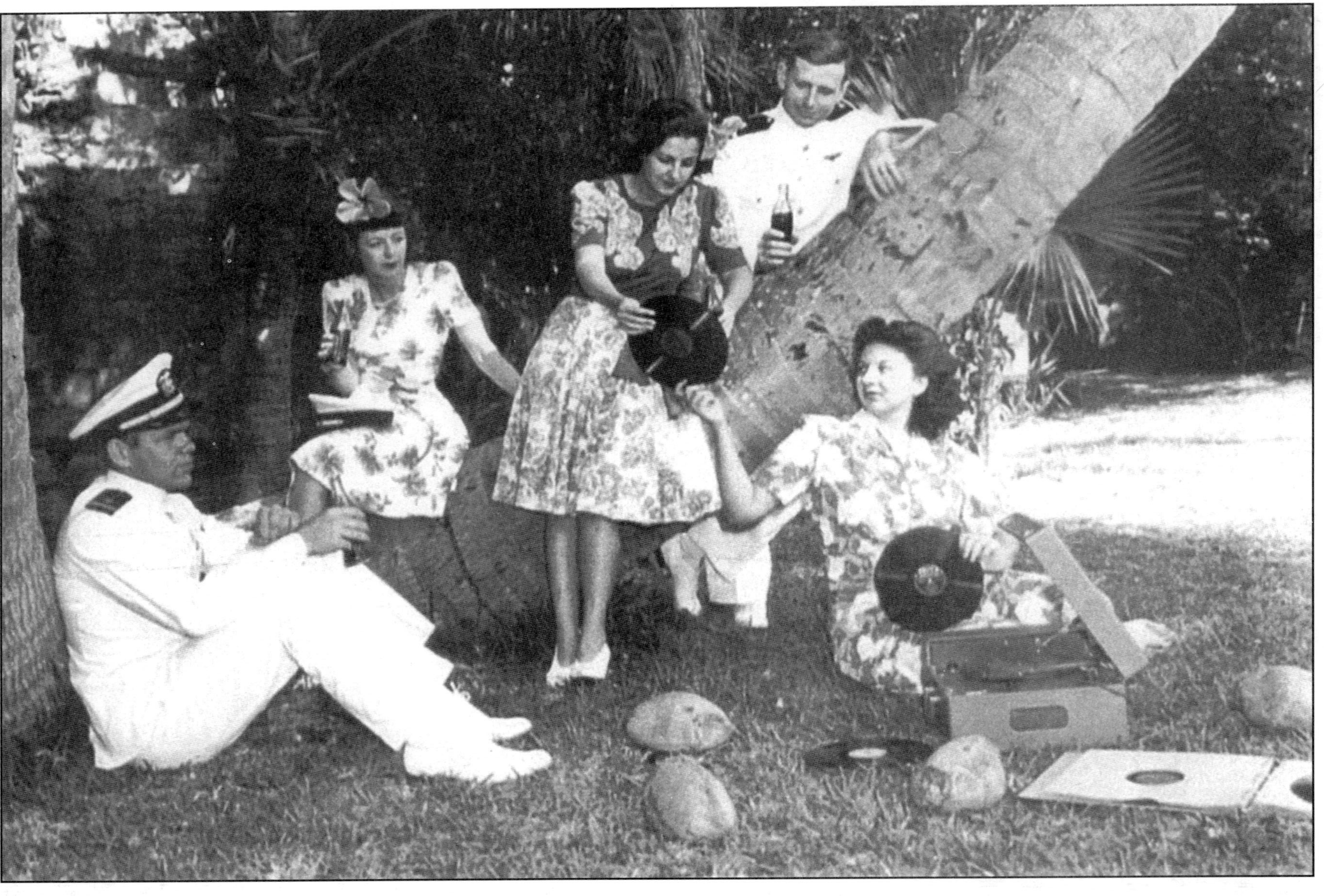

Naval officers and their wives and girlfriends relaxed and socialized as much as possible. Here a group is listening to 78 rpm records on a portable player and enjoying eight-ounce bottled Cokes.

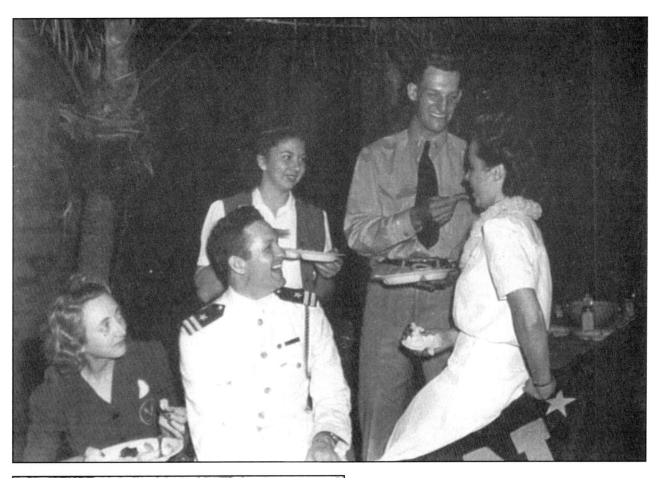

Harriett Weaver, *left*, Dad, *second from left*, and friends party in Honolulu. This was a part from one of Mother's photo layouts published in the *Los Angeles Times*.

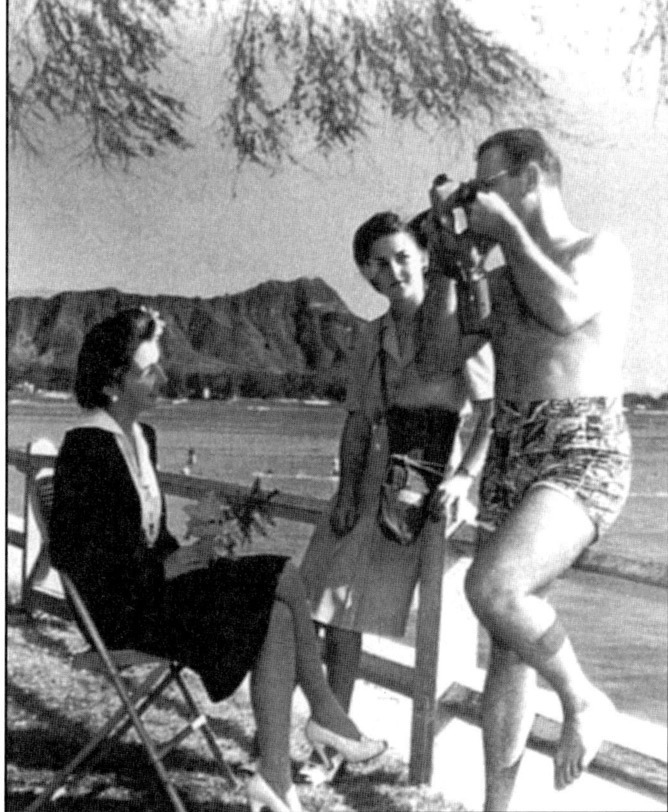

Waikiki was the scene of many social gatherings in the large navy community.

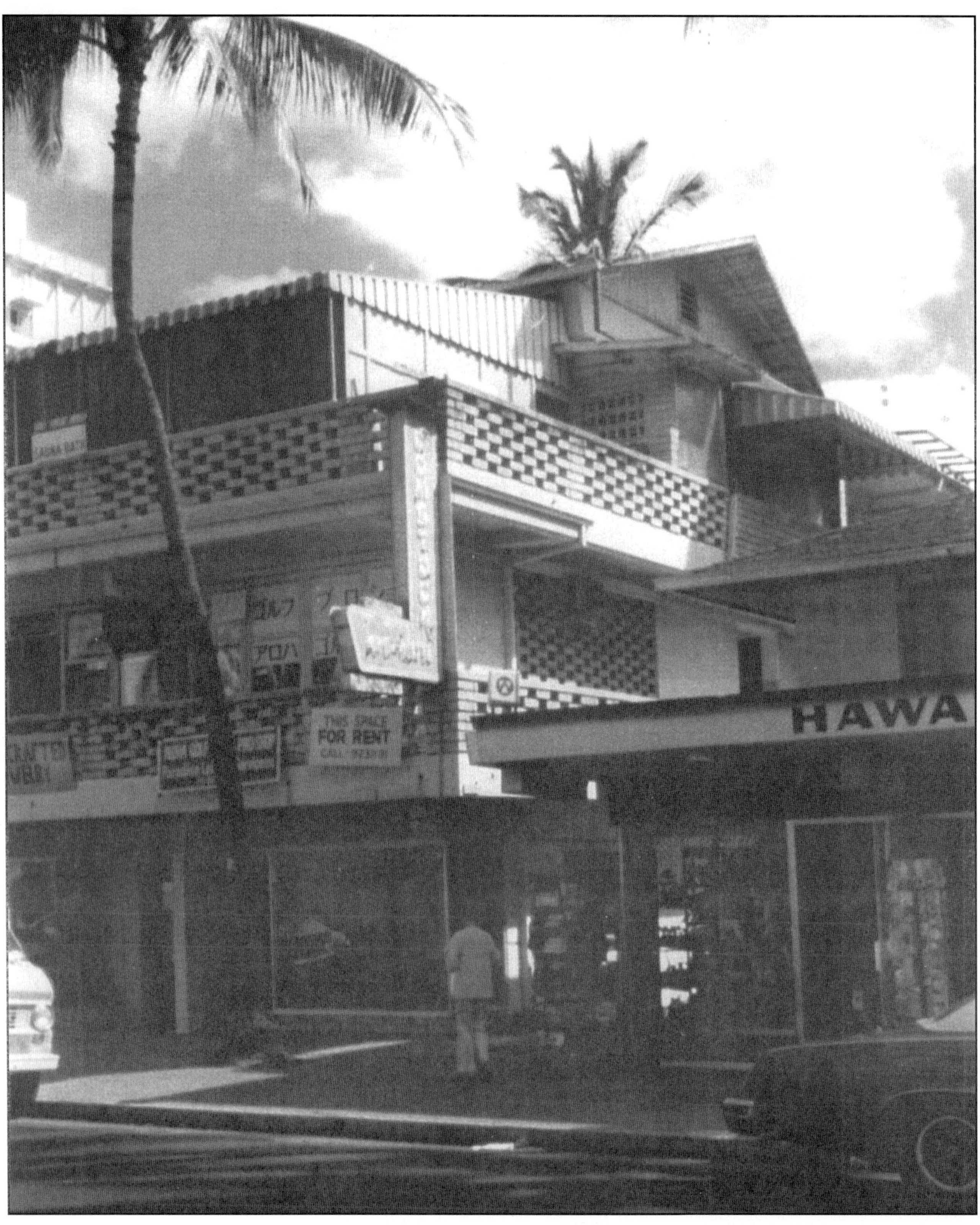

The Comstock Apartments Hotel in December 1975. Outwardly, it appeared to have changed greatly since we lived there. Then it was not so commercial and had lots of space around it. By pure luck and coincidence, Wilbur was able to see the place before it was scheduled for demolition a few weeks later.

Authors' collection

Our last picture of Dad just before he departed not long after the attack for duty as aide to Admiral "Poco" Smith on the cruiser USS *Chicago* (CA-29). We would see him once for the next three years while he fought in the Southwest and Central Pacific and the Aleutians.

We would spend a lot of time together in the coming years while Dad was away. This photo was taken at the Comstock.

Authors' collection

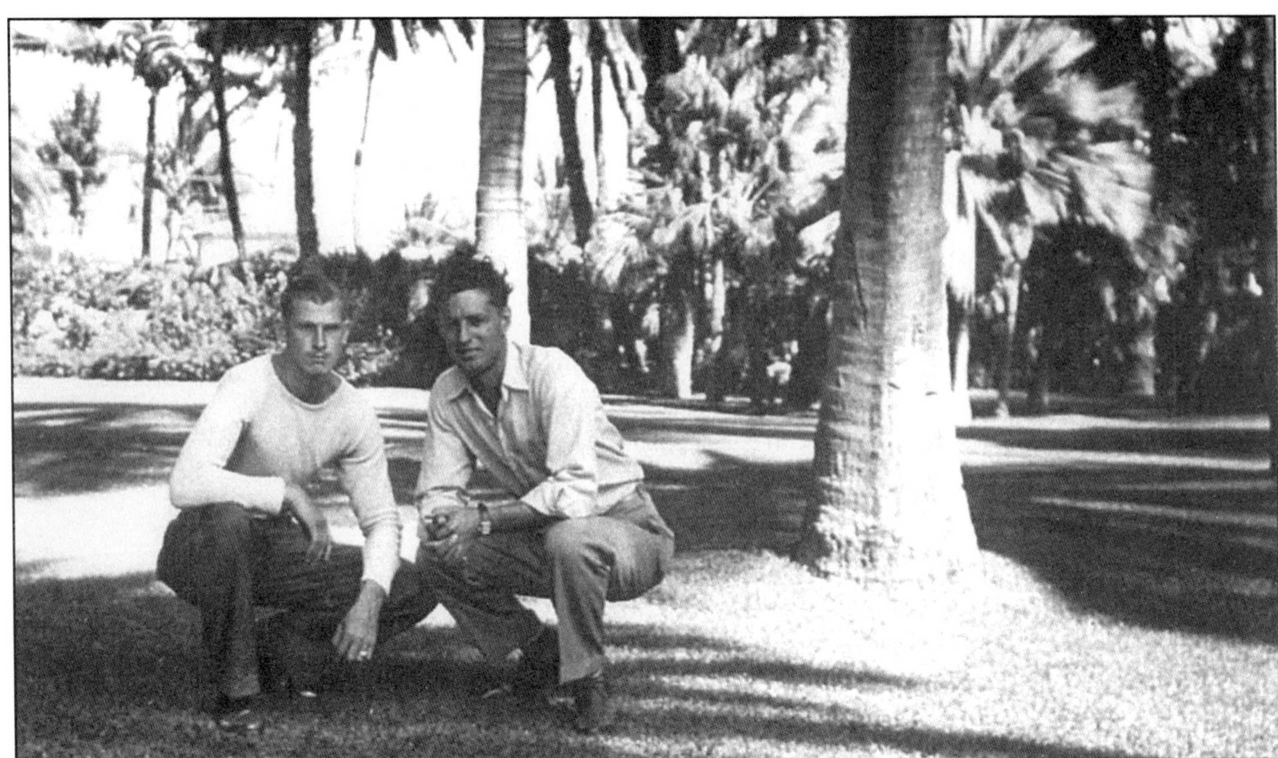

Fred S. Crane, *left*, army air forces, was stationed with a B-17 squadron at Hickam Field during the attack. In June 1942 he served on Midway during the battle there. Crane now lives in Wilmington, North Carolina.

Courtesy of Crane

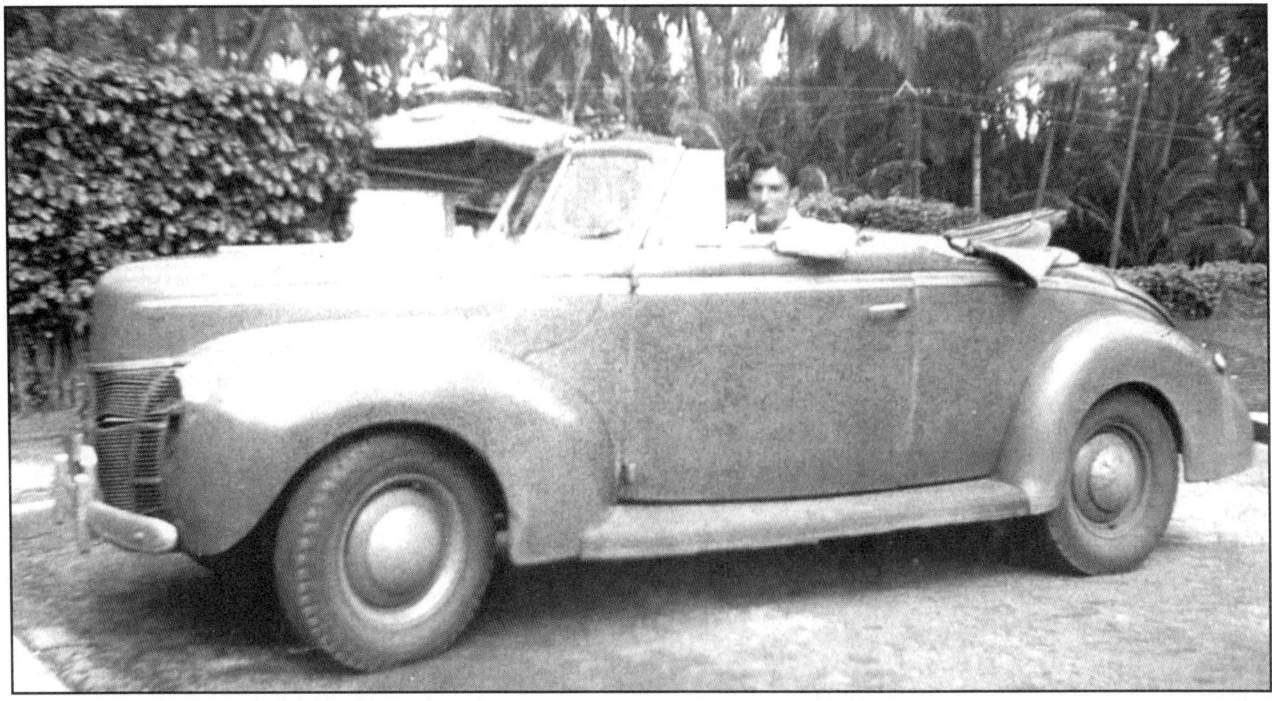

Wilmington native Taylor Marion Jeffords, Jr., and his 1940 Ford Convertible in Hawaii, December 1942. He still lives in Wilmington.

Courtesy of Jeffords

Hampstead, North Carolina, native Lawrence Homer Henderson, *left*, crewman on USS *California* (BB-44), shown prior to the attack. Henderson still lives in Hampstead.

Courtesy of Henderson

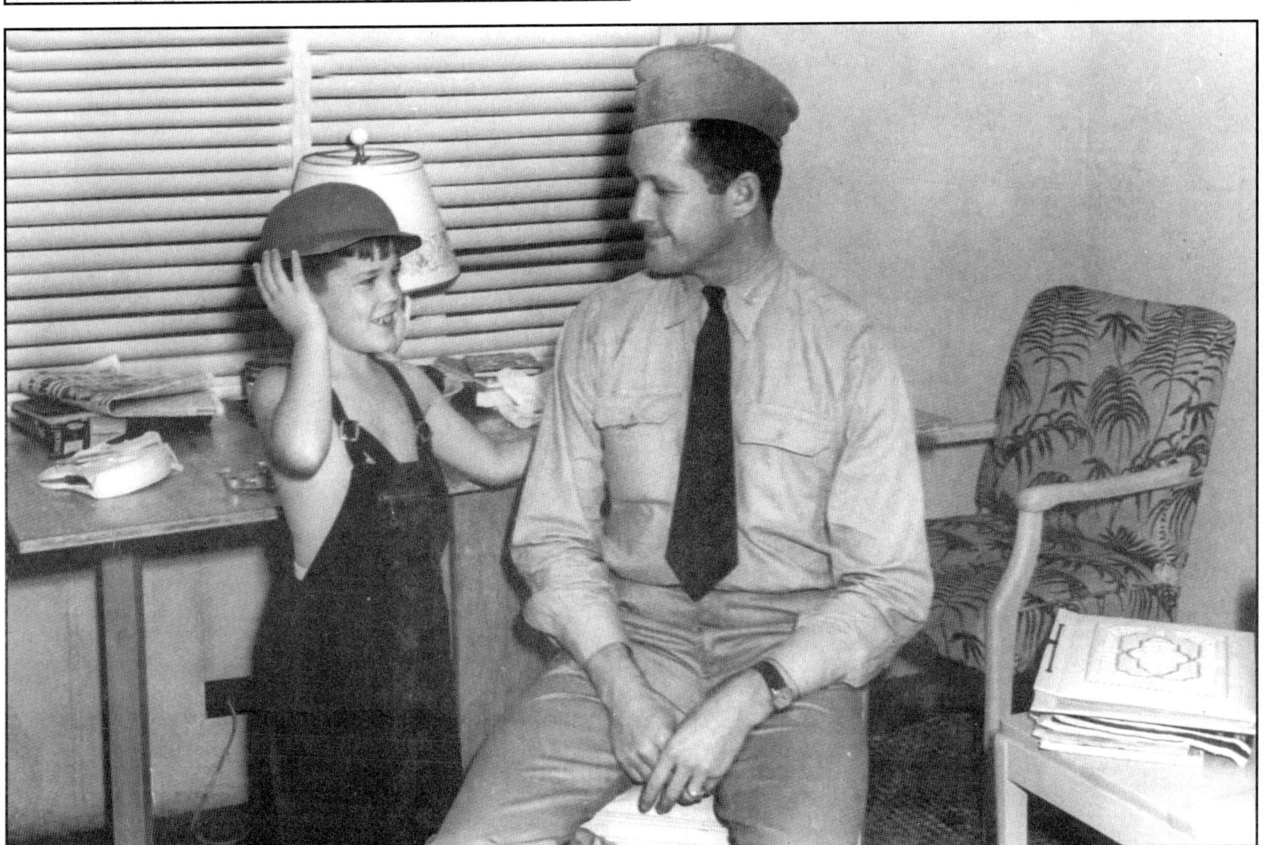

Berton and Dad right before he left for combat. December 1941.

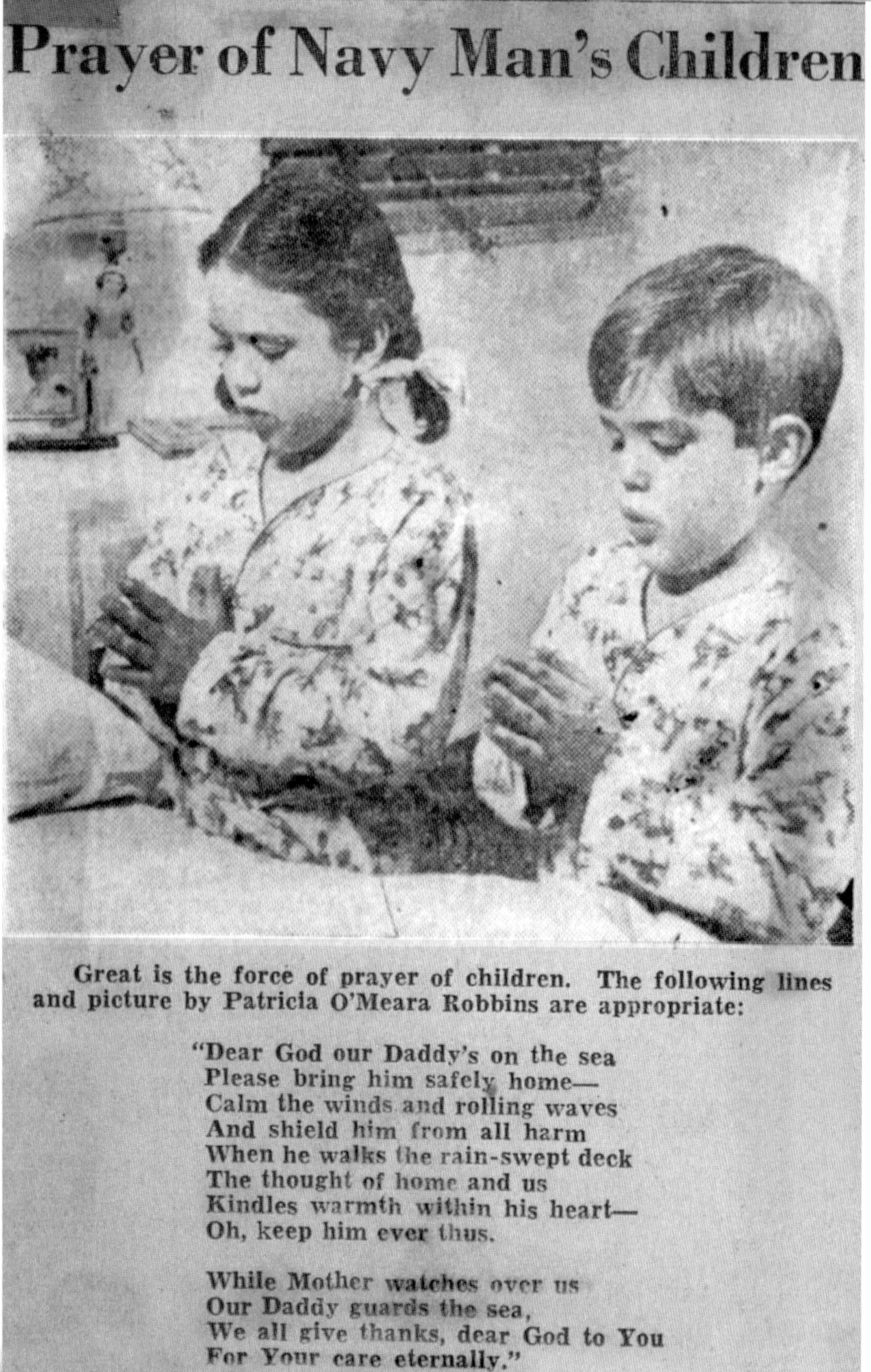

THE HONOLULU ADVERTISER, SUNDAY MORNING, DECEMBER 28, 1941

Prayer of Navy Man's Children

Great is the force of prayer of children. The following lines and picture by Patricia O'Meara Robbins are appropriate:

"Dear God our Daddy's on the sea
Please bring him safely home—
Calm the winds and rolling waves
And shield him from all harm
When he walks the rain-swept deck
The thought of home and us
Kindles warmth within his heart—
Oh, keep him ever thus.

While Mother watches over us
Our Daddy guards the sea,
We all give thanks, dear God to You
For Your care eternally."

Mother's photo of us and "Prayer of a Navy Man's Children" probably spoke for thousands of others like us.

The Honolulu Advertiser, December 28, 1941

President Gerald R. Ford, *center,* arrives on *Arizona* Memorial for 34th anniversary observance precisely at 0755 on 7 December 1975. First Lady Betty Ford, with top assistant Dick Cheney, are shown getting off the boat. Within seconds, and without advance notice, a reconstructed Japanese Mitsubishi A6M *Zero* zoomed close overhead, as if by fate. It startled all in the party including the president's advanceman, Wilbur, and the Secret Service, who reached for their pistols, which would have been little match.

Authors' collection

Dad had just been awarded the Navy Cross in 1945 for his service as commanding officer of the destroyer USS *Leutze* (DD-481) during action at Surigao Strait, Battle of Leyte Gulf, in which he helped sink a Japanese battleship. He was recovering in the Long Beach (California) Naval Hospital from severe wounds received at Iwo Jima.

My aunts Katherine and Muriel O'Meara, visiting Hawaii from Los Angeles, by chance ran into Wilbur while he was advancing President Ford's visit. Through the navy, he helped give them the "Cook's tour" of Pearl Harbor. Here they are at the Comstock where we lived in 1941–42 across the street from the Royal Hawaiian Hotel.

Authors' collection

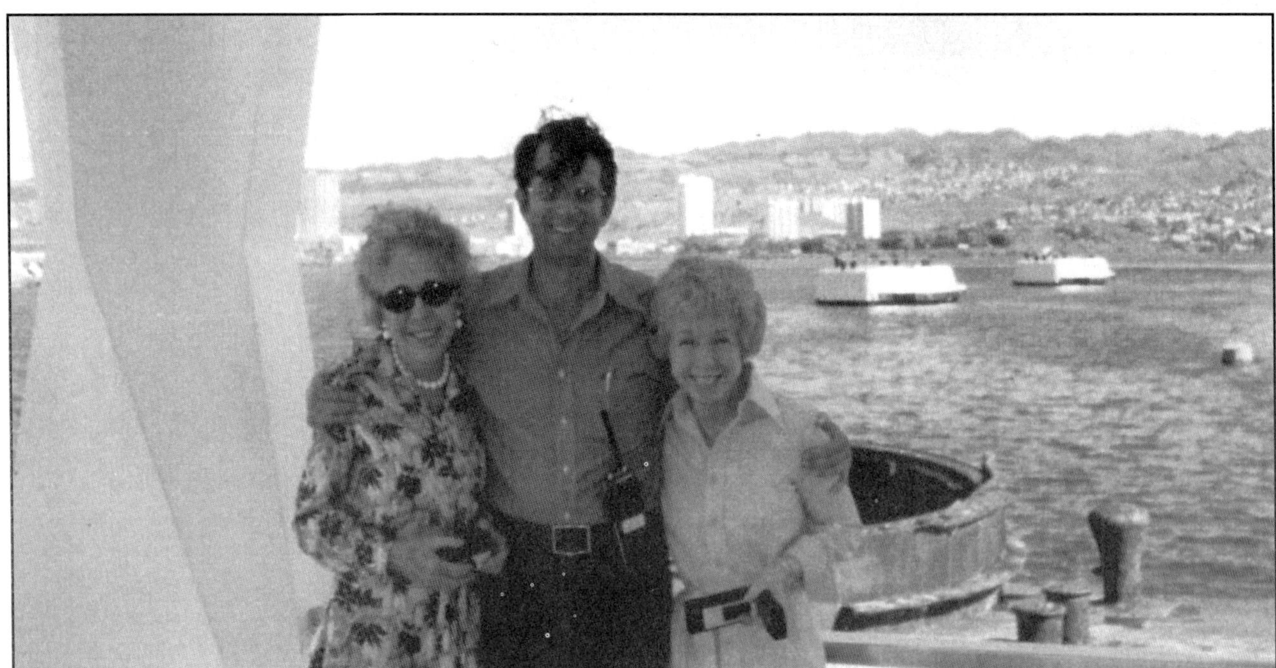

Wilbur with my Los Angeles aunts Katherine and Muriel O'Meara at the *Arizona* Memorial at Pearl Harbor in December 1975. As an advance representative to President Ford, he was in Hawaii preparing for Ford's visit there on 7 December. After numerous stops in Pearl during his navy career, Wilbur has not been back since except for passing through Honolulu.

Authors' collection

Baker 1st Class Taylor Marion Jeffords, Jr., of Wilmington, crew member of the USS *West Virginia* (BB-48) at Pearl Harbor.

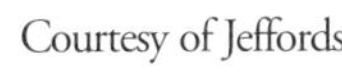

Courtesy of Jeffords

Dad was proudly promoted to rear admiral on his retirement in 1959 after 29 years of service. Photo ca. 1980.

Not quite the average Sunday in the park, but Berton and I loved visiting family friend Hazel Lewis on Diamond Head. Her father owned land and a pineapple plantation.

Chapter 5

"A Miserable Event": Evacuation to the Mainland

Steamship companies such as the Matson Lines which before the war sailed luxury passenger ships carrying tourists to Hawaii quickly modified the ships into troop and supply transports from West Coast ports. On their return voyages they took military dependents and the sick and wounded. "From all counts, the evacuation was a miserable event, but through no fault of the Matson Line," historian Archie Satterfield stated. "Officers' wives pulled rank on the enlisted men's wives, and one woman insisted that she would have stayed in Honolulu with the bombing raids, even troop landings, rather than make the voyage again with the hysterical, rank-pulling women and their undisciplined children." En route officials warned the women not to confirm or deny anything that had been reported about Hawaii, but newspapers got their stories anyway, some inaccurate.[1]

Officials on Hawaii urged as many persons as possible be evacuated to lessen defense problems, relieve crowded conditions, and reduce the quantity of required imports. About 20,000 army and navy dependents and 10,000 island women and children—of whom about 80 percent were Armed Forces dependents—left, most during first months. The first group reached San Francisco Christmas morning after a hectic voyage. About half of the remaining 10,000 canceled their plans after Midway.

Early in 1942, we kids were told we might have to *return to California. On the one hand that wasn't so bad. On the other, we had about completed our transformation to becoming natives, and with our new-found friends (lei makers, beach boys, theater manager, liquor store owner, piano players, and singers) and a certain amount of freedom, the thought of wearing shoes and going to school dimmed our enthusiasm for our partners in crime, our grampa, and now only one uncle, as the other was in the army. Apparently Mother had to show cause as to why she should be allowed to remain on the island, particularly with two youngsters, for an indefinite length of time. She was somehow always able to talk her way into and out of most anything, and this was no exception. Actually, one of the pieces she contracted to do before our arrival, but delayed due to major interference by the Japanese, was nearly complete, and the fact that she had been renewed with Associated Press for another short period was enough for our extension. Whew!*

Peggy Hughes Ryan, a navy wife, remembered, "The number of my friends being evacuated from Honolulu continued to grow. The first to go were those who had lost husbands; next came mothers with babies, and last, pregnant women. We had been warned by the military authorities that we would receive only 24 hours notice of departure, so we lived from day to day out of suitcases....By mid-April, our group had dwindled to the few who either had husbands based on shore duty or held defense jobs...." The navy ordered Ryan to leave on 20 April. She had shipped her household goods, mainly wedding presents, and had only her trunk and suitcases. "Friends drove me to the pier where the leave-taking was subdued. No bands, flower leis, and paper streamers—so customary in the pre-war years. Instead there was a mixed group, nearly all women and children, with the unmistakable look of refugees. Quite a few were of Oriental descent....Forty years later, as I look back on my Pearl Harbor experience, I remain convinced that most young navy wives who were there did what they had to do—adjusted to the unusual and accustomed themselves to the unexpected. Which, after all, is what a service wife must do in any era."[2]

We were not allowed to forget that no matter what Mother's professional standing was, she was still (and primarily) a navy wife. As the weeks passed, more and more friends were being forced to leave for the Mainland, or actively sought passage home. A pattern seemed to have set in of boredom with the sameness of each day, the struggle to conform to rigidity, and loneliness. There was nowhere to travel, and the only social life was as a volunteer or in the world of women, mostly alone. Many opted to leave by early summer and get on with their lives. Mother resisted, but there were no more assignments coming for life on Oahu, and AP and United Press now had more than enough photo journalists, as did the military. She was being pressured because of us kids; we had *to go to school, that was law. Evidently this pressure was somewhat relieved due to all passage being denied temporarily in late spring-early summer. Something was up, but civilians had no clue. Laws were tightened, rules enforced, and censorship of everything enforced. Several of "the girls" were denied travel for a time and asked to return to jobs having to do with the war effort. Rumors were rife of another impending attack or possible invasion.*

After the Battle of Midway, the island breathed easier that we were never going to be in danger. Many of the wives, Mother included, could pretty well figure where the husbands were, and only hope they were safe. She realized Dad was at Midway. The battle seemed to be also a turning point in our having a better idea of where he was, at least after the fact.

In the late summer of 1942 we learned we would return to Los Angeles in time to start school in the fall. By now I guess we were ready for a change, and I'm sure Mother was more than ready to get on with her life. It was pretty much a certainty that Dad was not going to return to Pearl Harbor for any reason in the near future, there was no work for her, and she was ready for family to take over in caring for us. In all honesty, Mother needed a break from constant strain. We kids needed the break from her anxious personality, and time had come to think ahead in a different direction, or in our case, having any *direction at all. We now waited to hear when passage would be available, and the long, sometimes difficult, goodbyes began.*

We sailed in August for California on a troop ship in convoy zigzagging across the Pacific. One of the ships escorting us in the convoy was the destroyer Shaw, *my dad's Pearl Harbor ship, a strange sight in the distance with its reconstructed bow. Mother tried taking pictures but I think it was too far to be clear. We kids found it hard to believe that a ship could sail with only half of it being real.*

The only event I recall on our return voyage was a biggie, and one memory that stayed with us all for many years. We kids were awakened late one night and told to quickly put on our life jackets. Since the convoy traveled in darkness at night, we had only little blue lights in the passageway on board, but could hear people hurriedly going by our room. The heavy doors to the rooms had been pulled open and secured and women with children had been given priority exit to the deck. As we approached the stairs going up to the deck where we had many times practiced life boat drills, I remember clearly to this day the slow creaking of chains as the boats were lowered into the water. We had all been assigned a station and a boat number. It was pitch black, but as we became accustomed to the dark we could make out what was going on immediately around us and who was next to us. Those chains, creaking and groaning, was the most menacing sound I ever heard. With the exception of the laborious, lumbering noise of ball bearings on the German tank in the movie Saving Private Ryan, *I have never heard since anything so utterly frightening. We were in the process of being lowered into the whaleboat, swinging side to side as we slowly dropped with the ominous creaking sound in pitch black, when suddenly everything stopped, and very quietly the word was passed that it was "all clear." Apparently a Japanese sub had been trailing us and got too close for comfort. Since our ship carried passengers and no heavy guns, we had become an easy target. I have no idea what happened to the sub, if it was sunk by one of the convoy ships, or turned away. It only mattered that we were not going to be on an open boat on the vast Pacific. I was too frightened to cry that night.*

There was an oddly eerie quietness about all movement and conversation, almost as if this was a surreal dream. It was many years before I had the courage to step into an open whaleboat, or onto any small boat or ship again.

Vignette describing how Ensign Herbert C. Jones was awarded the Medal of Honor for valor on-board *California*. By Mario Demarco for *Navy Times.*

Naval Historical Center

Vignette describing the award of the Medal of Honor to Captain Mervyn Sharp Bennion, commanding officer of the *West Virginia*, for valor on-board his ship during the attack. By Mario Demarco for *Navy Times.*

NavalHistorical Center

USS *West Virginia* Mess Attendant 2nd Class Doris "Dorie" Miller received the Navy Cross for heroism (the first black so honored in the war) for attending to his mortally wounded commanding officer, Captain Mervyn Sharp Bennion, and for manning an anti-aircraft weapon. Officially he was credited with downing two Japanese planes, and unofficially six. Miller was a shipmate and associate of ship's baker Taylor Marion Jeffords, Jr., of Wilmington. Miller was killed when his ship, the USS *Liscome Bay* (CVE-56), was sunk on Thanksgiving Day, 1943. The frigate USS *Miller* (FF-1091) was named for him in 1971.

Naval Historical Center

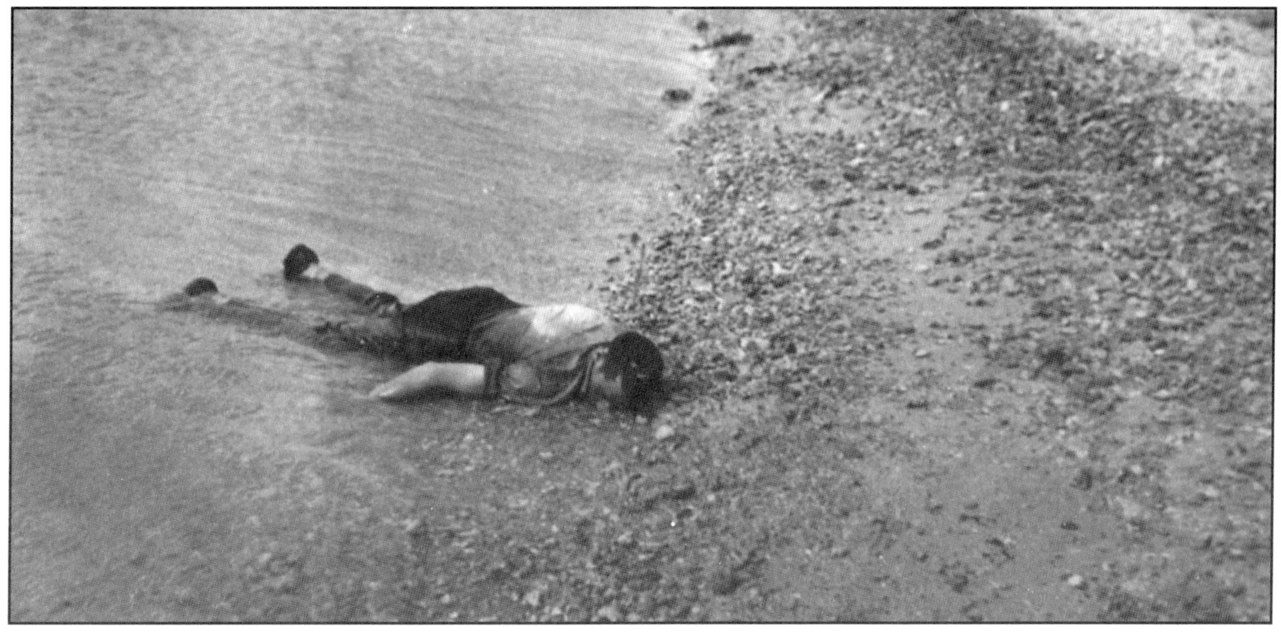

Body of U.S. sailor washed ashore at Naval Air Station Kaneohe after the attack.

Naval Historical Center

In the Hawaiian tradition of "Farewell to thee," sailors honor the dead killed at Naval Air Station Kaneohe. The men had been buried on 8 December 1941, and the ceremony took place later.

Naval Historical Center

Epilogue

War Refugees No Longer

The three of us stayed with my grandparents, William P. and Katherine McCormick O'Meara, at their Van Ness Avenue home in Los Angeles for a number of months after our return. The household at that time included two aunts, an uncle occasionally, one dog—"Susie Bomber," named by the donor, Uncle Dick, late of the Flying Tigers and now in the air force—assorted domestic help who never stayed too long, and so many gardeners we never bothered asking their names. Add to this mix the three of us and you have a recipe for high anxiety. It was good to be home, and good to have some reasonable rules to live by and faces to see and homes to visit. Berton and I were immediately enrolled at familiar St. Brendan's School, and even accepted wearing the required uniforms which included shoes.

I think the transition for my brother and me was made easy because we were living in the midst of a large family lauding attention on us as if we were war refugees. Actually, we were the only grandkids over the age of two who could talk, go places, and do things with all of them. Mother's involvement with us at this time tapered off, so the care and feeding and coping with the two of us fell to other family members. I have told and retold the humorous stories of life with Grampa to my own children and granddaughter Carrie, and so many happy vignettes of life with Uncle Bill, Uncle Carroll, Grandma Kitty, Aunt Katherine, and Aunt Mimi. Our world was Van Ness between Wilshire and Beverly Boulevards and Western Avenue and Larchmont Boulevard. This was safe. We knew the residents, the stores, the church, the parks, the vendor pulling his cart with fruits and vegetables, the Helms Bakery driver with his special whistle announcing his imminent arrival, and the teenager who delivered from the drug store.

Breakfast and lunch in the "morning room," dinner in the dining room, no eating in the "library," or as modern families would call it, the *family room.* Beggars often would come to the side door by the butler's pantry, and were never turned away and would be seated at the white wood table in the large, all white kitchen, given a sandwich or soup and bread, and if possible, given a bit of something to take away. We kids were always told about this as a lesson in gratitude.

Life for us was good, but for Mother a different story. Always high-strung and unconventional, it was difficult for her to adapt to such rigid routines as she felt existed in the house. Not one to rise in the morning, or retire at a reasonable hour at night, she caused more than annoyance with two aunts who worked regular schedules. Mother was not used to eating three regular meals, and felt only "farmers" ate dinner before eight o'clock. Between five and seven was the "cocktail hour," often spent visiting in the homes of friends. She did not feel comfortable having friends visit and could not be herself in her parents' home, proving once again "you can never go home again." News from Dad was irregular with long periods of no letters. The war news was often disturbing, and once again we could hear Mother crying at night and venting her frustrations during the day with anger toward family.

Finding a place to live was a real problem for everyone, and especially those with children. Priority was given those in defense work, but who among them would be looking at elegant high-rise apartments near the Wilshire Country Club, or in Westwood? The truth is, no one wanted children. Out of desperation Mother decided to put the two of us in the same boarding school in order not to be separated, and she in turn was able to rent a very nice apartment at The Hermoyne on Rossmore near the Wilshire Country Club. In retrospect this was a real turning point for all of us, and began one of the happiest, most stable periods for us kids, with the greatest influence in *my* life other than our parents.

Mother enrolled Berton and me as boarders at Marymount School for Girls on Sunset Boulevard in Bel-Air across from UCLA. Boys were admitted through second grade, but he was only one of two little boys who boarded. Many years later when Berton applied to the Naval Academy he had to list this school along with others, which caused him some embarrassment. We lived in very comfortable, orderly surroundings, administered by warm, even loving women, well educated and dedicated not only to a religious life, but educating youngsters in the classical manner which included languages, the arts, classical literature, ballet, along with sciences, math, history, and geography. We had classes once a week in "charm" as we called it, learning to stand and sit properly, make introductions, write "bread and butter" letters, the art of invitations and seating, how to speak in a well-modulated voice with breath control, and setting the table. We learned all these things just in time to witness the trashing of morals, patriotism, and manners across the country, and witness the growing Women's Lib movement.

Most all of us, both day students and boarders, had tremendous respect for the Madames, as they were called as young nuns of The Religious Of The Sacred Heart Of Mary, and learned quickly the simple rules we were expected to follow, and yet they understood we were still children and allowed us that privilege, often joining in our games and pranks. Fairness was paramount in all things. As we grew older and became teenagers, these same wonderful women were understanding of this most difficult period and were always available to hear our most intimate problems, giving advice with quiet good sense. I felt I could speak of anything on my mind, and did many times. To this day I thank my mother for the privilege of a Marymount education, a preparation for life.

In our second year back in Los Angeles, my brother attended St. John's Military Academy, and we saw each other only on weekends at our grandparents' home. Berton and I always considered the house on Van Ness Avenue as "home," as we were raised and influenced almost as much by aunts especially, and grandparents, particularly our grampa, that wily old bad-boy who adored us. It was in this house we went with mumps, whooping cough, measles. Here is where we dressed up for Halloween and went about the neighborhood for candy and annoyed the retired opera singer on the corner who kept her house in darkness to discourage children at the door, screaming "I know it's you, Billy O'Meara, sending those brats up here" (she was right), and here we celebrated a big family Christmas, and Easter. It was here I was fitted for my first communion dress, lovingly made by my grandmother. It was here we celebrated childhood. Mother was busy with more and more assignments and had become very much in demand, taking beautiful photos of daily activities of children of friends, and then celebrities and the wealthy, and continuing doing advertising shoots.

Our dad came home once that I recall, around November 1943. This was a happy time, although a bit strained for my brother and me, having another parent figure around, but he was such a calm, at times even remote personality, that we were more awed than resentful. Our parents were very social and were widely entertained welcoming Dad. He was not with us long and soon left for Bremerton, Washington, where he put into commission a new destroyer, the *Leutze*. Mother accompanied him north, staying for several months while we remained in our schools and spent many weekends on Van Ness. After she returned to Los Angeles, we moved into a new apartment complex where we remained for many years. We kids became day students and once again lived with just Mother.

Once again I would wake in the middle of the night seeing light from under my door and hearing tears from downstairs. It would be hard to sleep sometimes wondering why Mother was always so sad. Growing older now, we were expected to be more responsible in helping at home since she was gone so much. We were very privileged kids in many ways, attending good schools, Junior Assemblies, summer day camp at the Beverly Hills Hotel, ski trips, ballet lessons, private swimming classes held at one Beverly Hills address or another, elegant birthday parties, trips to the ranch, to Balboa, to Santa Barbara. Along with these privileges we were reminded constantly of our duty to "give back." It seemed to us for years that we "owed" our family for taking part in these activities. Actually, these lessons remained with us for life, almost to the point of feeling guilt enjoying life and having fun. I truly believe Mother was doing the best she could trying to be both mother and father, raising us in a culture she was used to but hoping to instill in us a sense of duty such as Dad might.

Berton and I were sent to public school for a while at the urging of Dad. Guess he felt we needed to experience a little more reality. We went to one of the best public elementary schools in the city and knew nearly everyone there from camps or dancing class or the Beach Club. We just didn't wear uniforms. One afternoon Eleanor Wasson, a dear friend of the family, picked Berton and me up from school and took us to her home in Beverly Hills. How curious! We were friends with the Wasson girls, but why did she do this? We were told Mother was "tied up" and we would have dinner at the Wasson home. Mother had received a government telegram suggesting, but not quite saying, that my father had been mortally wounded on the bridge of his ship while shelling the beaches at Iwo Jima, in order for the Marines to land. He had been hit by pieces of a shell and instantly paralyzed, and was not expected to live. Mother contacted everyone she knew in a position to help get more information on what was happening and if in fact Dad was alive. Bob Guggenheim, a close friend and at that time a naval officer, was able to determine Dad was on a hospital ship being taken to Wake Island, and then to be transferred to Oahu. Eventually, a letter arrived from the ship's executive officer, Leon Grabowski, who had taken command, filling in the details of 17 February 1945. Once again our family was hit square in the face with the realities of war. And once again we kids were asked to be brave and grown up.

By mid-April Dad was sent to the Long Beach Naval Hospital, where he spent a very long time recuperating from his injuries and several operations to remove shrapnel lying too close to his spinal cord. I was taken to see him the end of April, for my birthday, and didn't recognize him. I cried and had to be taken from the room. My brother had already seen Dad, and was far more stoic than I. After this initial shock of seeing this man in bed unable to move without assistance, partially paralyzed, we became used to spending Saturday or Sunday at the hospital while Mother stayed in the room with Dad. This was equally depressing and boring for us kids, and being normal we found ways to create mischief, mainly sneaking into the theater. Looking back, I don't think we behaved differently than any youngsters under those circumstances.

As months went by and summer came, we were able to spend our days at camp, and being with kids. This is when the hospital would release Dad home for an overnight occasionally. He had a walker and cane, and our household had to adjust to his not using his right side. Furniture was moved around to accommodate this. Stairs were most difficult and so Dad would often stay in the master bedroom during the day, coming down to see the many guests who stopped by in the evening. Mother devoted her life to Dad and his care and comfort and was determined he would come home to us on a permanent basis.

During that August of 1945, Berton and I were at the Beverly Hills Hotel Summer Day Camp, when it was announced the war was over. There was a lot of noise and laughter and tears of joy among the adults, and uncorking of champagne, hugs and kisses all around. Late in the afternoon we were called for, with Dad in the passenger seat and Mother driving. The mood was somber in the car going home, the radio announcers from major cities across the country relating what was happening in the streets, and both parents almost devoid of emotion. What a complete paradox to the elation we had just left! This was the first time, and one of only three in my life, I saw my father cry. When we reached home he was sobbing, his entire body shaking uncontrollably. His tears were for all those good people who would never again come home, who died miserably for this peace, for the many tragedies he witnessed, and for the senselessness of war. He felt that the joy in the streets should be thanks for being alive and our country not having to endure the brutality known in Europe and the Far East. That we should spend some time in prayer thanking God for our being saved and promise to always remember this lesson of how the war changed the very way we live forever. We did not understand this full meaning until years later, and once again we kids were given a lesson in gratitude and giving back in exchange for our blessings.

These years were bittersweet and certainly a force in our lives forever. When we first went to boarding school, we became somewhat a curiosity among our classmates and treated almost like war orphans. We were asked questions which we answered truthfully about our early experiences from 7 December on, and I remember two mothers particularly who stated that we certainly knew how to tell fairy tales. After awhile neither of us discussed anything to do with living in Honolulu, and put the bad times somewhere in the back of our memory bank, not to revisit them for many, many years.

In 1988, Berton and I were in Vista, California, as our mother lay dying in the Camp Pendleton Naval Hospital. Her house was full of "stuff," and one of our unhappy duties was in sorting through drawers, boxes, and closets of a lifetime of memories. This was the first time in years just the two of us had an opportunity to talk freely about our parents, their influence on us, and how our lives were shaped by them and history. We agreed that Mother would have been a fun aunt, a sort of "Auntie Mame," but was not meant to be a mother. We also agreed that although we were fairly responsible, patriotic and God-fearing citizens, we were also guilt-ridden, and not completely at ease enjoying life. My brother shared with me his feeling of failure in not living up to the stature of his father, the hero figure, and his lifelong battle for acceptance from our parents. I was determined to be a hands-on mother to my children, allowing them to be kids in a real neighborhood, enjoying their activities and excusing them certain human inadequacies. Perhaps, as a parent trying to make up for the roller coaster existence Berton and I lived, I was too lenient.

I know those years during World War II had a profound effect on people everywhere, changing the way we lived forever. We are the sum of our experiences, good or bad, and the rest is up to us. It is important that all generations that follow those years understand why we give thanks to all who fought and sacrificed not just their lives but in what they gave up, and what they lost: youth, certainly innocence, security, family.

I have great admiration for my mother and dad, and all they did, and thank them for what I have come to learn. The lessons of gratitude they so embraced have been learned.

CRJ

"The Man of the Family"

USS *Leutze* (DD-481)

23 November 1944
At Sea

My Dear Son:

This may not be a very long letter but I hope you won't mind....We have been so busy that this is the first time I have felt able to do it. We are having a short breathing spell for a few days. That is it is a few days breather out here. After all there aren't any Japs to speak of within two or three hundred miles right now. The way we operate that is a long way compared to the usual situation.

Mother's letters and the pictures she sends have kept me quite well posted on all the things that have been going on at home....We have been very busy out here as Mother can tell you and although it is impossible for me to be home Christmas I am sure it will all help to get me home sooner than might otherwise be expected.

In the meantime son I am still counting on you to be the man of the family. To be a man in the finer sense of the word is not easy, it requires many things. I have told you before some rules by which a gentleman is guided and lives. Now that you are getting around with many people here are some others. Be slow to anger but quick in the defense of your honor and your woman kind. Be quiet and polite in manner but strong and steadfast in the defense of your rights. Have pride in yourself and your family and country but he humble before God.

With My Love, Your Father

[Berton A. Robbins, Jr., to Berton III, 8, from a rest area following the Peleliu campaign and Battle of Leyte Gulf—Authors' Collection]

Sully Sullivan, owner of the Waikiki Fotoshop, who supplied Mother with her camera and photographic supplies.

One of the many naval officer weddings that used us as junior attendants.

Berton, *left*, cousin Kathleen O'Meara, grandmother Kitty O'Meara, aunt Jean Vander Pyl (Kathleen's mother and wife of Uncle Carroll), Carroll. Vander Pyl became a well-known radio and TV personality, including as the voice of Wilma Flintstone. August 1942, Los Angeles.

At our Waikiki home, the Comstock Apartments Hotel. Berton showed off the latest children's gas mask.

Authors' collection

Notes

Introduction

1. Item of January 20, 1942, in American Legion Post 10 (Wilmington, N.C.) Wartime Scrapbooks.

   The author's mother, Viola M. Jones, kept these scrapbooks for the post during the war. They are now in the Randall Library at the University of North Carolina at Wilmington.
2. Item of December 28, 1941, in American Legion Post 10 scrapbooks.
3. Wilmington (N.C.) *Morning Star*, May 5, 1942; Items of December 28, 1941, and August 27, 1949, in American Legion Post 10 scrapbooks.
4. Leatrice R. Arakaki and John R. Kuborn, *7 December 1941: The Air Force Story* (Hickam Air Force Base, Hawaii: Pacific Air Forces, 1991), 137.
5. Walter Lord, *Day of Infamy* (New York: Henry Holt and Co., 1957), 218.

Chapter 1

1. Arthur Zich and the Editors of Time-Life Books, *The Rising Sun* (Alexandria, Va.: Time-Life Books, 1977), 76.
2. Stanley D. Porteus, *And Blow Not the Trumpet: A Prelude to Peril* (Palo Alto, Calif.: Pacific Books, 1947), 160.
3. John J. Stephan, *Hawaii Under the Rising Sun: Japan's Plans for Conquest After Pearl Harbor* (Honolulu: University of Hawaii Press, 1984), vii.
4. Husband E. Kimmel quoted in Samuel Eliot Morison, *History of United States Naval Operations in World War II, v. III: The Rising Sun in the Pacific, 1931–April 1942* (Boston: Little, Brown and Co., 1951), 220.
5. W. A. Gabrielson quoted in Editors of *Army Times, Pearl Harbor and Hawaii* (New York: Walker and Co., 1971), 123.
6. Editors of *Army Times, Pearl Harbor and Hawaii* (New York: Walker and Co., 1971), 134.
7. Paul H. Backus quoted in Paul Stillwell, ed., *Air Raid: Pearl Harbor! Recollections of a Day of Infamy* (Annapolis, Md.: Naval Institute Press, 1981), 167.
8. Cornelius C. Smith, Jr., quoted in Stillwell, 224–25.
9. Lawson P. Ramage quoted in Stillwell, 201.
10. Smith quoted in Stillwell, 226.
11. Gwenfread Allen, *Hawaii's War Years 1941–1945* (Reprint: Westport, Conn.: Greenwood Press, 1971), 147.
12. Wilfred Jay Holmes quoted in Stillwell, 252.
13. Blake Clark, *Remember Pearl Harbor* (New York: Harper & Brothers, 1943), 180.
14. Evelyn W. Guthrie quoted in Stillwell, 241.
15. Clark, 228–29.
16. Porteus, 161.
17. Peggy Hughes Ryan quoted in Stillwell, 233.
18. Allen, 112.
19. Clark, 227–28.
20. Porteus, 161.
21. Ryan quoted in Stillwell, 234.
22. Allen, 95.
23. Porteus, 173.
24. *Honolulu Advertiser* quoted in *Army Times*, 131.
25. Clark, 233.
26. Backus quoted in Stillwell, 168.
27. Interview with Justus Sistrunk, October 26, 2000.

Chapter 2

1. Walter Karig and Welbourn Kelley, *Battle Report: Pearl Harbor to Coral Sea* (New York: Rinehart and Co., Inc., 1944), 249.
2. Samuel Eliot Morison, *History of United States Naval Operations in World War II, v. III: The Rising Sun in the Pacific, 1931–April 1942* (Boston: Little, Brown and Co., 1951), 222.
3. Chester Nimitz quoted in Editors of *Army Times, Pearl Harbor and Hawaii* (New York: Walker and Co., 1971), 132.
4. Morison, 256.
5. Karig and Kelley, 250.
6. Morison, 262.
7. Karig and Kelley, 251, 254.
8. Ibid., 251, 254–55.
9. Ibid., 270.
10. Morison, 262–65.
11. Ibid., 391.
12. Ibid., 394.
13. Ibid., 396, 398.
14. Harry A. Gailey, *The War in the Pacific: From Pearl Harbor to Tokyo Bay* (Novato, Calif.: Presidio Press, 1995), 133.
15. James F. Dunnigan and Albert A. Nofi, *Victory at Sea: World War II in the Pacific* (New York: Quill, 1995), 23.

16. Gwenfread Allen, *Hawaii's War Years 1941–1945* (Reprint: Westport, Conn.: Greenwood Press, 1971), 62–63.
17. Ibid., 63–64.
18. Dunnigan and Nofi, 162–63.
19. Morison, 267–68; O'Hare Medal of Honor citation, 17 April 1942; Robert Crossman e-mail to author, 19 March 2001.

Chapter 3

1. Walter Karig and Welbourn Kelley, *Battle Report: Pearl Harbor to Coral Sea* (New York: Rinehart and Co, Inc., 1944), 95.
2. Editors of *Army Times, Pearl Harbor and Hawaii* (New York: Walker and Co., 1971), 137.
3. Homer N. Wallin, *Pearl Harbor: Why, How, Fleet Salvage and Final Appraisal* (Washington, D.C.: Naval History Division, 1968), 281.
4. Ibid., 151.
5. Samuel Eliot Morison, *History of United States Naval Operations in World War II, v. III: The Rising Sun in the Pacific, 1931–April 1942* (Boston: Little, Brown and Co., 1951), 166.
6. Ibid., 145.
7. Blake Clark, *Remember Pearl Harbor* (New York: Harper & Brothers, 1942), 161.
8. *Army Times*, 103.
9. Wallin, 104–5.
10. Homer N. Wallin quoted in Karig and Kelley, 95.
11. Wallin, 284.
12. Ibid., 233.
13. Interview with Lawrence Homer Henderson, October 12, 2000.
14. Interview with Taylor Marion Jeffords, Jr., October 13, 2000.

Chapter 4

1. Blake, Clark, *Remember Pearl Harbor* (New York: Harper & Brothers, 1942), 215–16.
2. Ibid., 216–17.
3. Stanley D. Porteus, *And Blow Not the Trumpet: A Prelude to Peril* (Palo Alto, Calif.: Pacific Books, 1947), 185.
4. Gwenfread Allen, *Hawaii's War Years 1941–1945* (Reprint: Westport, Conn.: Greenwood Press, 1971), 246.
5. Clark, 237.
6. Porteus, 185–86.
7. Editors of *Army Times, Pearl Harbor and Hawaii* (New York: Walker and Co., 1971), 155.
8. Allen, 246–47.
9. Porteus, 183.
10. Allen, 349.
11. Ibid., 352.
12. Ibid., 167.
13. Clark, 218.
14. Allen, 239–40, 242.
15. Ibid., 305–7.
16. Porteus, 180–81.
17. Cornelius C. Smith, Jr., quoted in Paul Stillwell, ed., *Air Raid: Pearl Harbor! Recollections of a Day of Infamy* (Annapolis, Md.: Naval Institute Press, 1981), 226.
18. Allen, 57.
19. Peggy Hughes Ryan quoted in Stillwell, 234–35.
20. Porteus, 182.
21. James G. Carroll, *Sopac Holiday* (Self-published monograph, 1986), 4.
22. Interview with Fred S. Crane, October 13, 2000.
23. Interview with Rufus Stewart, October 24, 2000.
24. Interview with Raymond Owsley, October 24, 2000.
25. Interview with Don Jenkins, October 24, 2000.
26. Interview with Ted Tipper, October 24, 2000.
27. Interview with Johnny Johnson, October 24, 2000.
28. Interview with John Egan, October 24, 2000.
29. Allen, 351–52.
30. John J. Stephan, *Hawaii Under the Rising Sun: Japan's Plans for Conquest After Pearl Harbor* (Honolulu: University of Hawaii Press, 1984), 5.
31. Allen, 131.

Chapter 5

1. Archie Satterfield, *The Home Front: An Oral History of the War Years in America: 1941–45* (Playboy Press, 1981), 31.
2. Peggy Hughes Ryan quoted in Paul Stillwell, ed., *Air Raid: Pearl Harbor!; Recollections of a Day of Infamy* (Annapolis, Md.: Naval Institute Press, 1981), 235.

Bibliography and Suggested Further Reading

Agawa, Hiroyuki (Translation by Bester, John). *The Reluctant Admiral: Yamamoto and the Imperial Navy.* Tokyo: Kodansha International Ltd., 1979.

Albright, Harry. *Pearl Harbor: Japan's Fatal Blunder.* New York: Hippocrene Books, 1988.

Allen, Gwenfread. *Hawaii's War Years 1941–1945.* Reprint: Westport, Conn.: Greenwood Press, 1971.

Arakaki, Leatrice R., and John R. Kuborn. *7 December 1941: The Air Force Story.* Hickam Air Force Base, Hawaii: Pacific Air Forces, 1991.

Barker, A. J. *Pearl Harbor: Tora, Tora, Tora.* New York: Ballantine Books, 1988.

Carroll, James G. *Sopac Holiday.* Self-published, 1986.

Chambers, John Whiteclay II, ed. in chief. *The Oxford Companion to American Military History.* New York: Oxford University Press, 1999.

Clark, Blake. *Remember Pearl Harbor.* New York: Harper & Brothers Publishers, 1942.

Clausen, Henry C., and Lee Bruce. *Pearl Harbor: Final Judgment.* New York: Crown Books, 1992.

The Correspondents of *Time, Life,* and *Fortune. December 7, the First Thirty Hours.* New York: Alfred A. Knopf, 1942.

Dear, I. C. B., and M. R. D. Foot, eds. *The Oxford Companion to World War II.* New York: Oxford University Press, 1995.

Dickinson, Clarence Earle. *The Flying Guns: The Cockpit Record of a Naval Pilot from Pearl Harbor through Midway.* New York: Charles Scribner's Sons, 1942.

Dull, Paul S. *A Battle History of the Imperial Japanese Navy. 1941–1945.* Annapolis, Md.: Naval Institute Press, 1978.

Dunnigan, James F., and Albert A. Nofi. *Victory at Sea: World War II in the Pacific.* New York: Quill, 1995.

Editors of *Army Times. Pearl Harbor and Hawaii.* New York: Walker and Co., 1971.

Forte, Robert S., and Ronald E. Marcello. *Remembering Pearl Harbor: Eyewitness Accounts by U.S. Military Men and Women.* Wilmington, Del.: Scholarly Resources Imprint, 1991.

Fuchida, Mitsuo. *Shinjuwan Sakusen No Shinso: Watakushi Wa Shinjuwan Joku Ni Ita.* Nara, Japan: Yamato Taimusa Sha, 1949.

Gailey, Harry A. *The War in the Pacific: From Pearl Harbor to Tokyo Bay.* Novato, Calif.: Presidio Press, 1995.

Genda, Minoru. *Shinjuwan Sakusen Kaikoroku.* Tokyo: Yomiuri Shimbun, 1972.

Goldstein, Donald M., and Katherine V. Dillon. *The Pearl Harbor Papers: Inside the Japanese Plans.* McLean, Va.: Brassey's U.S., 1993.

Griess, Thomas E., ed. *The West Point Military History Series: Atlas for the Second World War; Asia and the Pacific.* Wayne, N.J.: Avery Publishing Group, 1985.

Halsey, William F., and J. Bryan, III. *Admiral Halsey's Story.* New York: McGraw-Hill Book Co., 1947.

Hard, Tameichyi, Fred Saito, and Roger Pineau. *Japanese Destroyer Captain.* New York: Ballantine Books, 1961.

Hata, Ikuhiko, and Yasuho Izawa (Translation by D. C. Gorham). *Japanese Naval Aces and Fighter Units in World War II.* Annapolis, Md.: Naval Institute Press, 1989.

Hoehling, A. A. *The Week Before Pearl Harbor.* New York: W. W. Norton & Co., 1963.

Ienaga, Saburo (Translation by Frank Baldwin). *The Pacific War 1931–1945.* New York: Pantheon Books, 1978.

Karig, Walter, and Welbourn Kelley. *Battle Report: Pearl Harbor to Coral Sea.* New York: Rinehart and Co., Inc., 1944.

Lilienthal, David E. *Hawaii's Japanese: An Experiment in Democracy.* Princeton, N.J.: Princeton University Press, 1946.

Lord, Walter. *Day of Infamy*. New York: Henry Holt and Co., 1957.

The "Magic" Background of Pearl Harbor. Washington: Department of Defense and Government Printing Office, 1977.

Morison, Samuel Eliot. *History of United States Naval Operations in World War II, v. III: The Rising Sun in the Pacific; 1931–April 1942*. Boston: Little, Brown and Co., 1951.

———. *History of United States Naval Operations in World War II, v. IV: Coral Sea, Midway, and Submarine Actions, May 1942–August 1942*. Boston: Little, Brown and Co., 1949.

———. *The Two Ocean War*. New York: Ballantine Books, 1963.

Motley, John J., and Philip R. Kelly. *Now Hear This!*. Washington: Infantry Journal Press, 1947.

Naval Historical Center Web site, *www.history.navy.mil.*

Porteus, Stanley D. *And Blow Not the Trumpet: A Prelude to Peril.* Palo Alto, Calif.: Pacific Books, 1947.

Prange, Gordon W. *Pearl Harbor: Verdict of History*. New York: McGraw-Hill Book Co., 1985.

Prange, Gordon W., with Donald M. Goldstein, and Katherine V. Dillon. *At Dawn We Slept: The Untold Story of Pearl Harbor*. New York: Penguin Books USA, 1982.

———. *Dec. 7 1941: The Day the Japanese Attacked Pearl Harbor.* New York: Wings Books, 1991.

Sakamaki, Kazuo. *I Attacked Pearl Harbor*. New York: Association Press, 1949.

Satterfield, Archie, *The Home Front: An Oral History of the War Years in America: 1941–45*. Playboy Press, 1981.

Smith, Carl. *Classic Battles: Pearl Harbor: The Day of Infamy*. Oxford, England: Osprey Publishing, 1999.

Smith, S. E., ed. *The United States Navy in World War II*. New York: Quill Books, 1966.

Smurthwaite, David. *The Pacific War Atlas: 1941–1945*. New York: Facts on File, 1995.

Sommerville, Donald. *World War II Day by Day*. Greenwich, Conn.: Dorsett Press, 1989.

Spector, Ronald H., *Eagle Against the Sun: The American War with Japan.* New York: Random House, 1985.

Stephan, John J. *Hawaii Under the Rising Sun: Japan's Plan for Conquest After Pearl Harbor*. Honolulu: University of Hawaii Press, 1984.

Stillwell, Paul, ed. *Air Raid: Pearl Harbor! Recollections of a Day of Infamy*. Annapolis, Md.: Naval Institute Press, 1981.

Stinnett, Robert B. *Day of Deceit: The Truth About FDR and Pearl Harbor.* New York: The Free Press, 2000.

Toland, John. *But Not in Shame*. New York: Ballantine Books, 1961.

———. *Infamy: Pearl Harbor and its Aftermath*. New York: Berkeley Publishing, 1983.

———. *The Rising Sun: The Decline and Fall of the Japanese Empire, 1936–1945, vols. 1–2*. New York: Random House, 1970.

Travers, Paul Joseph. *Eyewitness to Infamy: An Oral History of Pearl Harbor*. New York: Madison Books, 1991.

Wallin, Homer N. *Pearl Harbor: Why, How, Fleet Salvage and Final Appraisal.* Washington: Naval History Division, 1968.

Watts, Anthony J. *Japanese Warships of World War II.* Garden City, N.Y.: Doubleday & Co., 1966.

Weintraub, Stanley. *Long Days Journey into War: December 7, 1941*. New York: Truman Talley Books, 1991.

Zich, Arthur, and the eds. of *Time-Life* Books. *The Rising Sun*. Alexandria, Va.: Time-Life Books, 1977.

Index

Photographs in *italics.*

Q

R

S

V

W

Y

Z